# FLY ON THE WALL

## THE BEST OF KEVIN TOBIN

# FLY ON THE WALL

## THE BEST OF KEVIN TOBIN 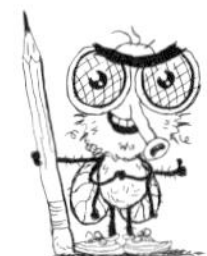

### FOREWORD BY MARK CRITCH

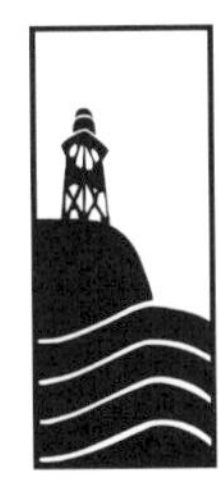

BREAKWATER BOOKS LTD.

P.O. Box 2188, St. John's, NL   Canada   A1C 6E6

WWW.BREAKWATERBOOKS.COM

COPYRIGHT © 2025 Kevin Tobin



LIBRARY AND ARCHIVES CANADA CATALOGUING IN PUBLICATION

Fly on the wall : the best of Kevin Tobin / cartoons by Kevin Tobin.

Tobin, Kevin, 1958– author, artist

Canadiana (print) 20250154749 | Canadiana (ebook) 20250154757

ISBN 9781778530494 (softcover) | ISBN 9781778530500 (ePUB)

Canadian wit and humor, Pictorial. | Newfoundland and Labrador—History—20th century—Caricatures and cartoons. Newfoundland and Labrador—History—21st century—Caricatures and cartoons. | Canadian wit and humor, Pictorial. Editorial cartoons.

LCC NC1449.T61 A4 2025 | DDC 971.8/040207—dc23

IMAGE CURATION   Jocelyne Thomas, Branwen Books and Beth Oberholtzer, Oberholtzer Design

DESIGN & IMAGE MANAGEMENT   Beth Oberholtzer, Oberholtzer Design

THE PUBLISHER GRATEFULLY ACKNOWLEDGES THE SUPPORT OF

The Canada Council for the Arts

The Government of Canada through the Department of Heritage, and

The Government of Newfoundland and Labrador through the Department of Tourism, Culture, Arts and Recreation

PRINTED AND BOUND IN CANADA

Breakwater Books is committed to choosing papers and materials for our books that help to protect our environment. To this end, this book is printed on a recycled paper.

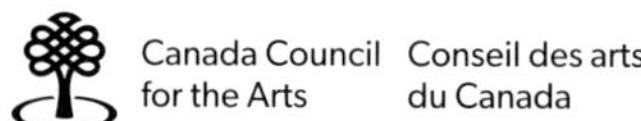 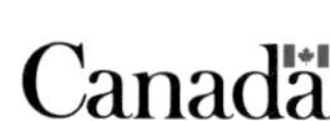 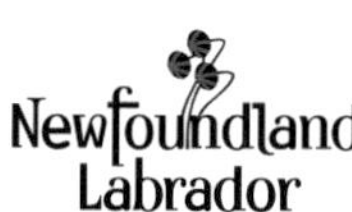 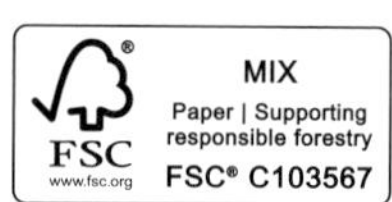

# DEDICATION

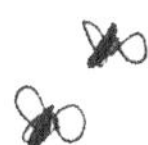

Most people have heard the phrase "ink in the blood". It means to have a natural predisposition toward or passion for the written word and the way it captures life. For me, the ink in my blood is what gives life to the cartoons I draw.

As a child, I had a passion for doodling, and soon discovered an interest in the written word. Comics. Books. Newspapers. I have fond memories of my father reading the Western Star *daily* newspaper after supper each evening, and I particularly enjoyed the coloured comic strips in the Saturday morning edition, the sweet smell of newsprint and ink coming from the pages. At school, I was a notorious doodler, the margins in my books filled with epic battles of super heroes, robots, and hockey players. After school, I even joined the forces of child-labour, now extinct, the proud neighbourhood paperboy.

Over a decade later, in the mid-1980s, my editorial cartoons would appear each week in the local Robinson-Blackmore newspapers. At first, it was one editorial cartoon a week, eventually appearing in The Evening Telegram. *In the 1990s it snowballed to six days a week, and then more recently it went down to three cartoons a week.*

But technology changes, and with it the way people consume media. It's a deadline journalists and printing press staff in St. John's have been dreading . . . the final edition of The Telegram daily newspaper. The presses have stopped in Newfoundland and Labrador. The Telegram *is now a weekly, and I am honoured to contribute each week to their Opinion Page. After a 145-year run, the People's Paper is now fully embracing the fast-paced world of online daily news. But I think of all the talented people who worked at the daily newspaper over the years: Reporters. Editorial staff. Press operators. Columnists. Newspaper carriers. Writing, printing, and delivering the stories of Newfoundland and Labrador. All born with ink in their blood.*

I dedicate this collection of 40 years of my editorial cartoons to my hard-working colleagues at The People's Paper.

Note to Reader—Choosing a representative selection of cartoons from a collection spanning 40 years is not easy, nor is deciding how to sort them. We—the author and the publisher—decided on the broad categories of Culture, Politics, Industry, Healthcare, and News, and chose cartoons that we felt reflected these topics over the years. We also felt that some of these cartoons required a little context; those cartoons are marked with a ✏ and a note on page 156. For all of these images, we invite you to consider not only the events they represent, but the thoughts and emotions they evoke. For a picture, as the saying goes, is worth a thousand words.

# FOREWORD
## MARK CRITCH

*I am a comedian. For over 20 years I have been a writer and cast member for CBC's 22 minutes. Before that, I had the same gig for Rising Tide's Revue. I basically made fun of politicians for a living. And how could I not? In Newfoundland and Labrador, politics is like pro wrestling. Family members view some politicians as heroes and some as villains. People argue at the dinner table over which is which. To be a legend, you have to be big and bold. John Crosbie and Danny Williams would have made fine wrestlers. Long John Crosbie and Whipper Danny Williams. It's a cartoonist's dream.*

*What would take me minutes of babbling to convey, Kevin Tobin can do in a brushstroke. His work was always the first thing I turned to in the paper.*

*To play the villain in a Kevin Tobin cartoon was a deadly blow to many a politician. It meant you had lost the hearts of people. For Kevin is a barometer of the winds of change.*

He makes us laugh. But he also can break our hearts. The loss of life at sea, or at war, are often marked by his pen. Those cartoons are monuments that will last forever. When my own father passed, Mike Critch of the VOCM news service earned a place in one of Kevin's cartoons. 'You made it, Dad', I thought.

I love to count the flies in Kevin's work. You'll see flies in many classic paintings. A fly over an official may indicate disfavour with the king or a dereliction of duty.

They will often circle the heads of the subjects in Kevin's work. The number of flies seen may be an indication of how the artist feels about them. I have been in a few cartoons myself. I believe my number of flies is three. I s'pose that's not so bad.

There were no flies in the cartoon of my father. Kevin never puts them in his drawings of the departed. That's because Kevin is a class act. His work is never cruel. But like all good humour, it is honest. I guess you could say, 'There's no flies on he.

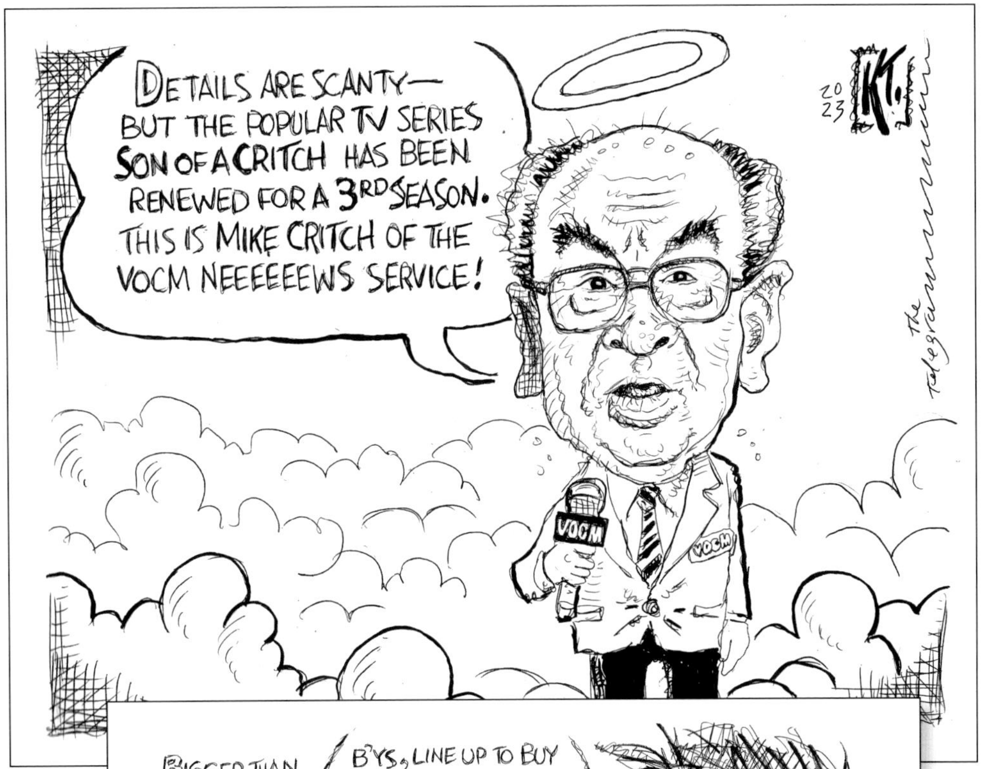

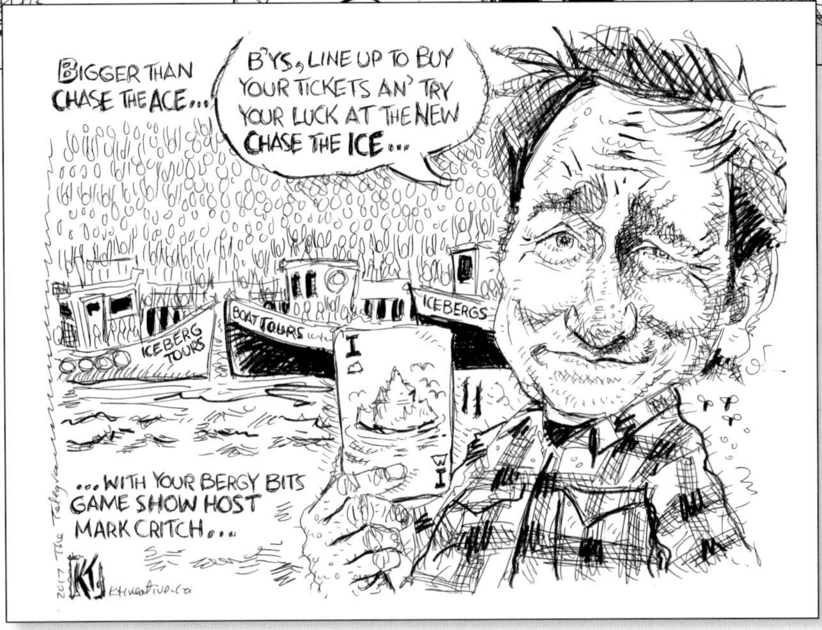

# SKETCHY BEGINNINGS

*How did I get into cartooning, anyway? In 1977, I got my first job laying out community newspapers with Robinson-Blackmore in Grand Falls-Windsor. The company's managing editor Bern Bromley and editor Ron Ennis saw some of my rough sketches and encouraged me to draw the odd political cartoon for the local Robinson-Blackmore newspapers from time to time.*

*In 1978, Bell Islander Paul Bickford was hired as a reporter and we became fast friends. Five years later, Paul and I were working at different jobs in St. John's; we met up again, and collaborated to create* Glut, The Newfoundland Humour Magazine.

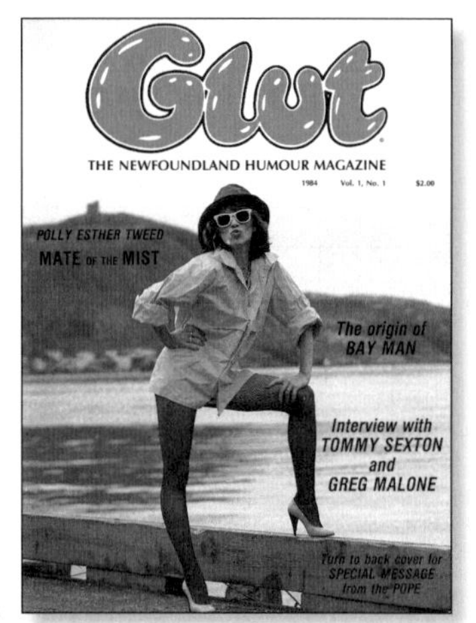


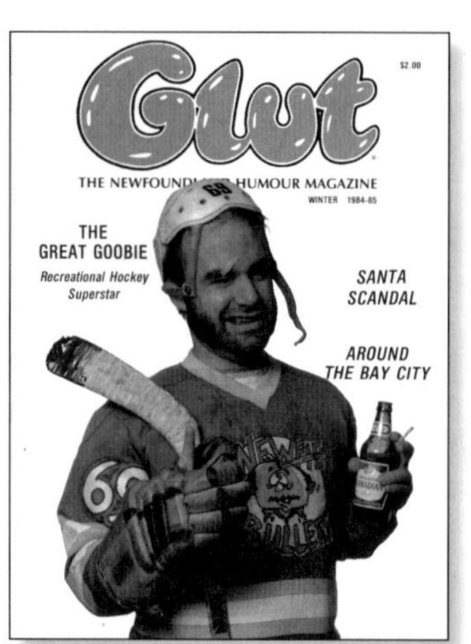


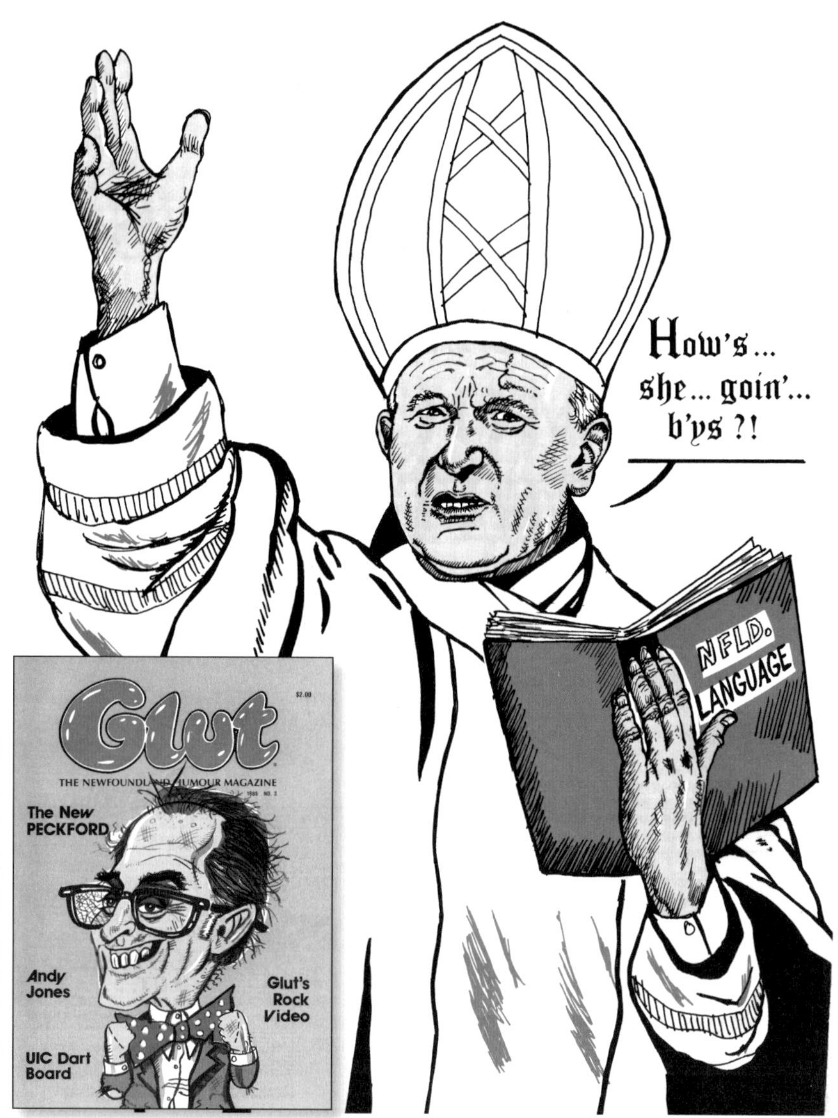

After three issues of Glut and being now broke, we decided to join forces once again to write and draw political cartoons for the local newspapers. Like so many before him, Paul left the Rock in 1985, seeking his fortune on the mainland. I approached The Evening Telegram publisher Steve Herder with my editorial cartoons; he turned me down. "Nice sketches, young feller," he said, "but needs more work on the ideas." My ego was bruised,

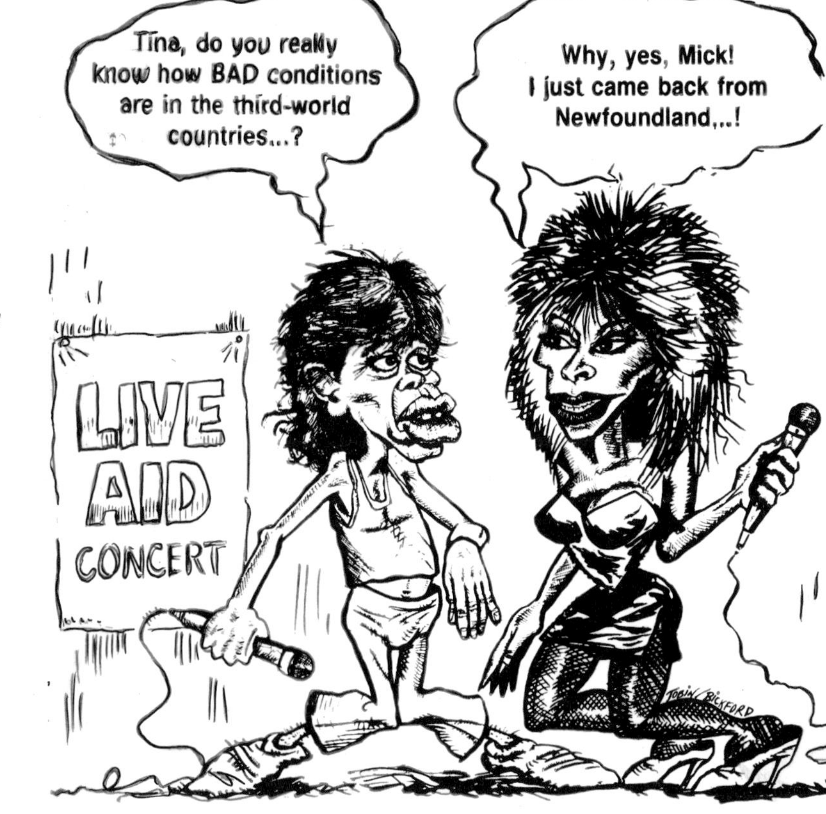




but I took another stab at the ideas, putting more thought into them, and approached Herder again. It worked.

In the mid-1990s, the odd fly started appearing in my cartoons, catching the buzz around politicians and celebrities. Forty years later, I'm still at it . . .

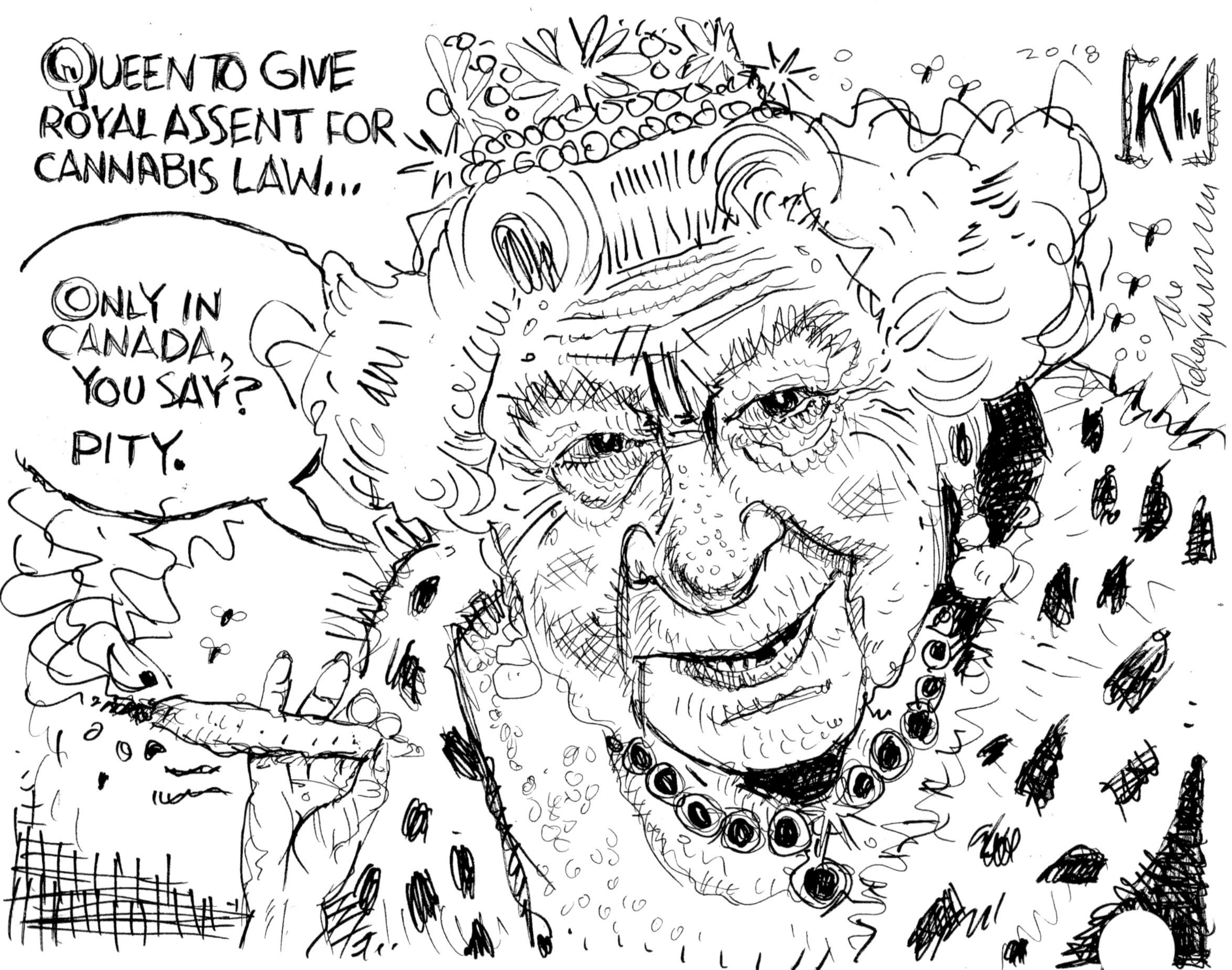
QUEEN TO GIVE ROYAL ASSENT FOR CANNABIS LAW...
ONLY IN CANADA, YOU SAY? PITY.
2018
The Telegram

# CULTURE

Believe it or not, flies have culture. Some fruit flies have cultural traditions passed down across generations; unfortunately, a fruit fly generation is about two weeks, so folk entomologists are always in a rush trying to document these traditions. In fact, the writer of the rowdy folk song "I'se the B'y" was a passionate entomologist who initially called the traditional song "I'se the Fly."

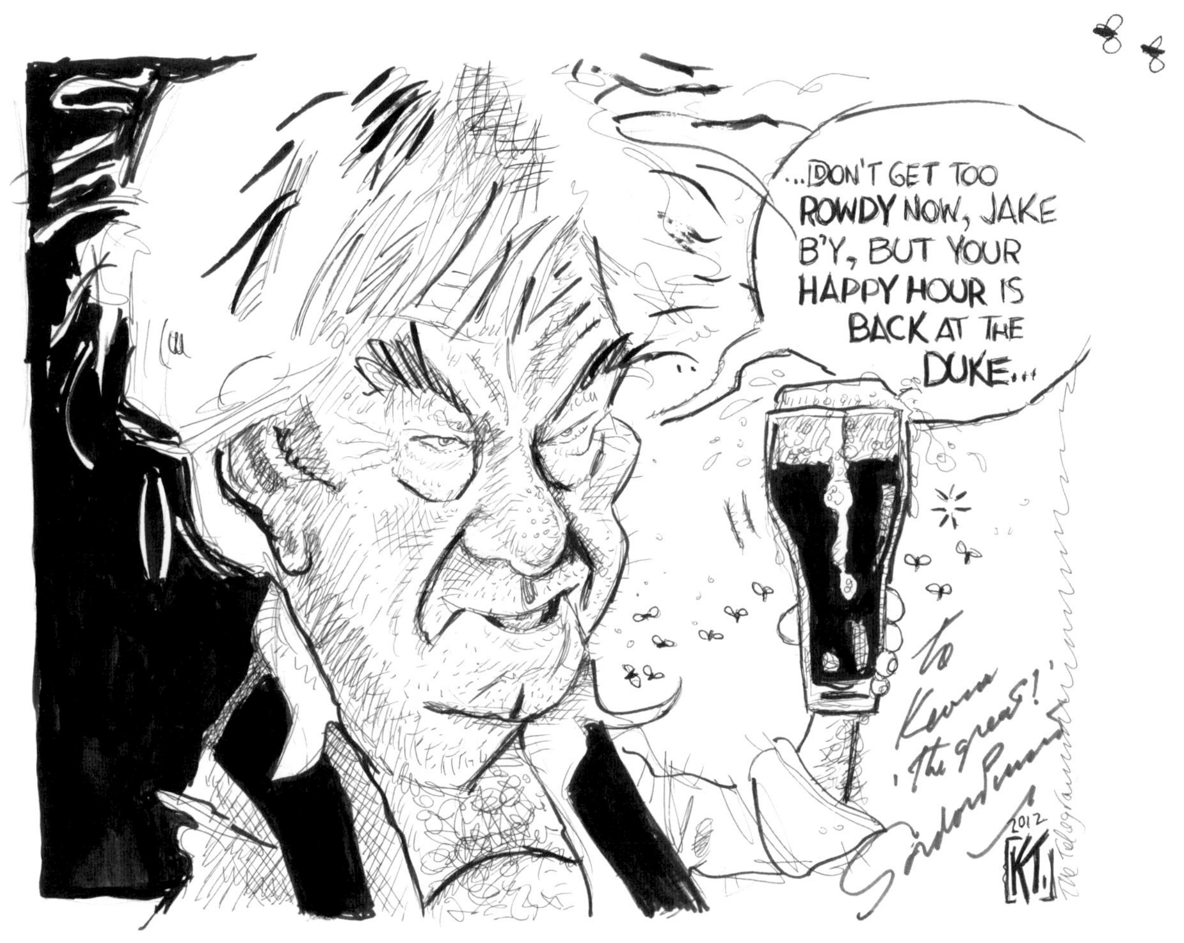

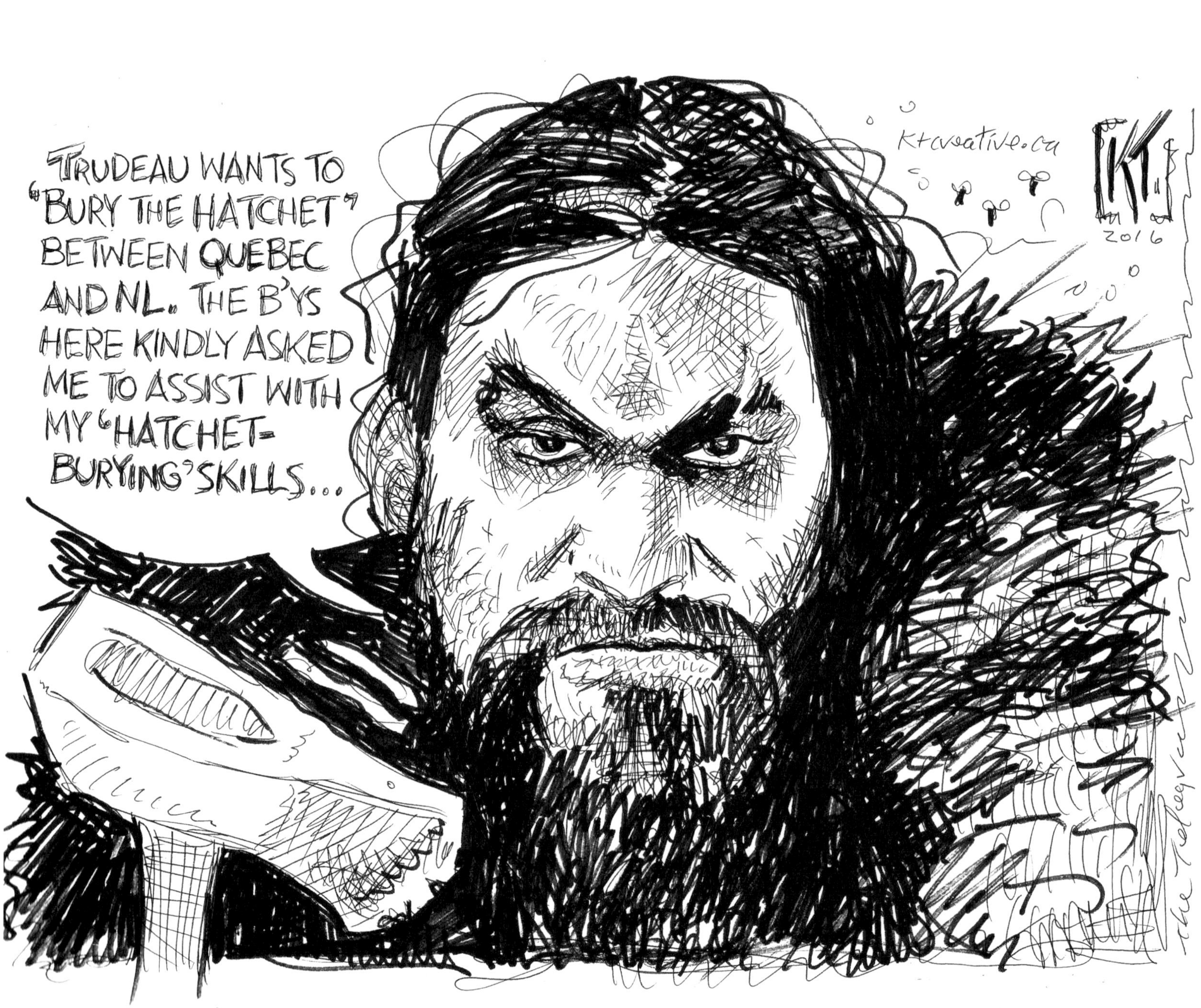

TRUDEAU WANTS TO "BURY THE HATCHET" BETWEEN QUEBEC AND NL. THE B'YS HERE KINDLY ASKED ME TO ASSIST WITH MY "HATCHET-BURYING" SKILLS...
ktcreative.ca
KT
2016
The Telegram

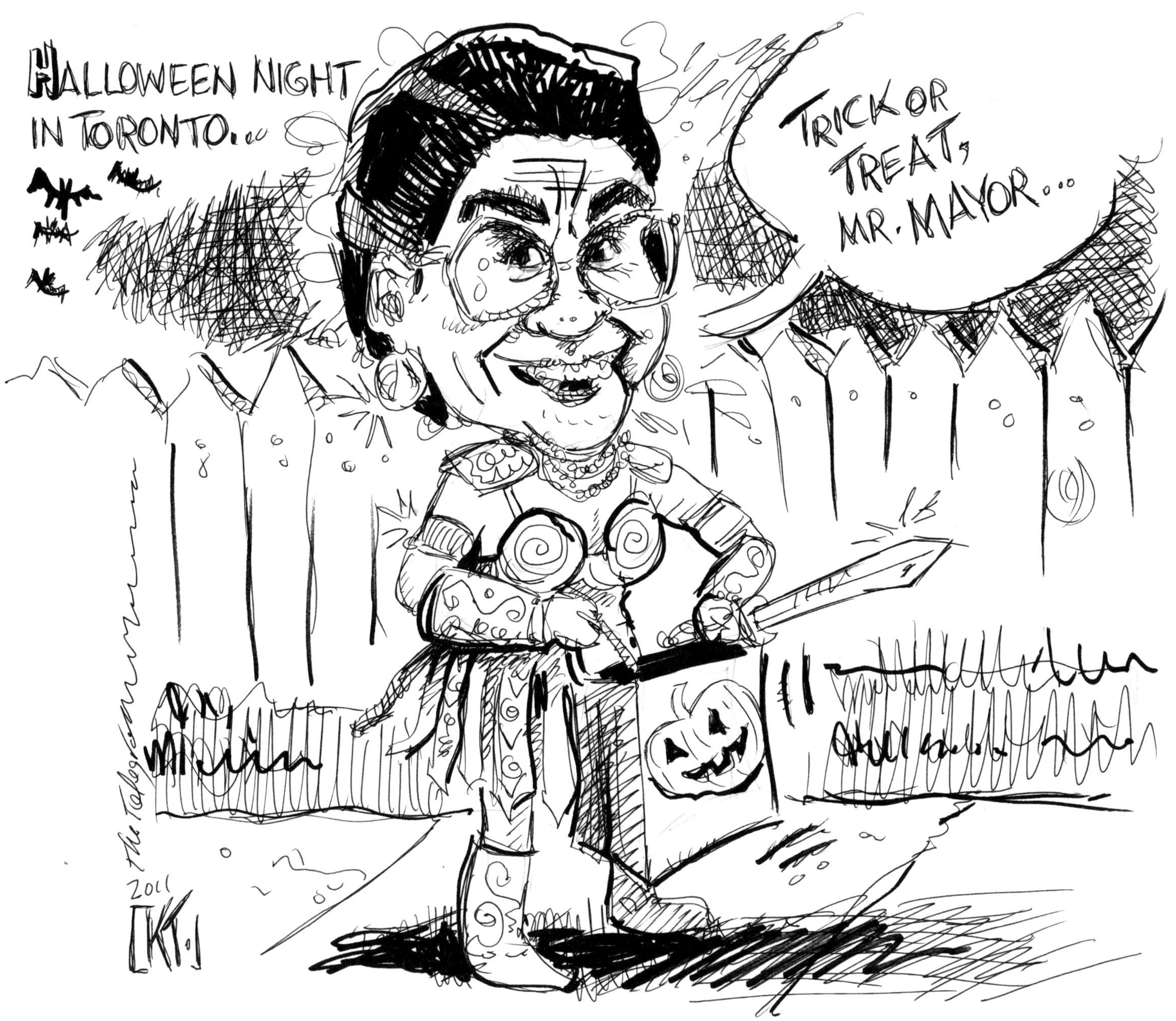

HALLOWEEN NIGHT IN TORONTO...
TRICK OR TREAT, MR. MAYOR...
The Tolorgram
2011

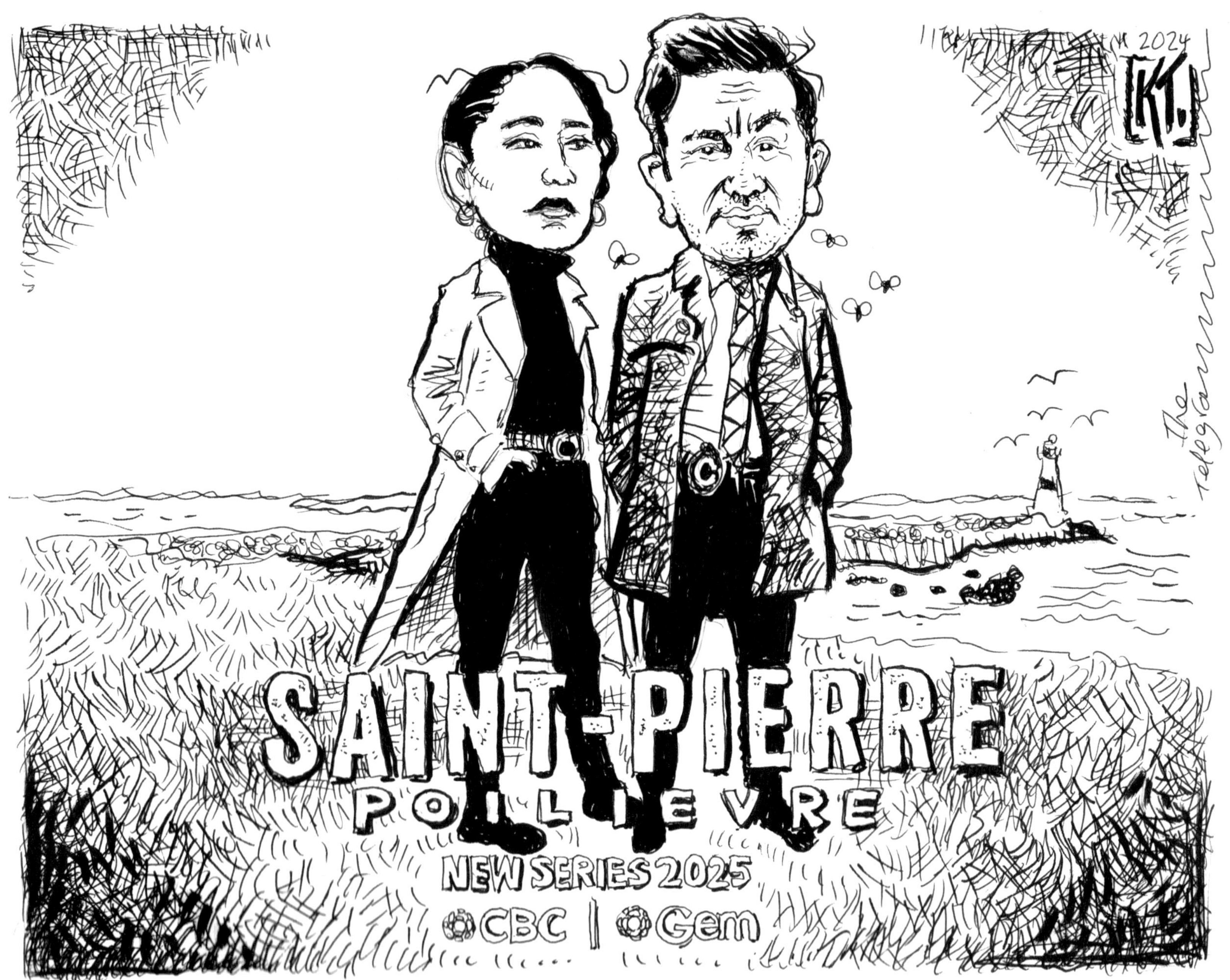
2024
SAINT-PIERRE
POILIEVRE
NEW SERIES 2025
CBC | Gem
The Telegram

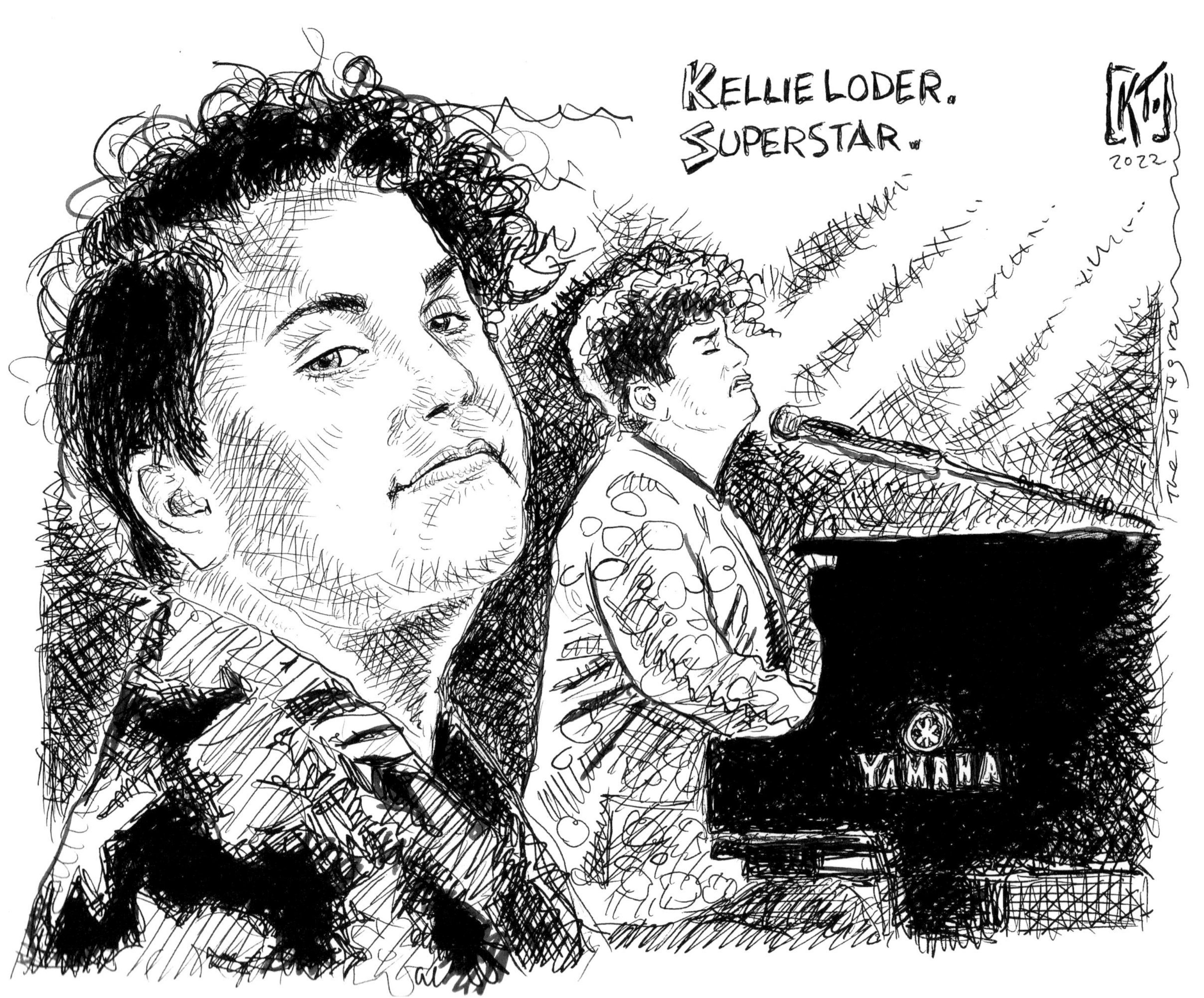
KELLIE LODER,
SUPERSTAR.
[KT]
2022
YAMAHA

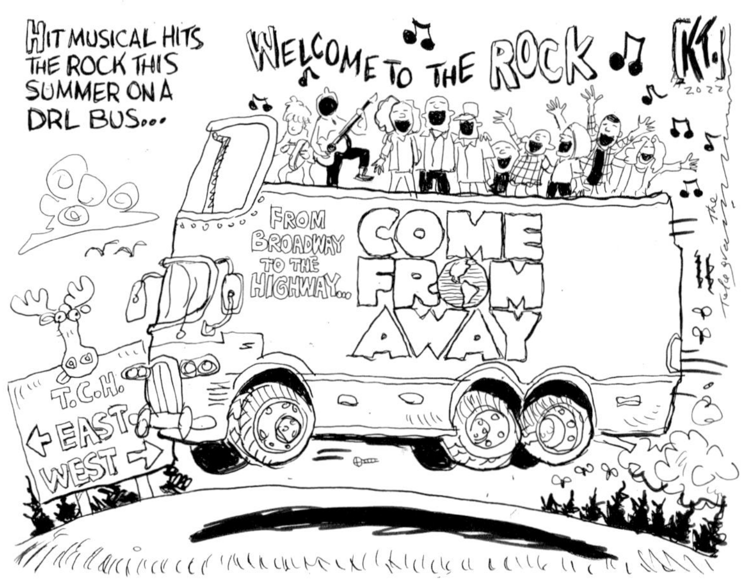

HIT MUSICAL HITS THE ROCK THIS SUMMER ON A DRL BUS...
WELCOME TO THE ROCK
FROM BROADWAY TO THE HIGHWAY...
COME FROM AWAY
T.C.H.
EAST
WEST


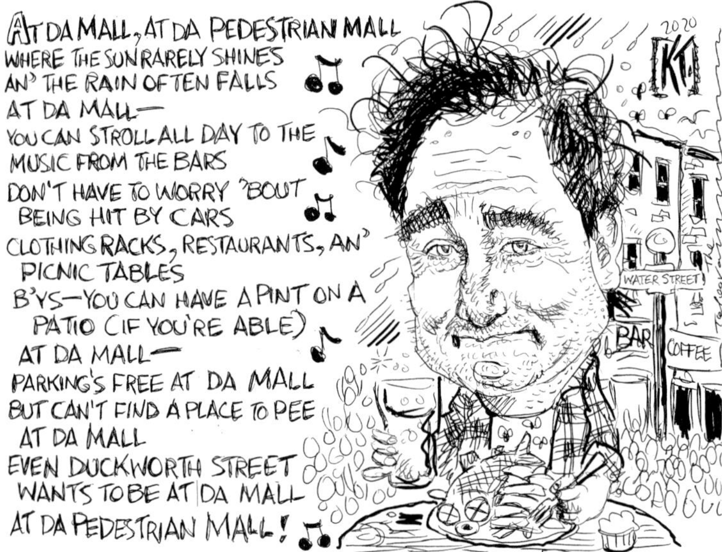

AT DA MALL, AT DA PEDESTRIAN MALL
WHERE THE SUN RARELY SHINES
AN' THE RAIN OFTEN FALLS
AT DA MALL—
YOU CAN STROLL ALL DAY TO THE
MUSIC FROM THE BARS
DON'T HAVE TO WORRY 'BOUT
BEING HIT BY CARS
CLOTHING RACKS, RESTAURANTS, AN'
PICNIC TABLES
B'YS—YOU CAN HAVE A PINT ON A
PATIO (IF YOU'RE ABLE)
AT DA MALL—
PARKING'S FREE AT DA MALL
BUT CAN'T FIND A PLACE TO PEE
AT DA MALL
EVEN DUCKWORTH STREET
WANTS TO BE AT DA MALL
AT DA PEDESTRIAN MALL!
WATER STREET
BAR
COFFEE

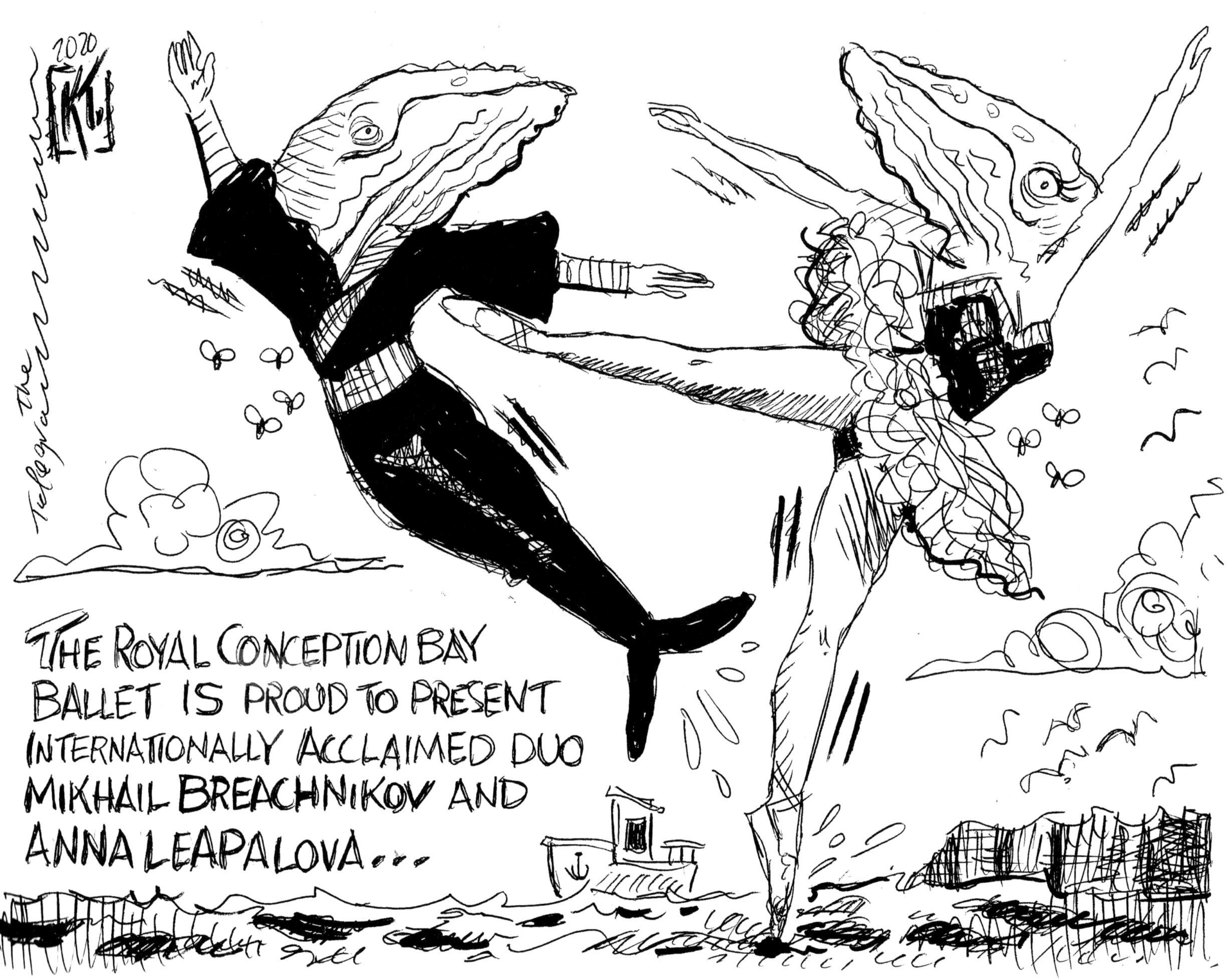

The Royal Conception Bay
Ballet is proud to present
Internationally Acclaimed Duo
Mikhail Breachnikov and
Anna Leapalova...

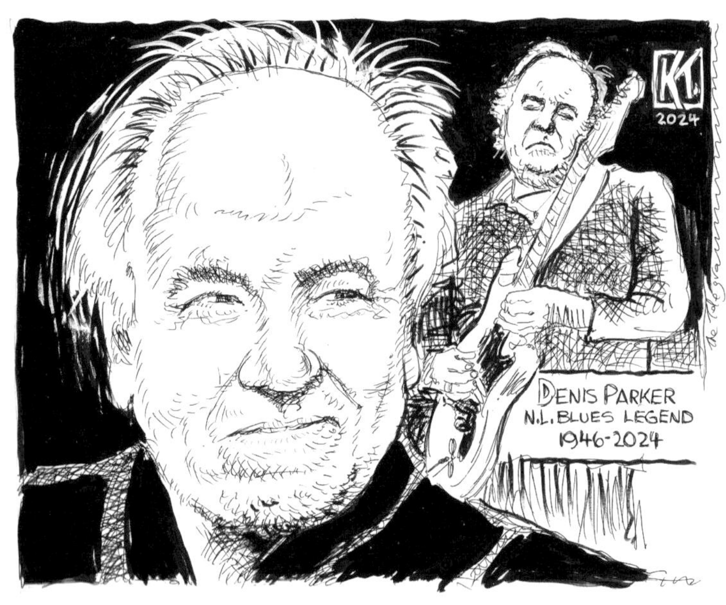
DENIS PARKER
N.L. BLUES LEGEND
1946-2024
KT
2024

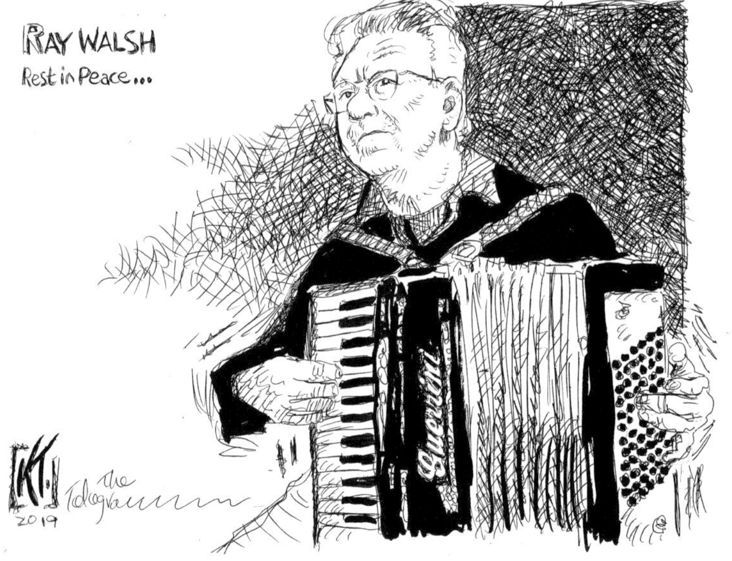
RAY WALSH
Rest in Peace...
KT
2019

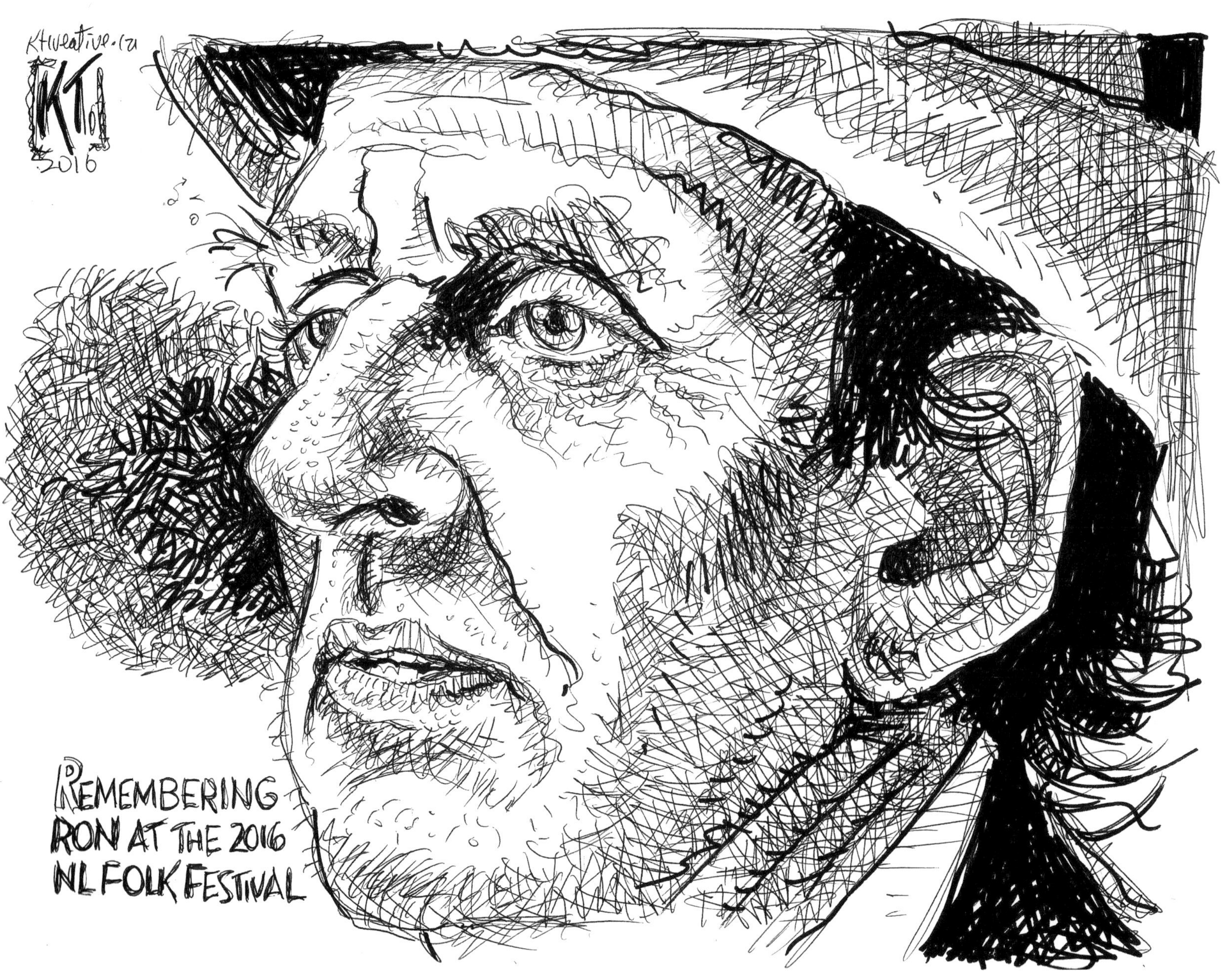

KTKreative.'21
KT
2016
REMEMBERING
RON AT THE 2016
NL FOLK FESTIVAL

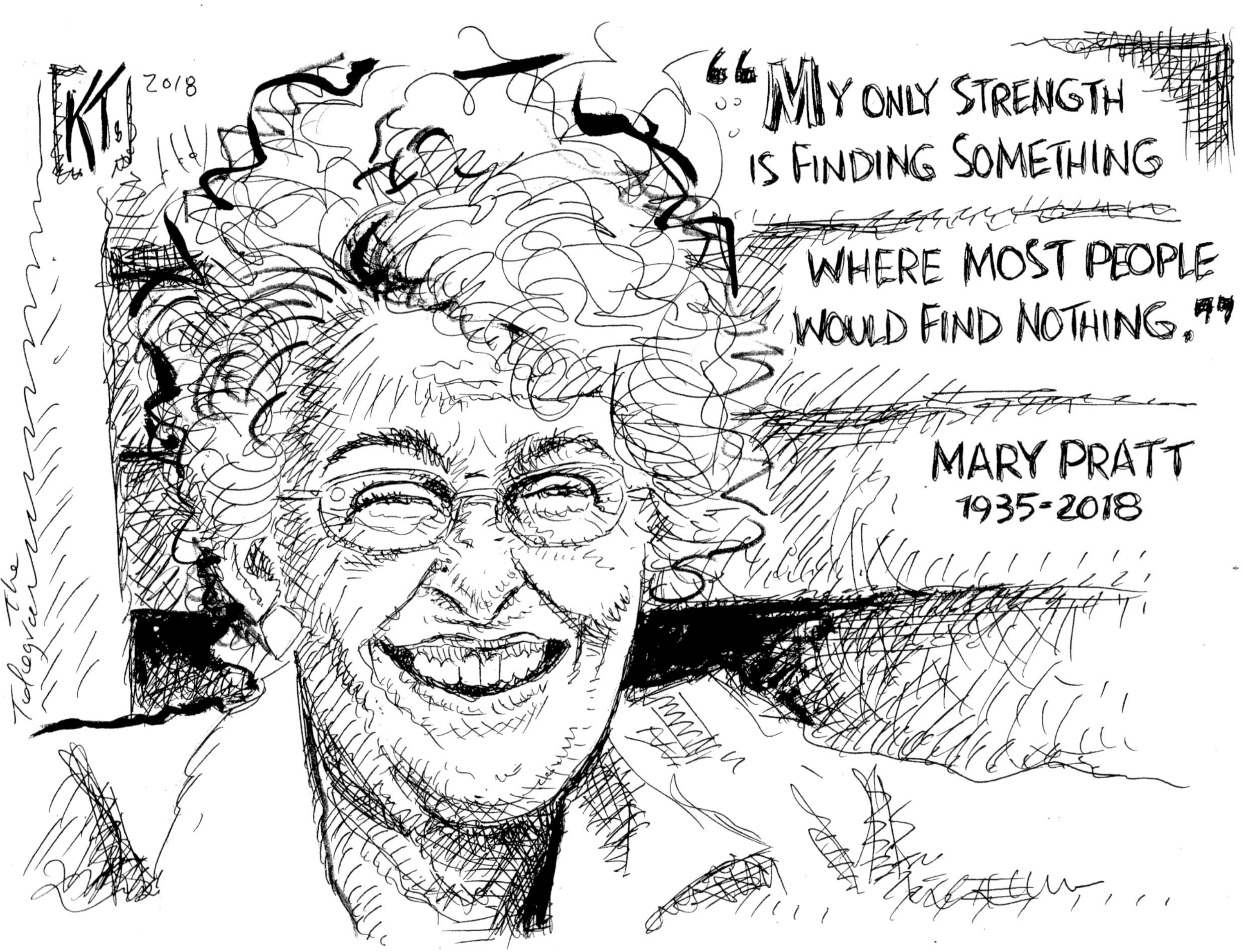

KT 2018
My only strength is finding something
where most people would find nothing.
Mary Pratt
1935-2018
The Telegram

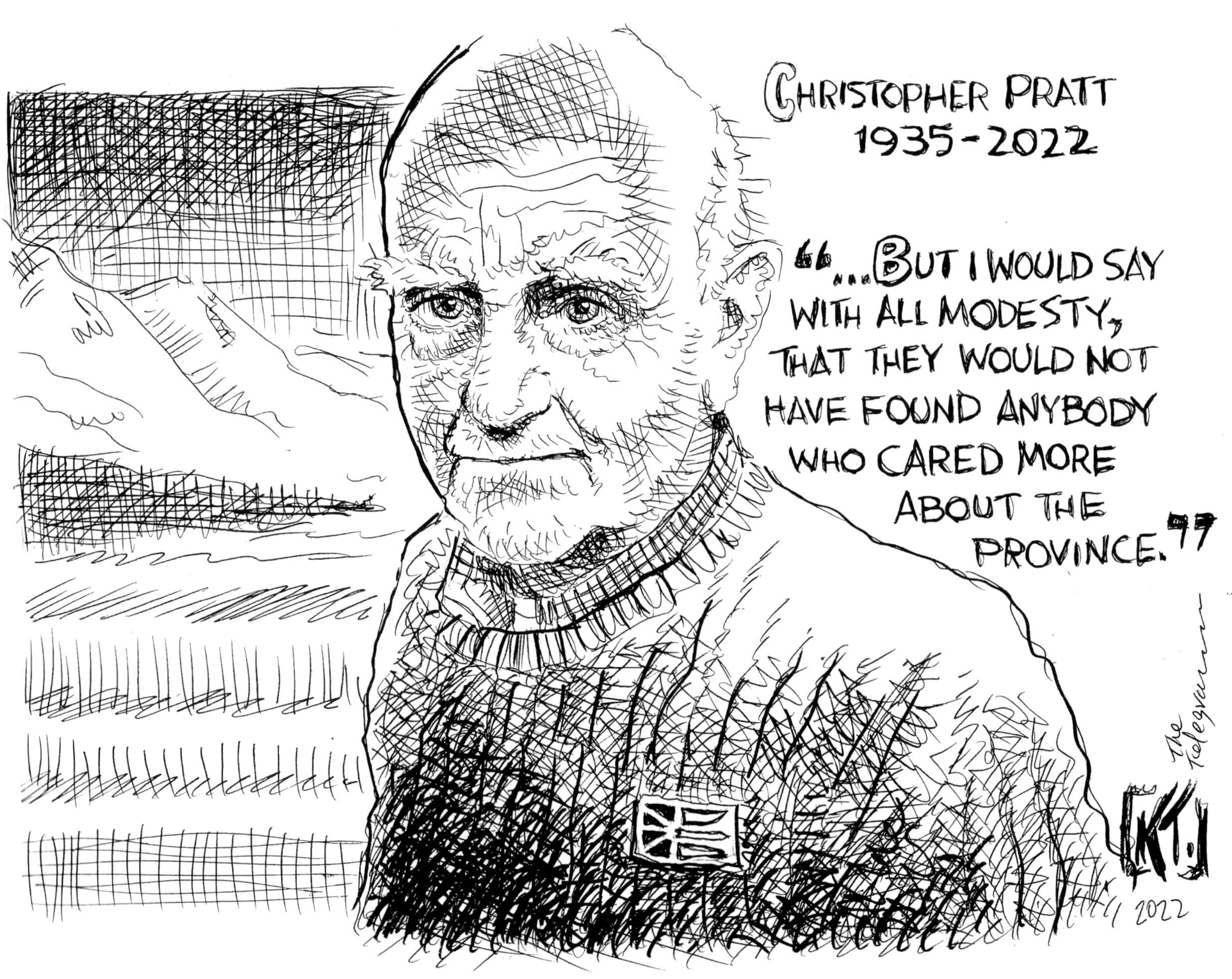

CHRISTOPHER PRATT
1935-2022

"...BUT I WOULD SAY WITH ALL MODESTY, THAT THEY WOULD NOT HAVE FOUND ANYBODY WHO CARED MORE ABOUT THE PROVINCE."

The Telegram

2022

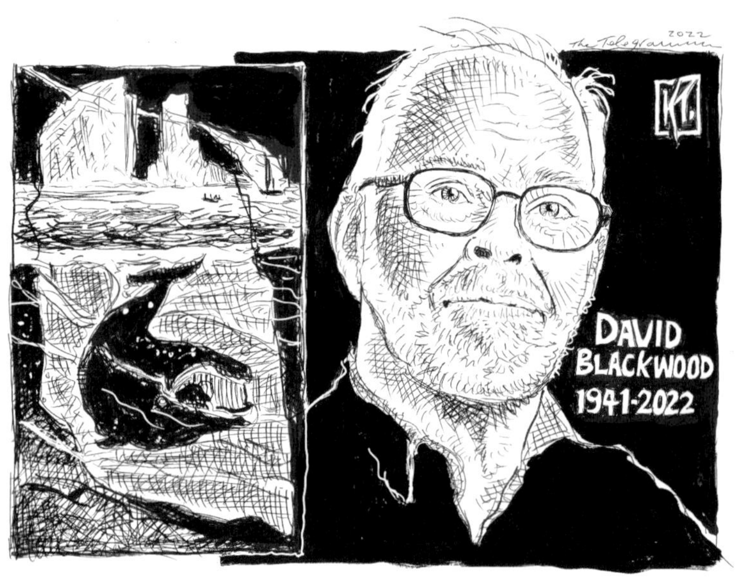

DAVID
BLACKWOOD
1941-2022


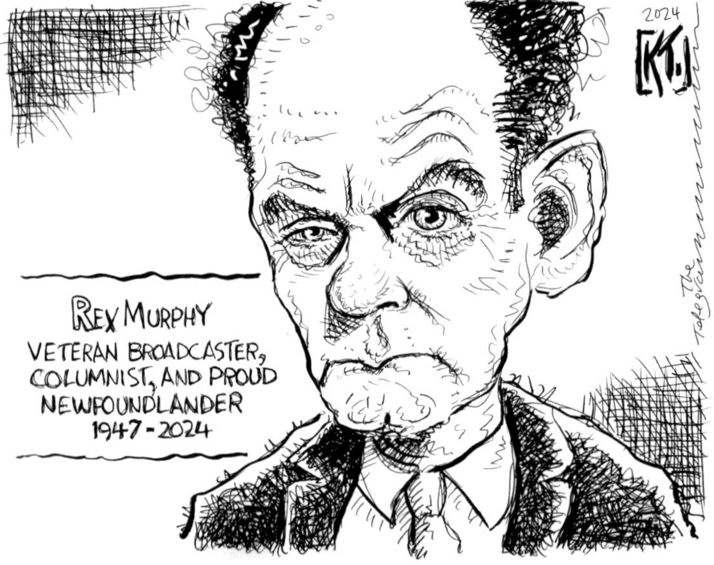

REX MURPHY
VETERAN BROADCASTER,
COLUMNIST, AND PROUD
NEWFOUNDLANDER
1947 - 2024

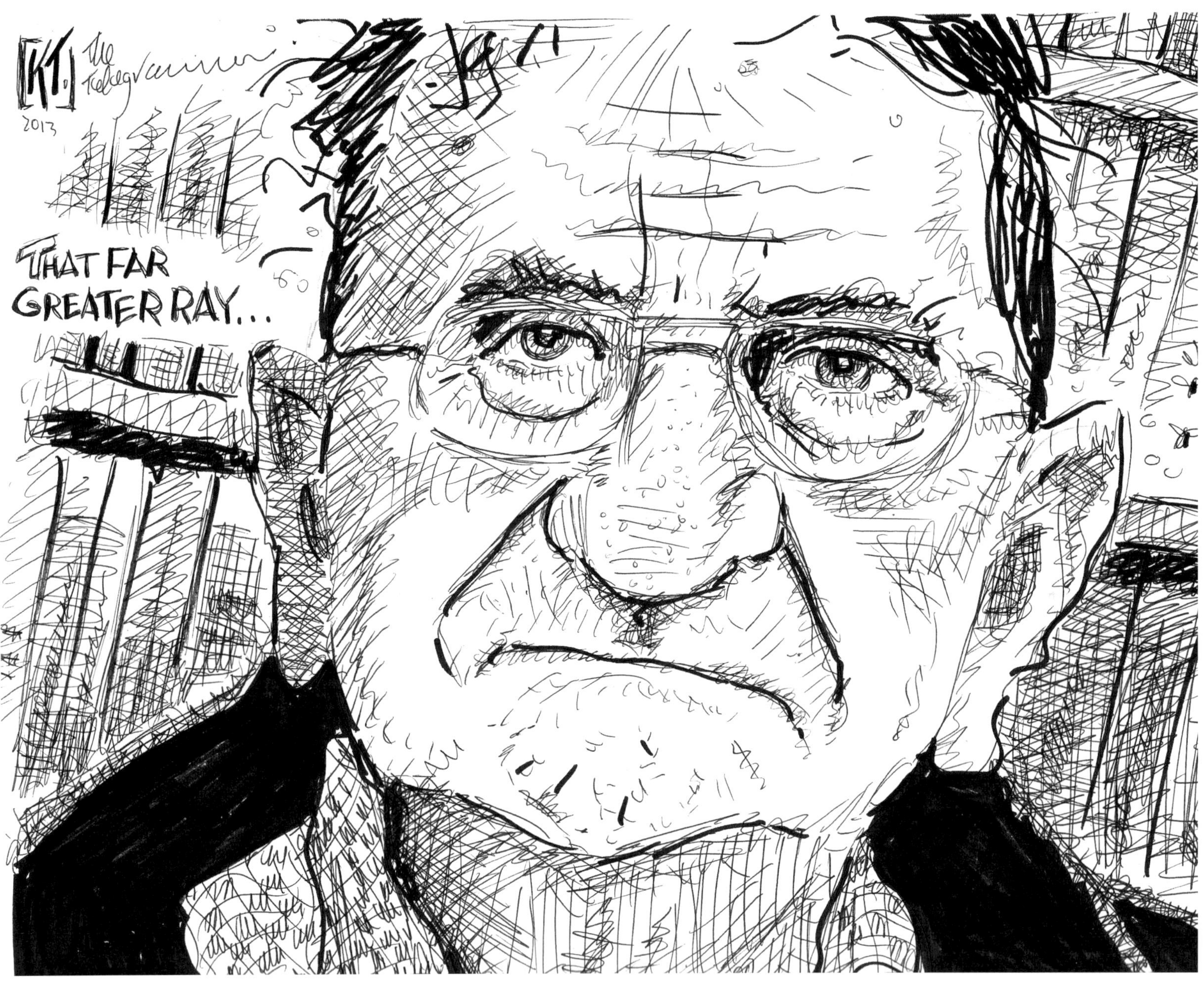

THAT FAR GREATER RAY...
2013

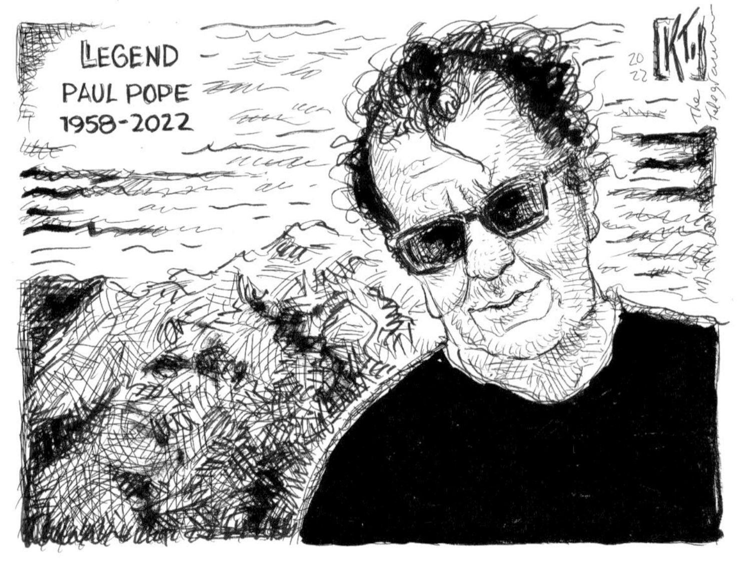
LEGEND
PAUL POPE
1958-2022

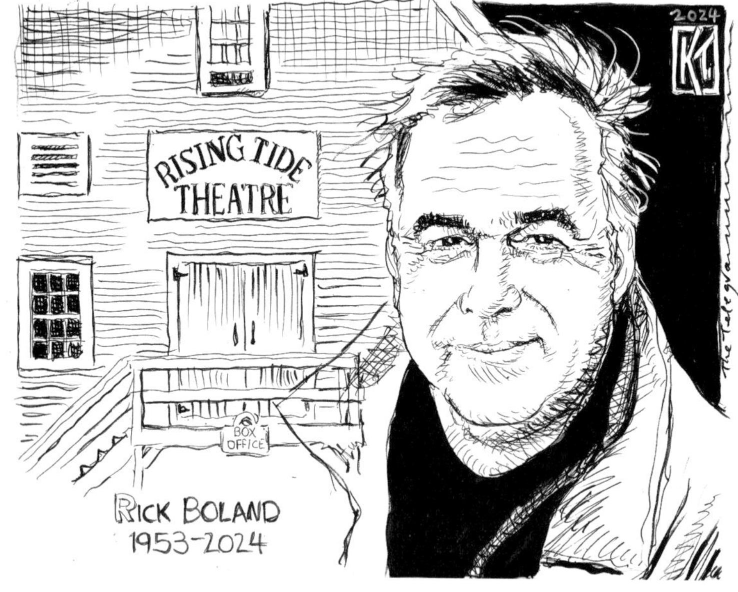
2024
RISING TIDE
THEATRE
BOX
OFFICE
RICK BOLAND
1953-2024

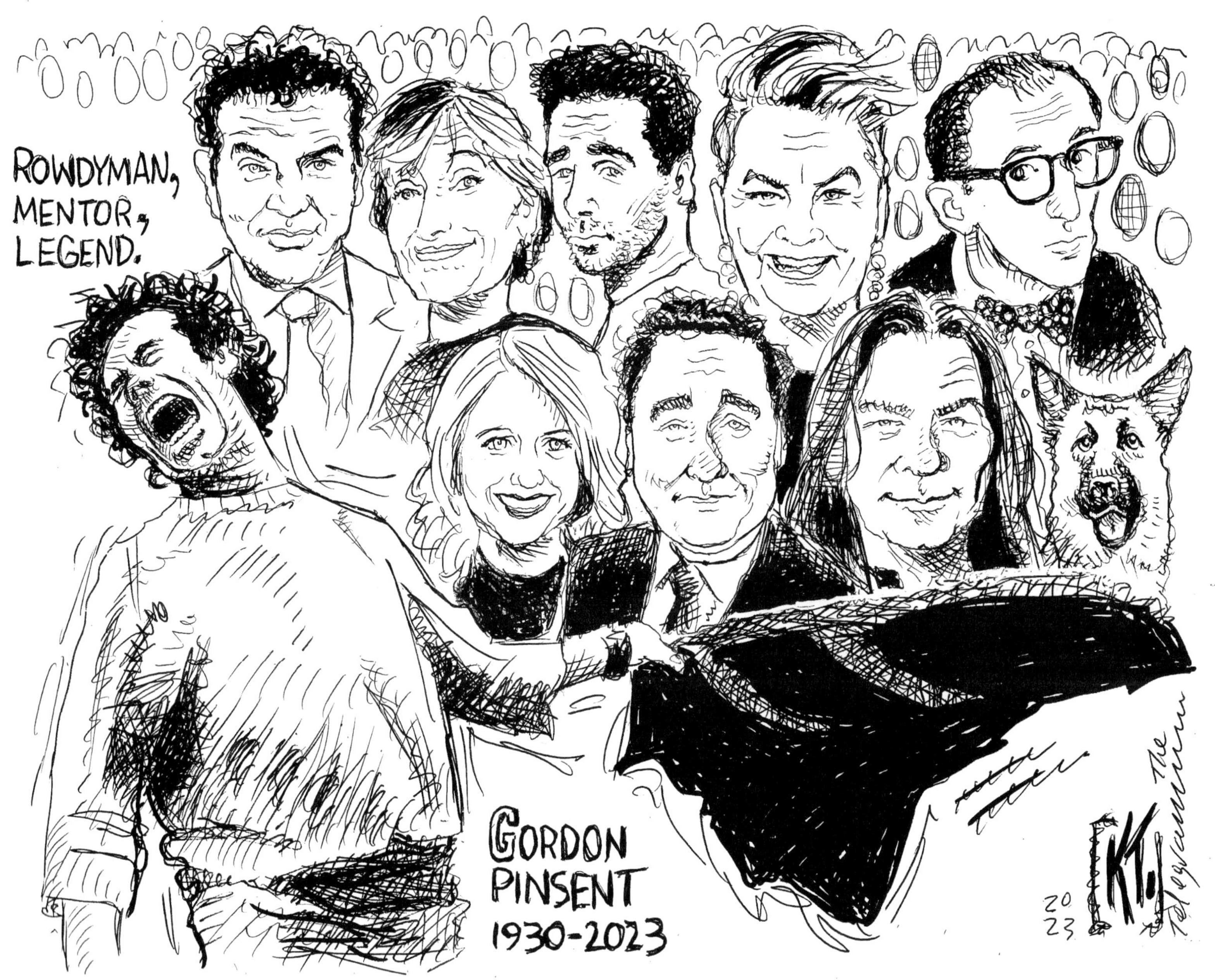

ROWDYMAN, MENTOR, LEGEND.
GORDON PINSENT 1930-2023

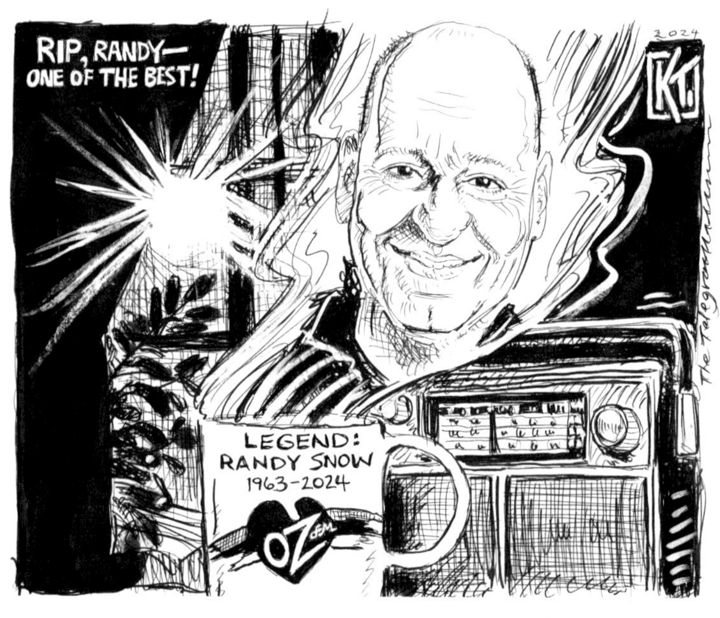
RIP, RANDY—
ONE OF THE BEST!
LEGEND:
RANDY SNOW
1963-2024
OZ.fm
The Telegram

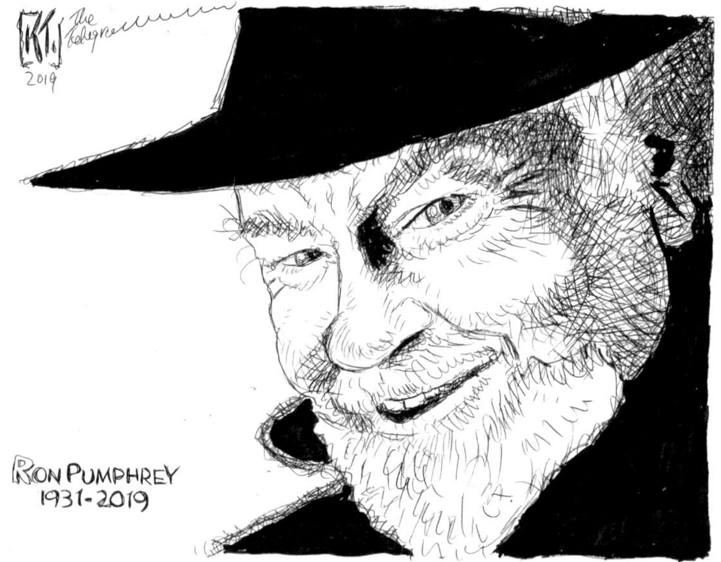
The Telegram
2019
RON PUMPHREY
1931-2019

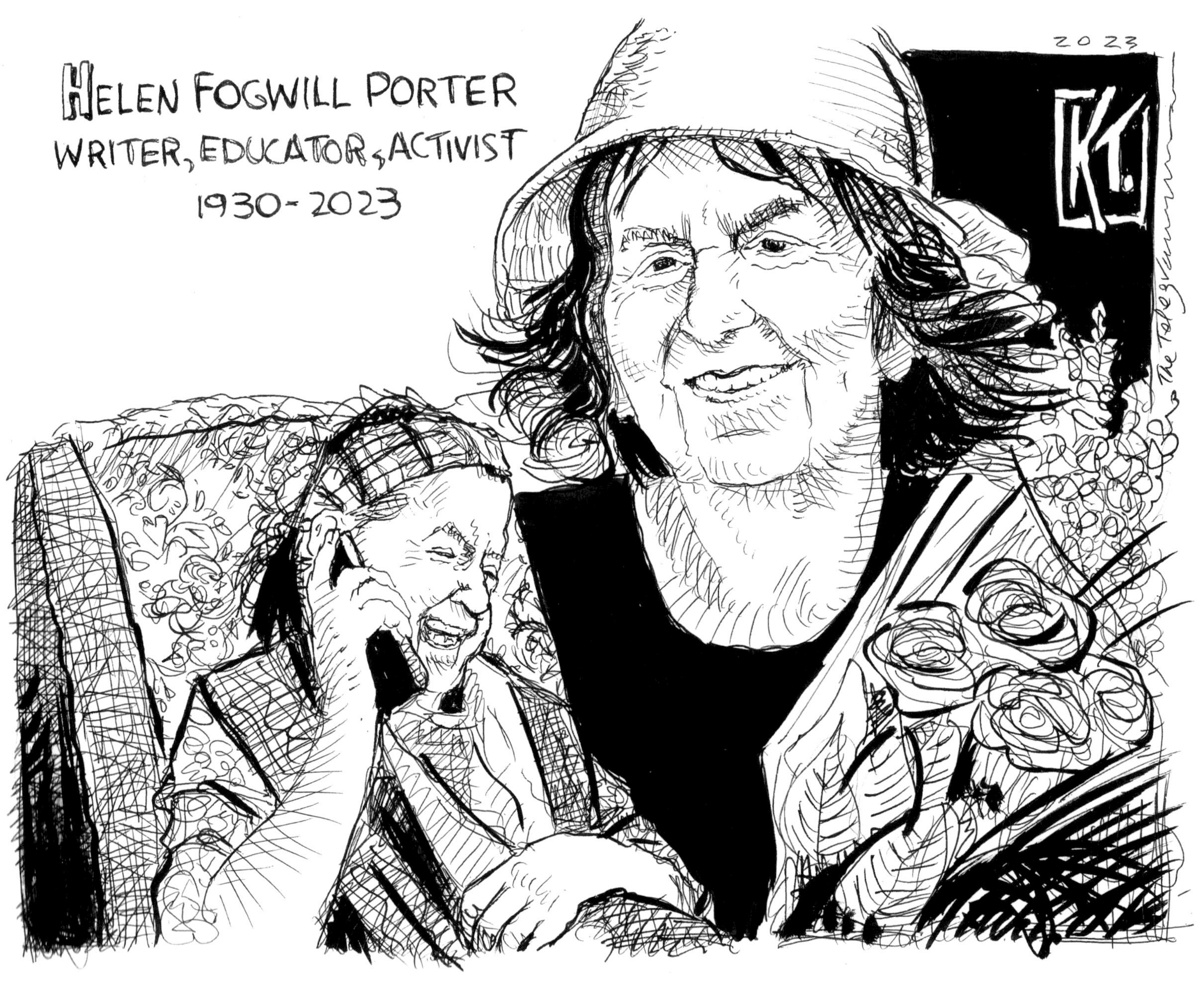
HELEN FOGWILL PORTER
WRITER, EDUCATOR, ACTIVIST
1930-2023
2023

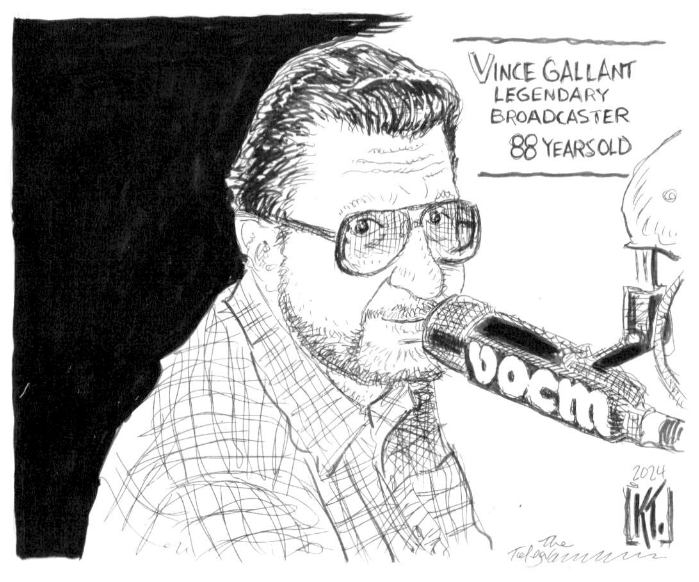

VINCE GALLANT
LEGENDARY
BROADCASTER
88 YEARS OLD
VOCM
2024


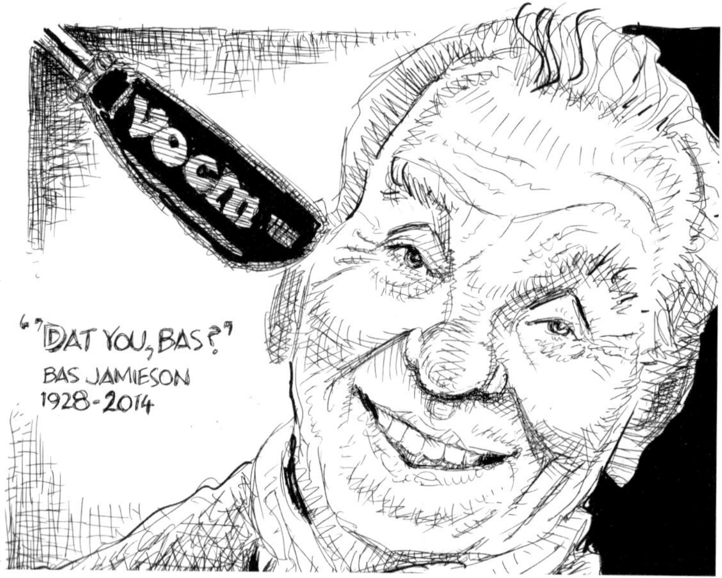

VOCM
" DAT YOU, BAS?"
BAS JAMIESON
1928 - 2014

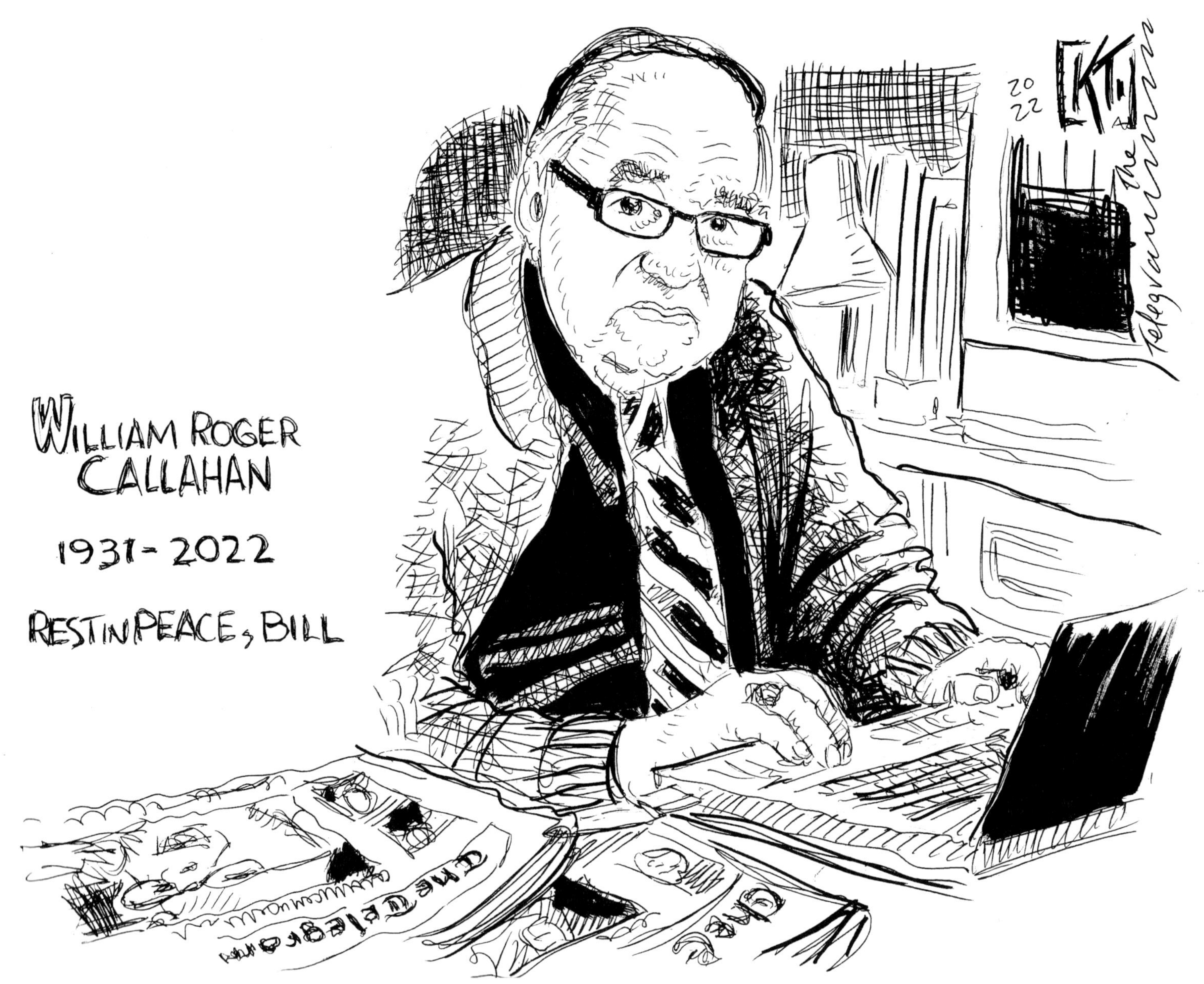
William Roger
Callahan

1931 - 2022

Rest in Peace, Bill

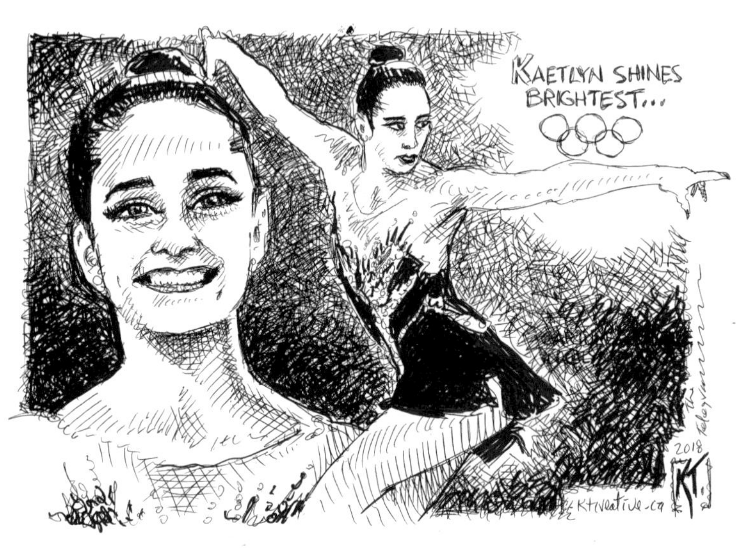
KAETLYN SHINES
BRIGHTEST...
2018

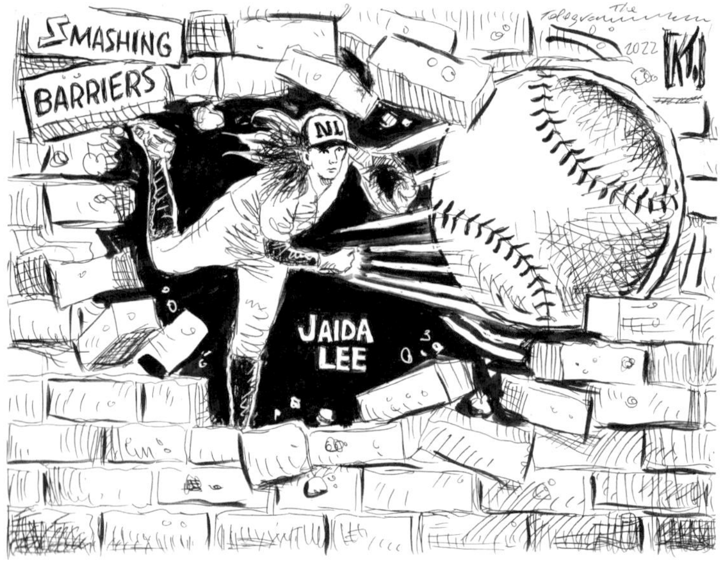
SMASHING
BARRIERS
NL
JAIDA
LEE
2022

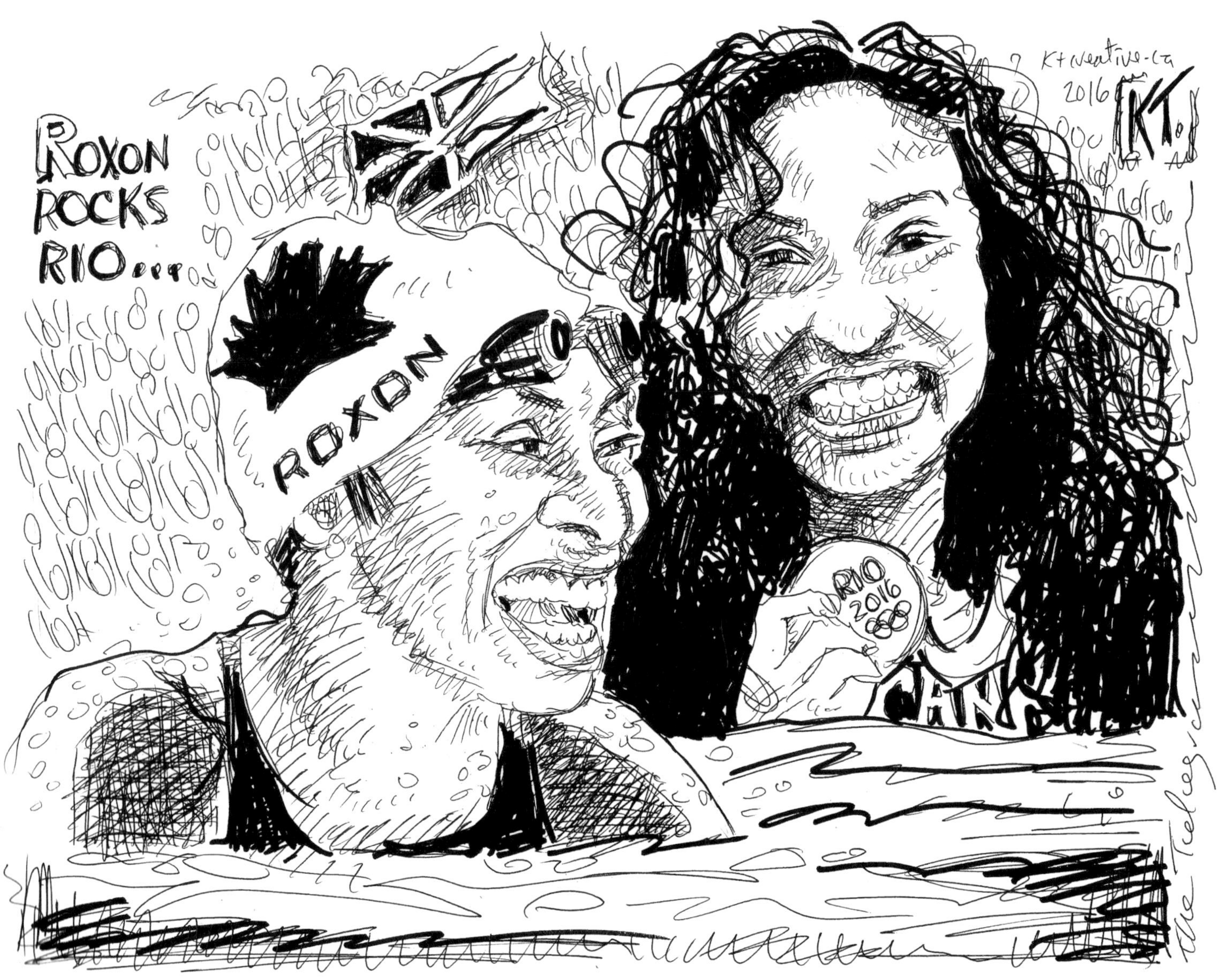

ROXON
ROCKS
RIO...
ROXON
RIO 2016
CANA
KtNeative.ca
2016
KT

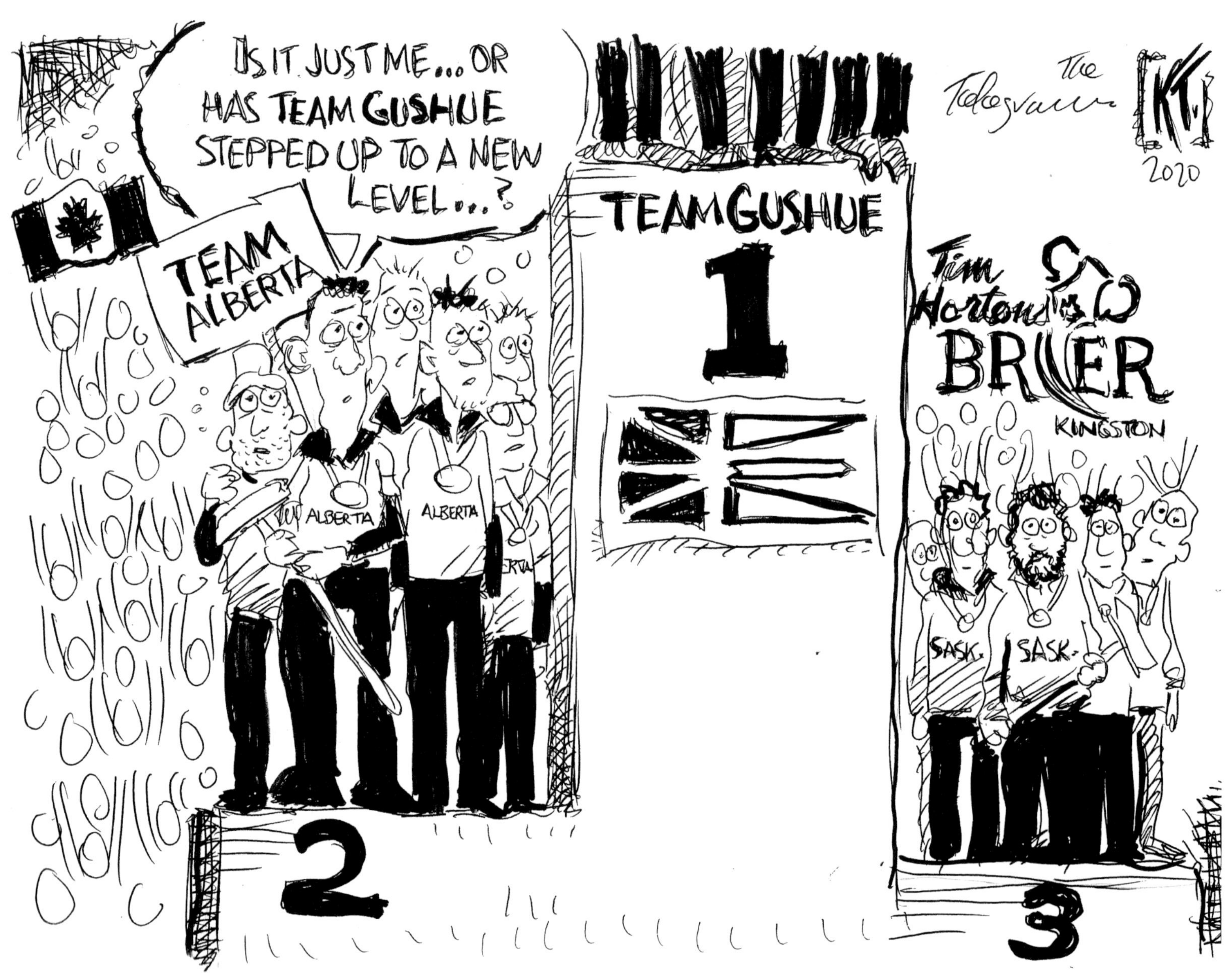
IS IT JUST ME... OR HAS TEAM GUSHUE STEPPED UP TO A NEW LEVEL...?
TEAM ALBERTA
The Telegram
KT
2020
TEAM GUSHUE
1
Tim Horton's
BRIER
KINGSTON
ALBERTA
ALBERTA
2
SASK.
SASK.
3

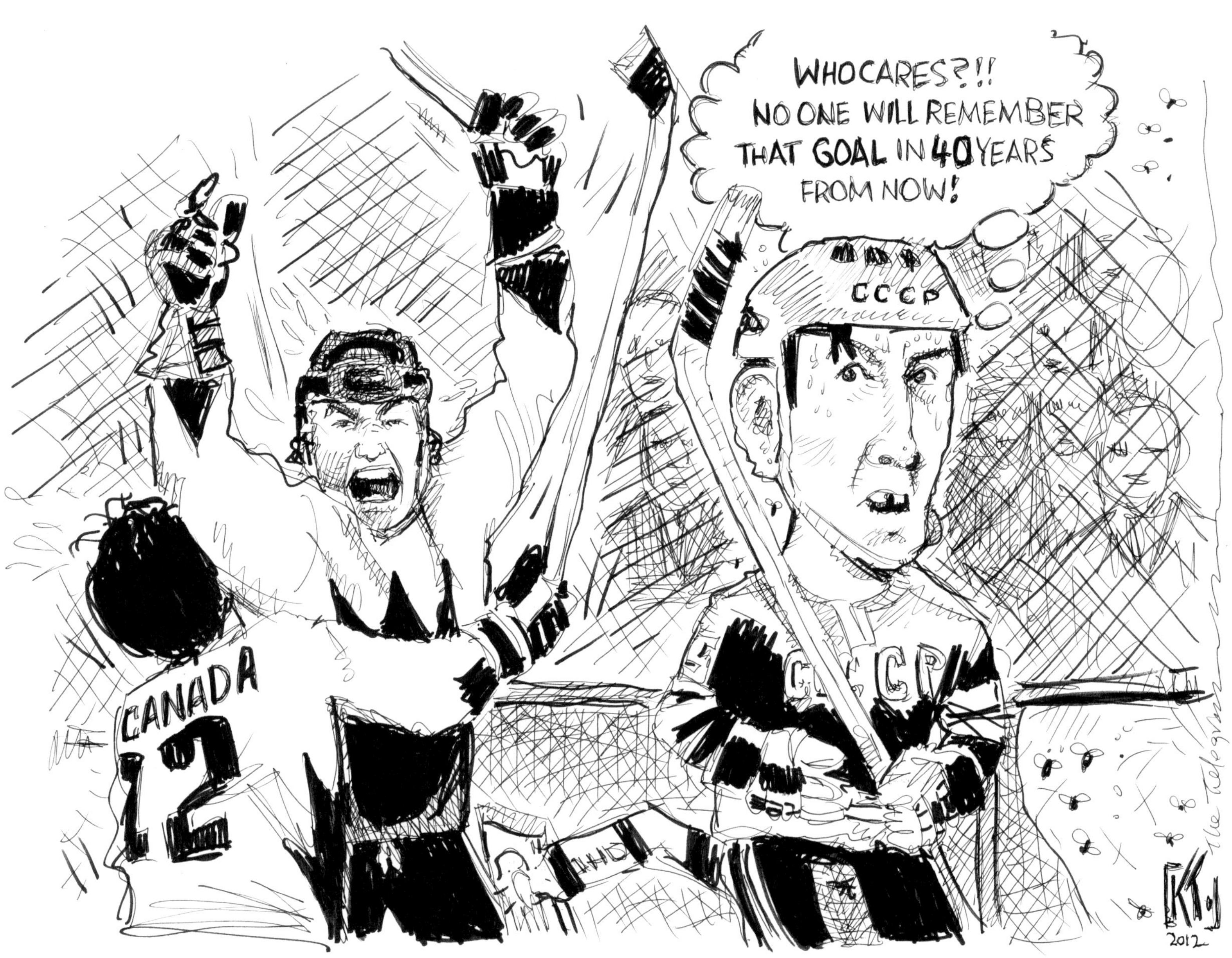

WHO CARES?!! NO ONE WILL REMEMBER THAT GOAL IN 40 YEARS FROM NOW!
CCCP
CANADA 12
CCCP
2012

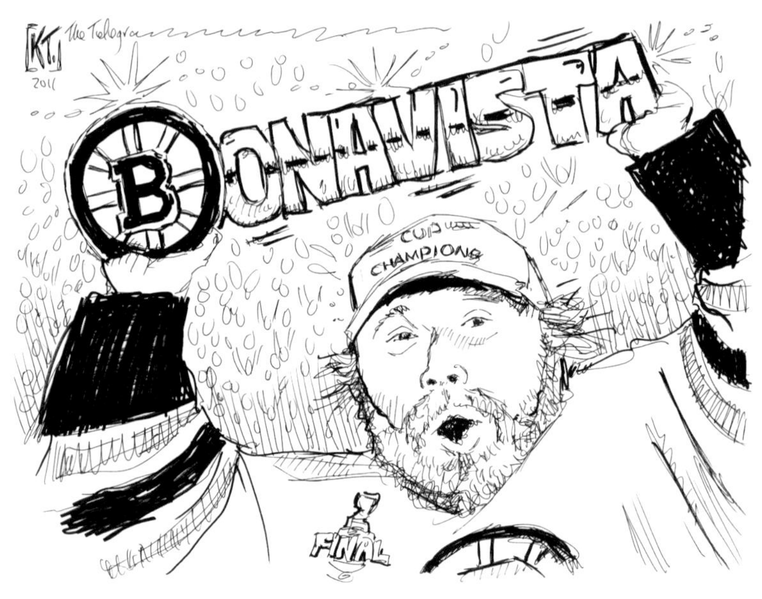
The Telegram
2011
BONAVISTA
CUP
CHAMPIONS
FINAL

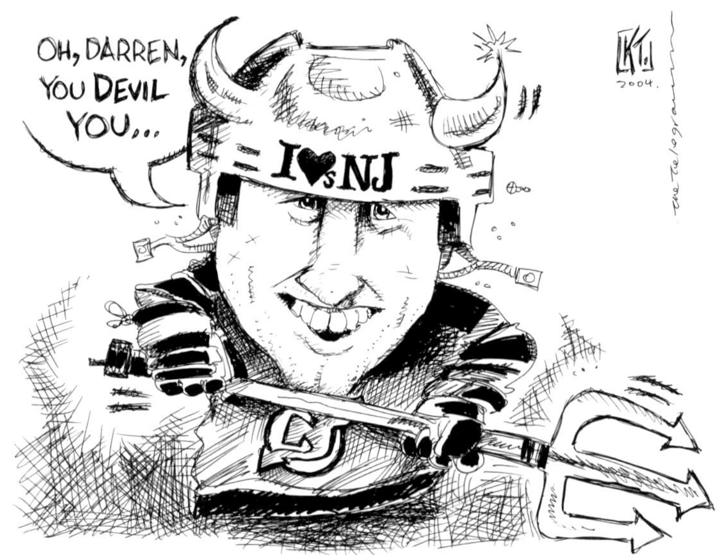
OH, DARREN,
YOU DEVIL
YOU...
I ♥s NJ
2004.

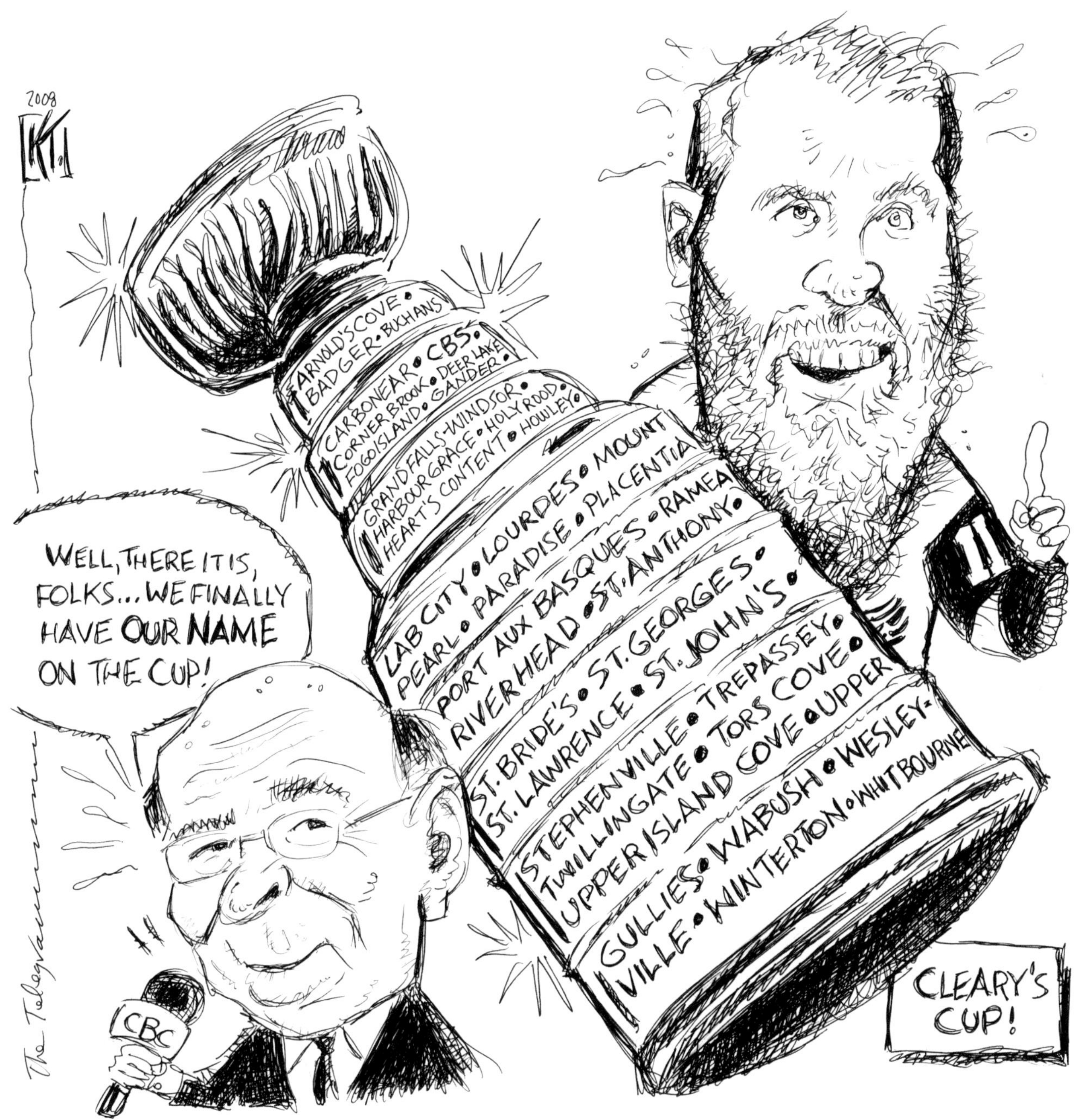

2008

WELL, THERE IT IS, FOLKS... WE FINALLY HAVE OUR NAME ON THE CUP!

CBC

ARNOLD'S COVE • BADGER • BUCHANS
CARBONEAR • CBS • CORNER BROOK • DEER LAKE • FOGO ISLAND • GANDER
GRAND FALLS-WINDSOR • HARBOUR GRACE • HOLYROOD • HEART'S CONTENT • HOWLEY
LAB CITY • LOURDES • MOUNT PEARL • PARADISE • PLACENTIA
PORT AUX BASQUES • RAMEA • RIVERHEAD • ST. ANTHONY
ST. BRIDE'S • ST. GEORGES • ST. LAWRENCE • ST. JOHN'S
STEPHENVILLE • TREPASSEY • TWILLINGATE • TORS COVE • UPPER ISLAND COVE • UPPER
GULLIES • WABUSH • WESLEY-VILLE • WINTERTON • WHITBOURNE

CLEARY'S CUP!

The Telegram

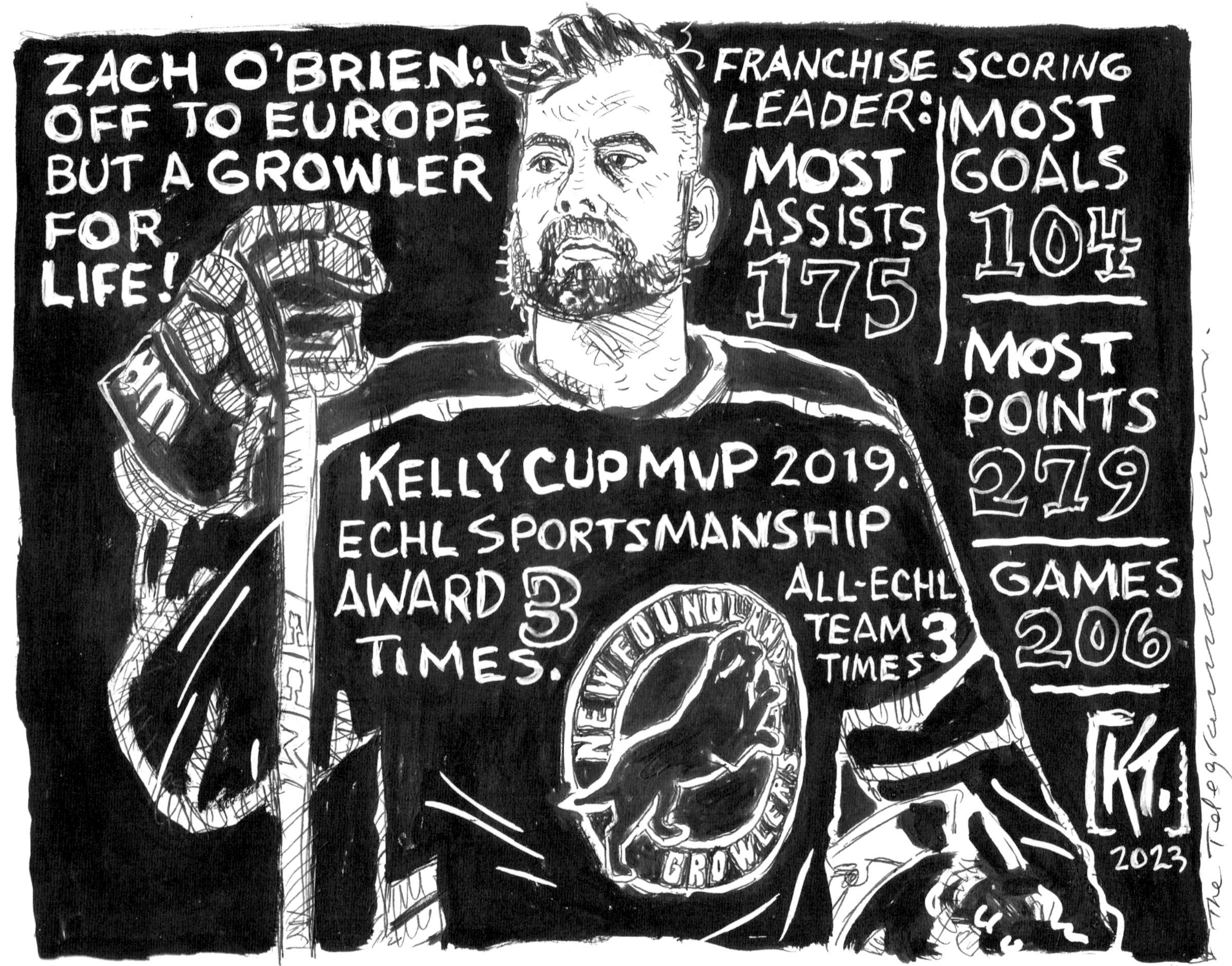

ZACH O'BRIEN: OFF TO EUROPE BUT A GROWLER FOR LIFE!
FRANCHISE SCORING LEADER:
MOST ASSISTS 175
MOST GOALS 104
MOST POINTS 279
GAMES 206
KELLY CUP MVP 2019.
ECHL SPORTSMANSHIP AWARD 3 TIMES.
ALL-ECHL TEAM 3 TIMES
NEWFOUNDLAND GROWLERS
KT.
2023
The Telegram

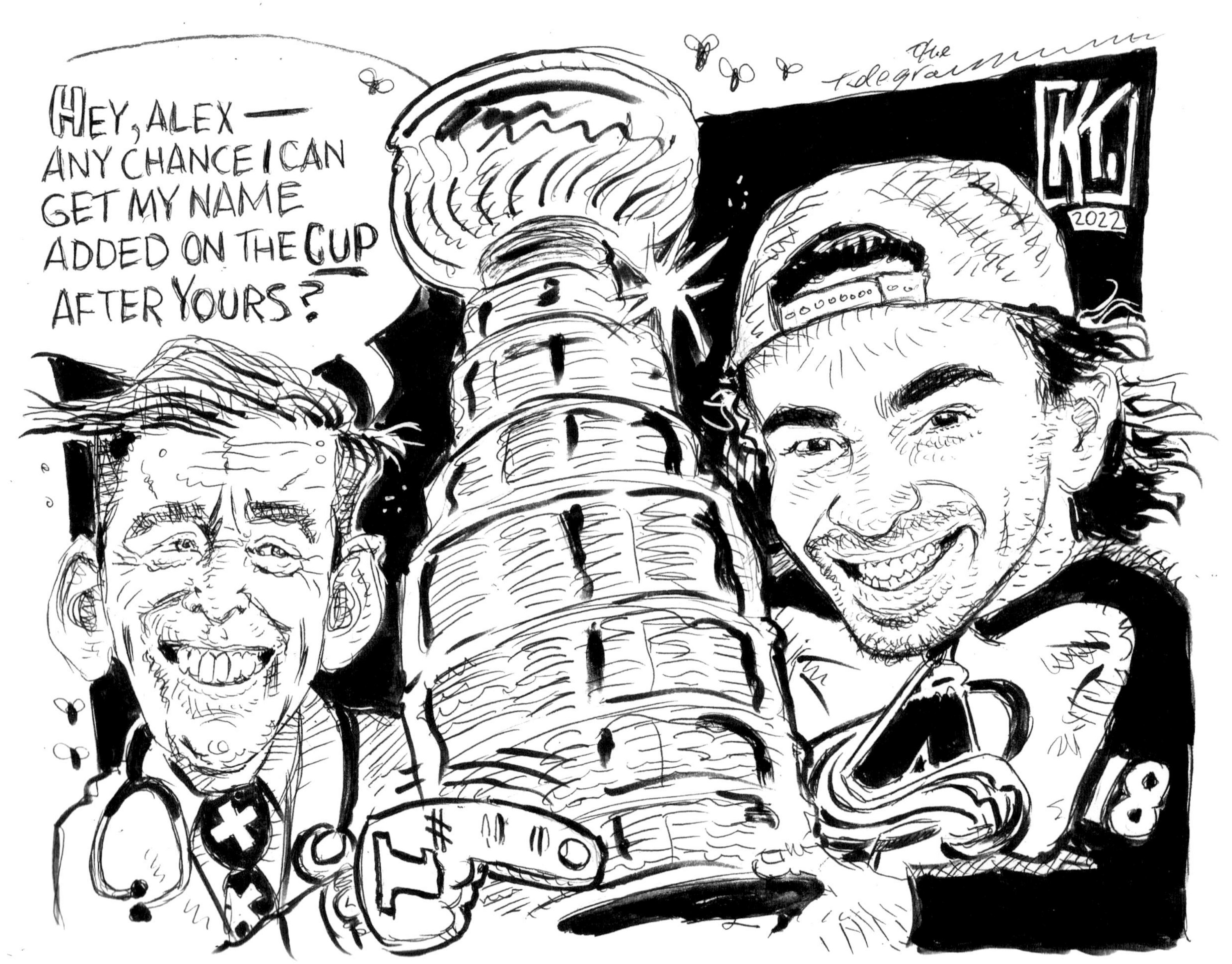

HEY, ALEX — ANY CHANCE I CAN GET MY NAME ADDED ON THE CUP AFTER YOURS?
the Telegram
2022
18

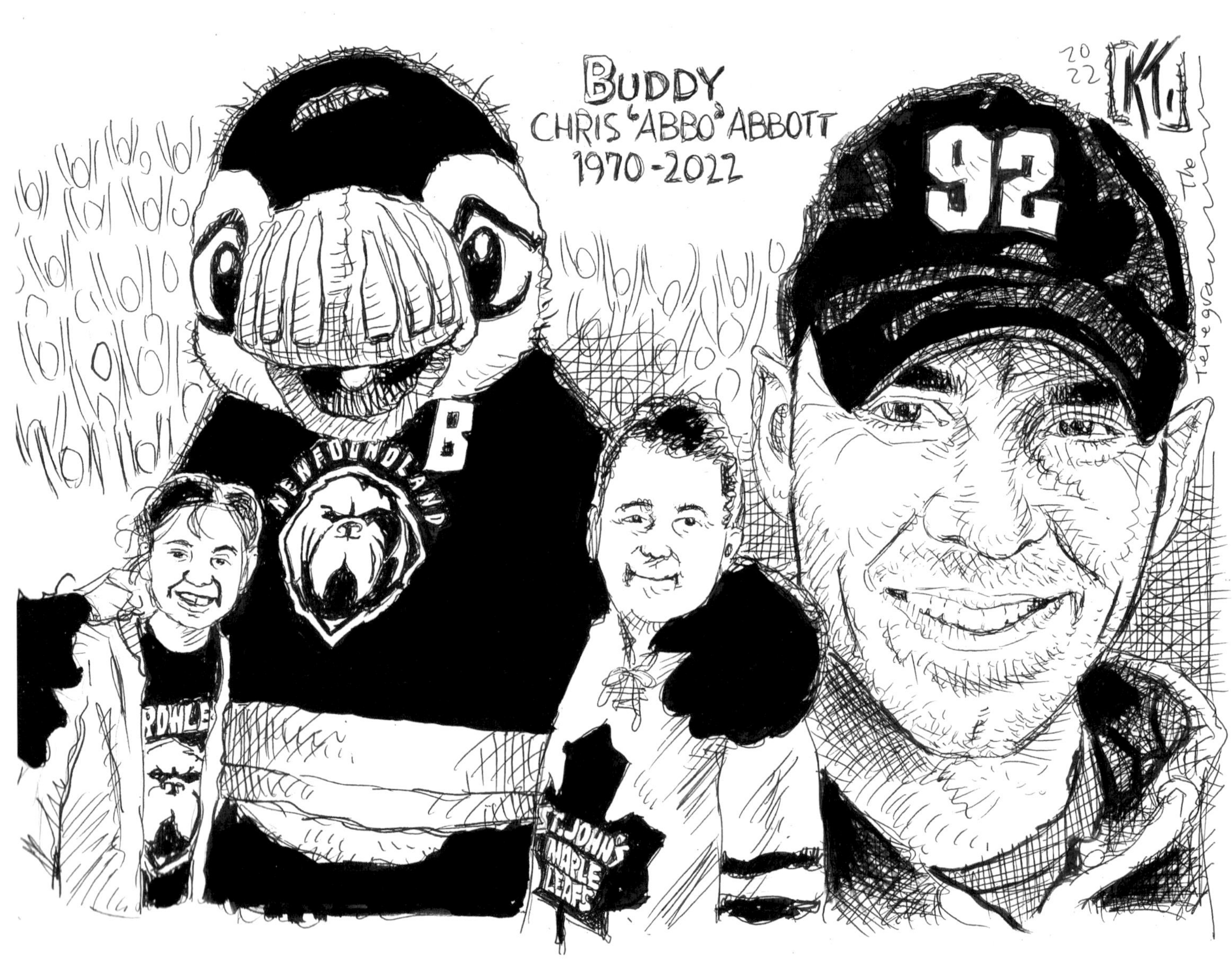
BUDDY
CHRIS 'ABBO' ABBOTT
1970 -2022
92
NEWFOUNDLAND
B
GROWLE
ST. JOHN'S MAPLE LEAFS
The telegram
2022

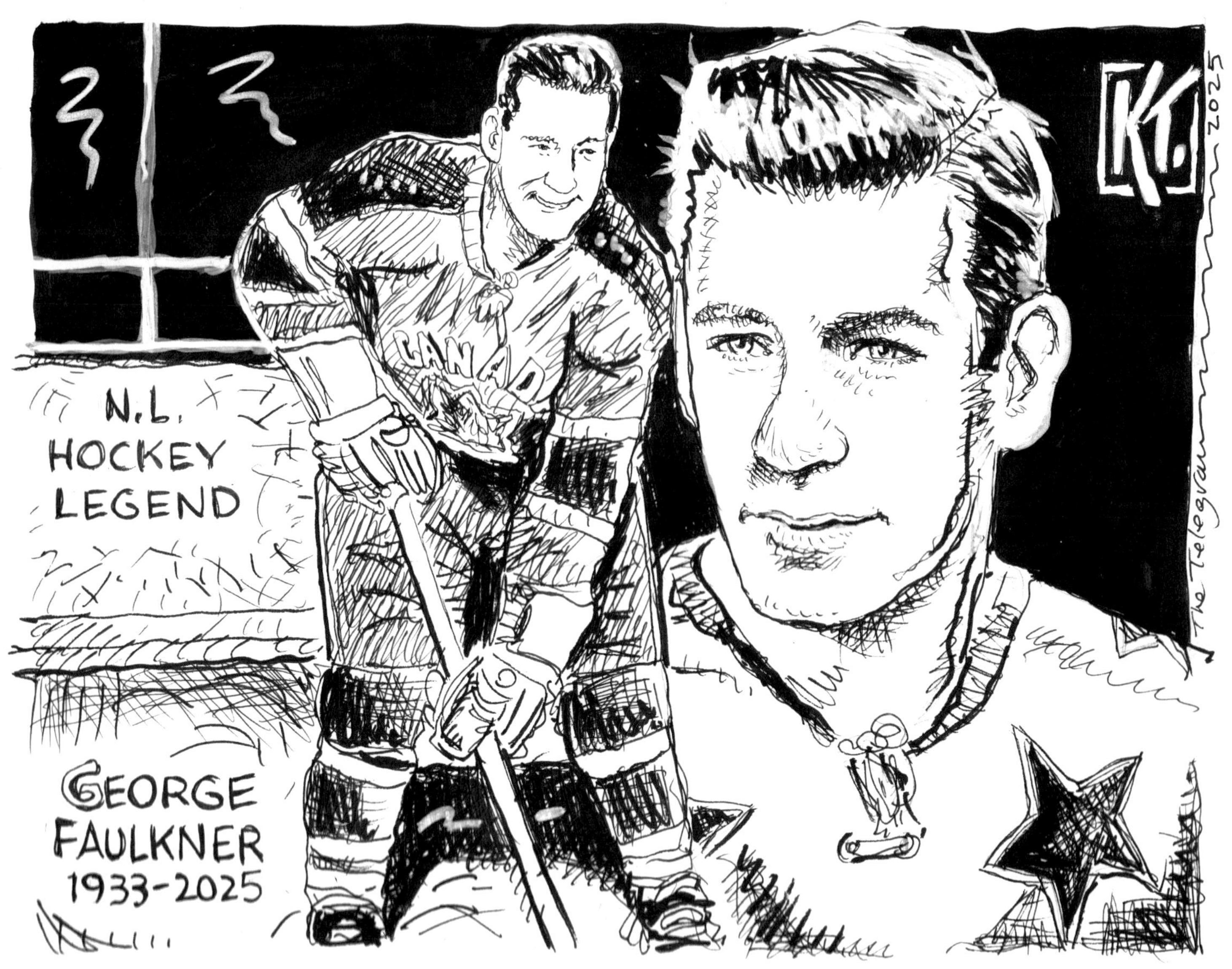
N.L.
HOCKEY
LEGEND
GEORGE
FAULKNER
1933-2025
CANADA
The Telegram
2025

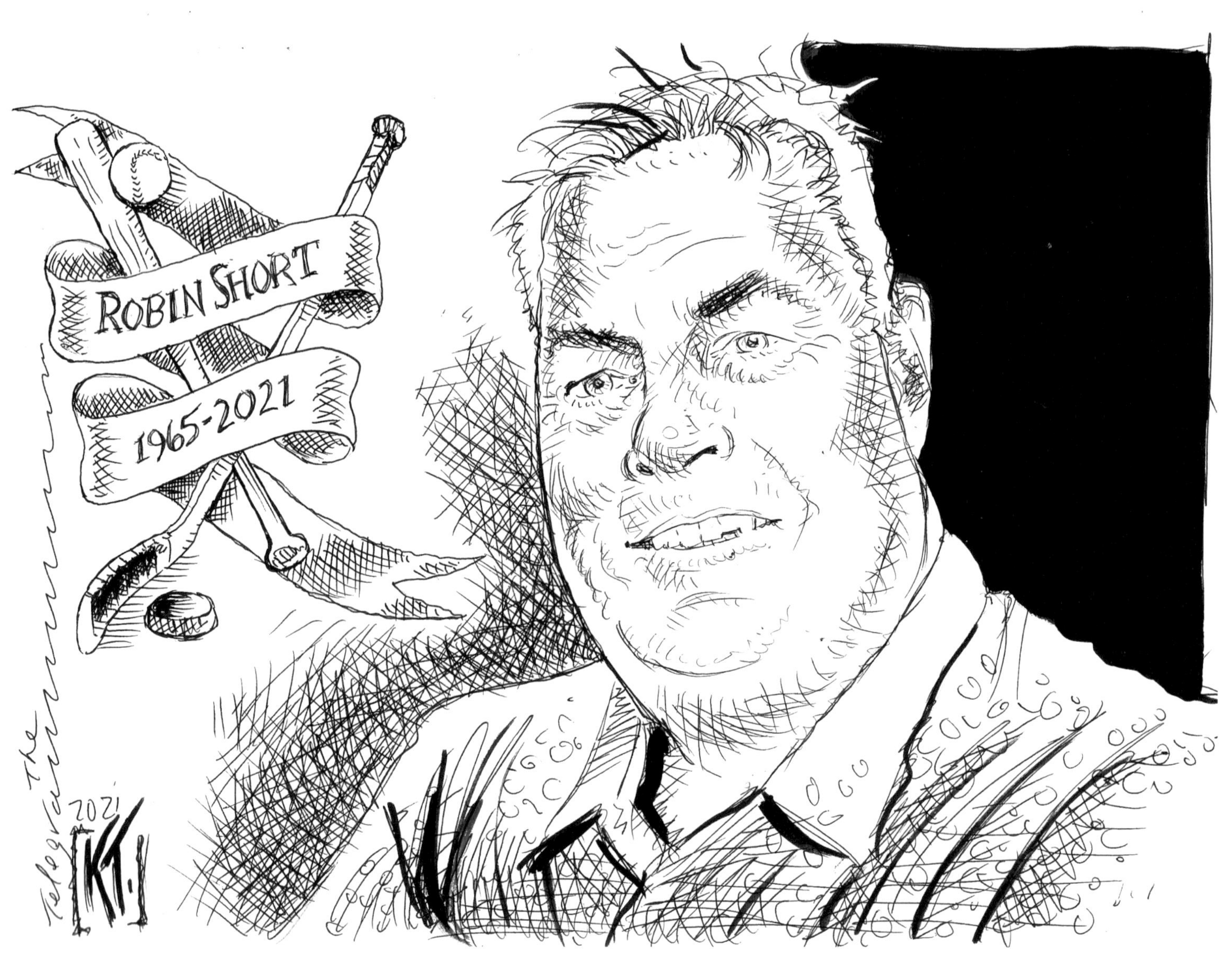

ROBIN SHORT
1965-2021

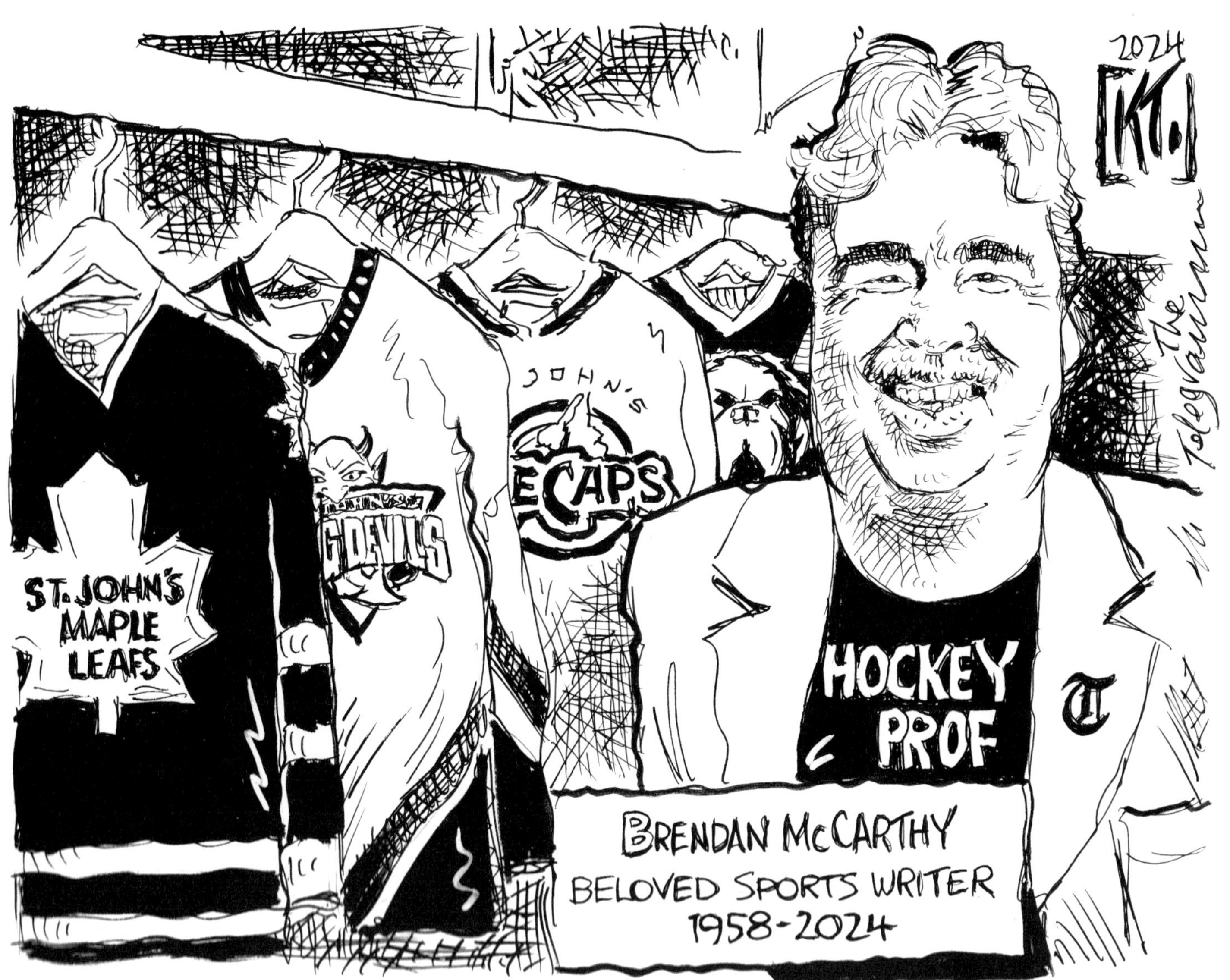


BRENDAN McCARTHY
BELOVED SPORTS WRITER
1958 - 2024

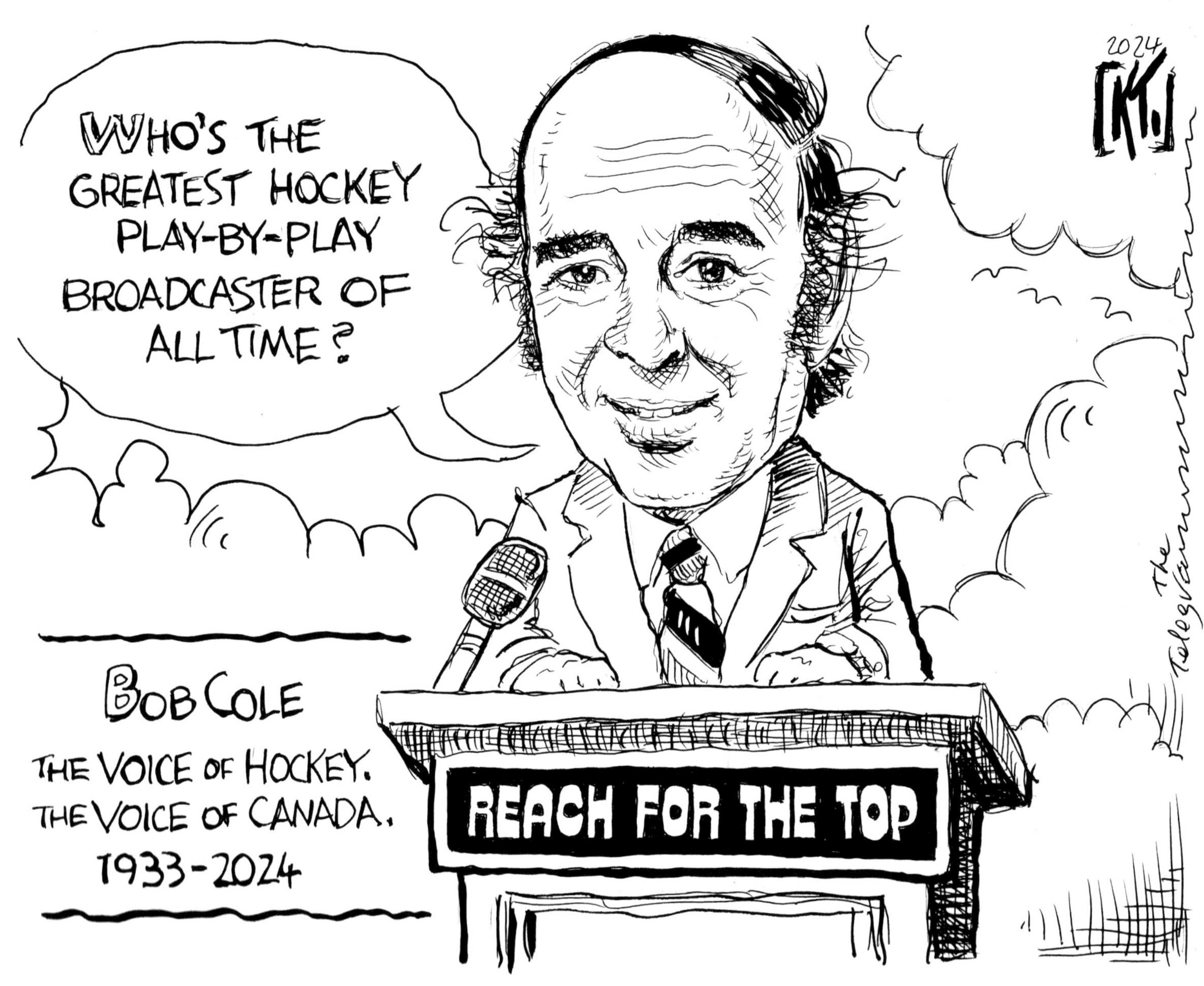

WHO'S THE GREATEST HOCKEY PLAY-BY-PLAY BROADCASTER OF ALL TIME?
2024
BOB COLE
THE VOICE OF HOCKEY. THE VOICE OF CANADA.
1933-2024
REACH FOR THE TOP

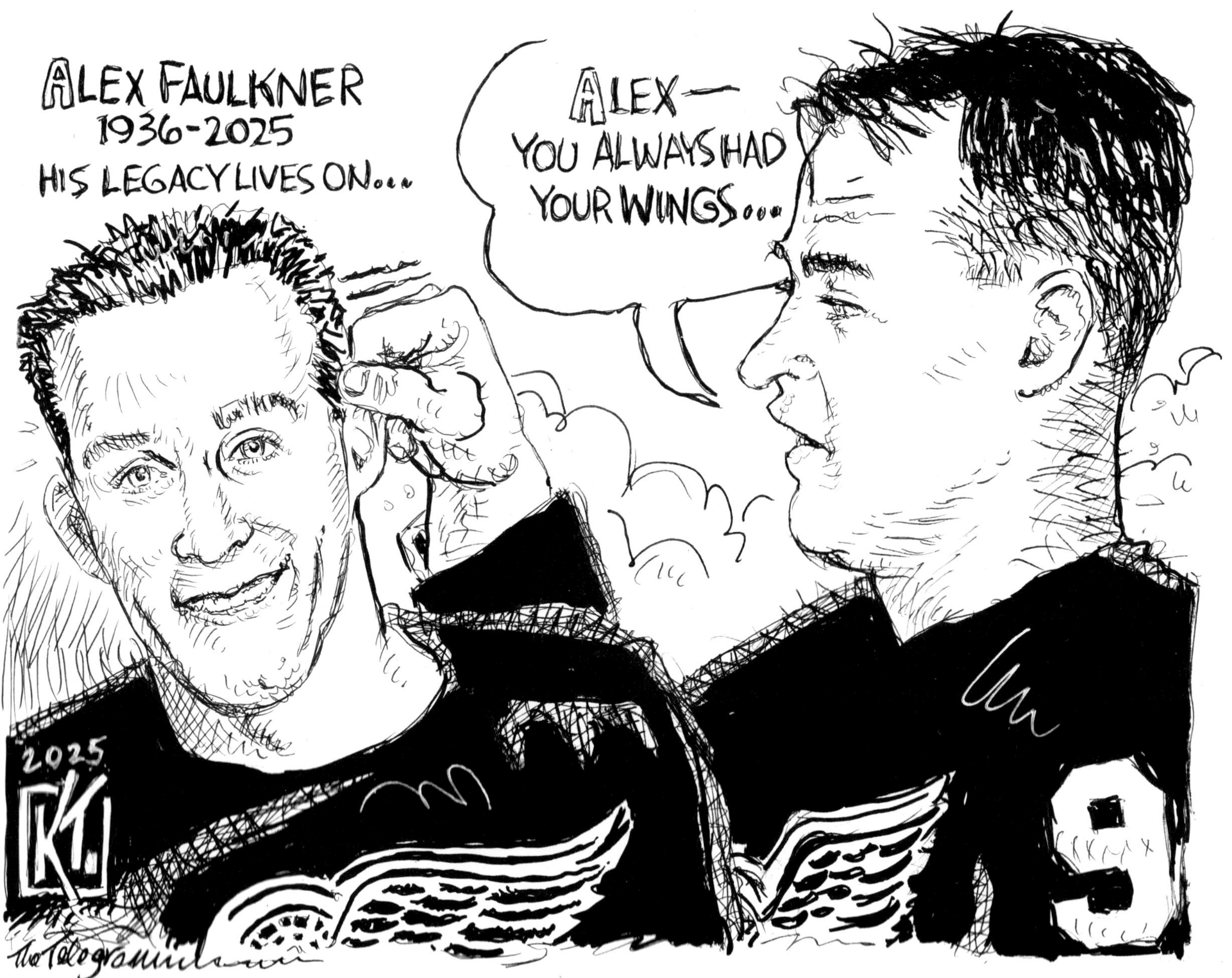

ALEX FAULKNER
1936-2025
HIS LEGACY LIVES ON...
ALEX—
YOU ALWAYS HAD
YOUR WINGS...
2025

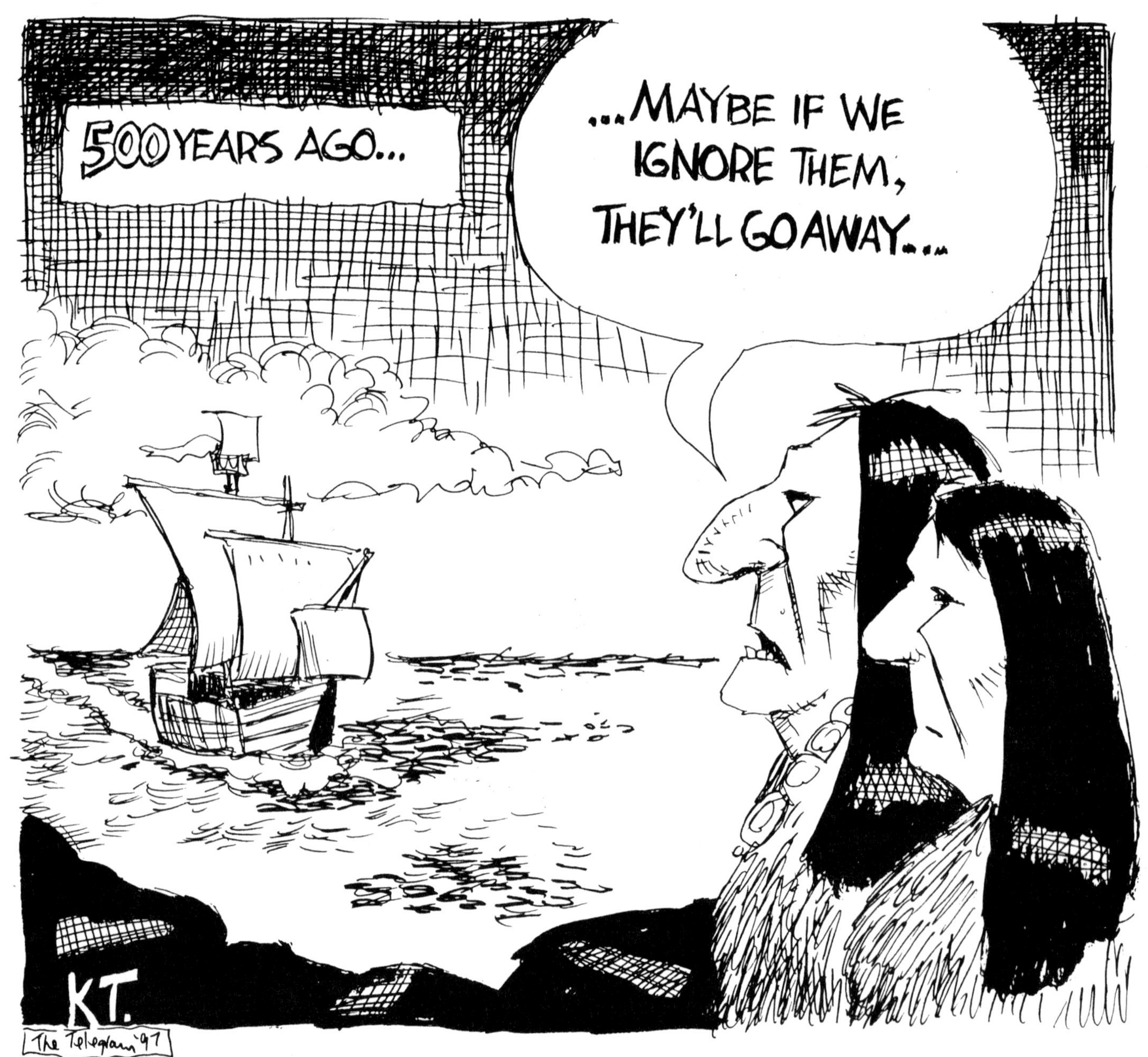

500 YEARS AGO...
...MAYBE IF WE IGNORE THEM, THEY'LL GO AWAY...
KT.
The Telegram '97

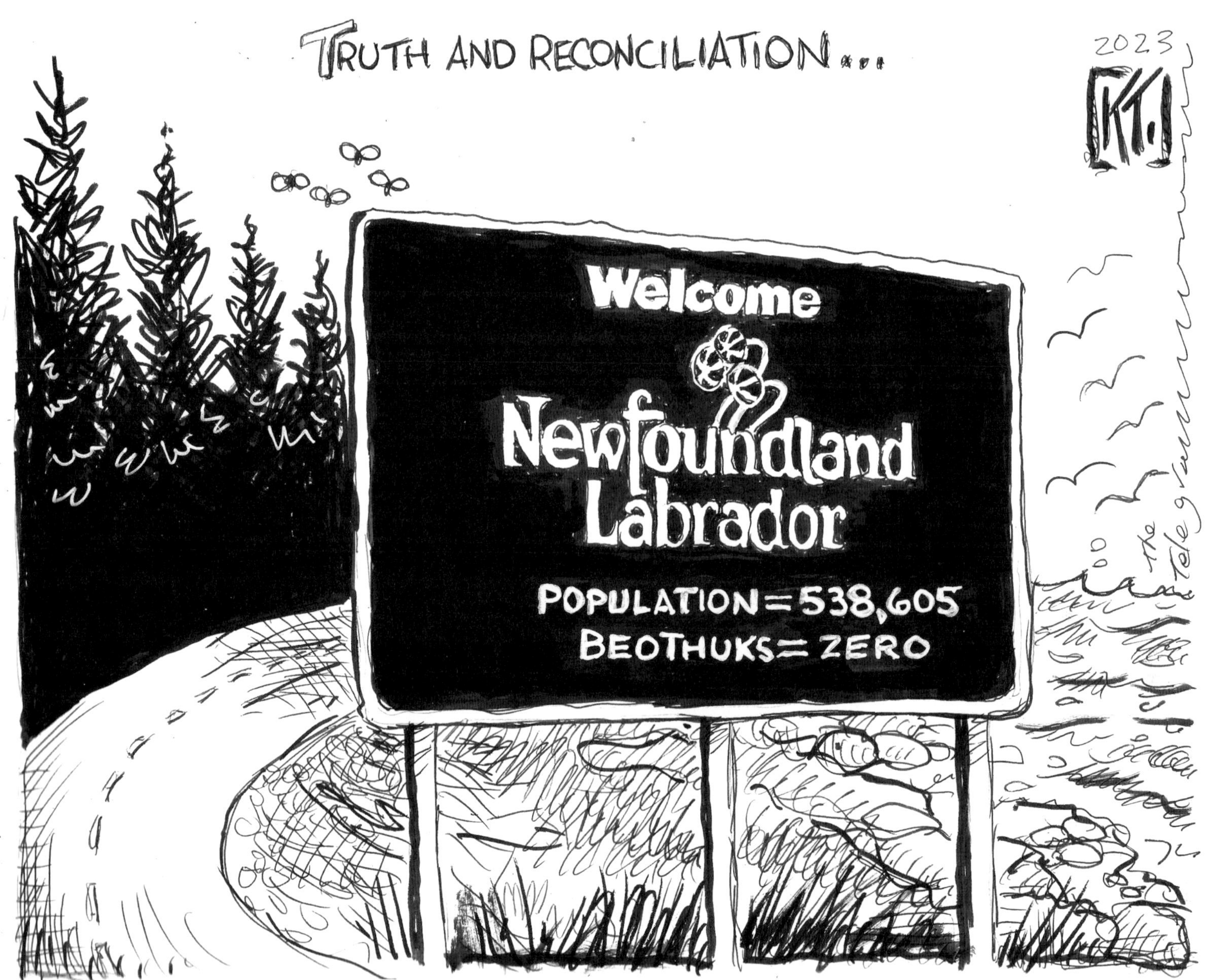

TRUTH AND RECONCILIATION...
2023
Welcome
Newfoundland
Labrador
POPULATION = 538,605
BEOTHUKS = ZERO

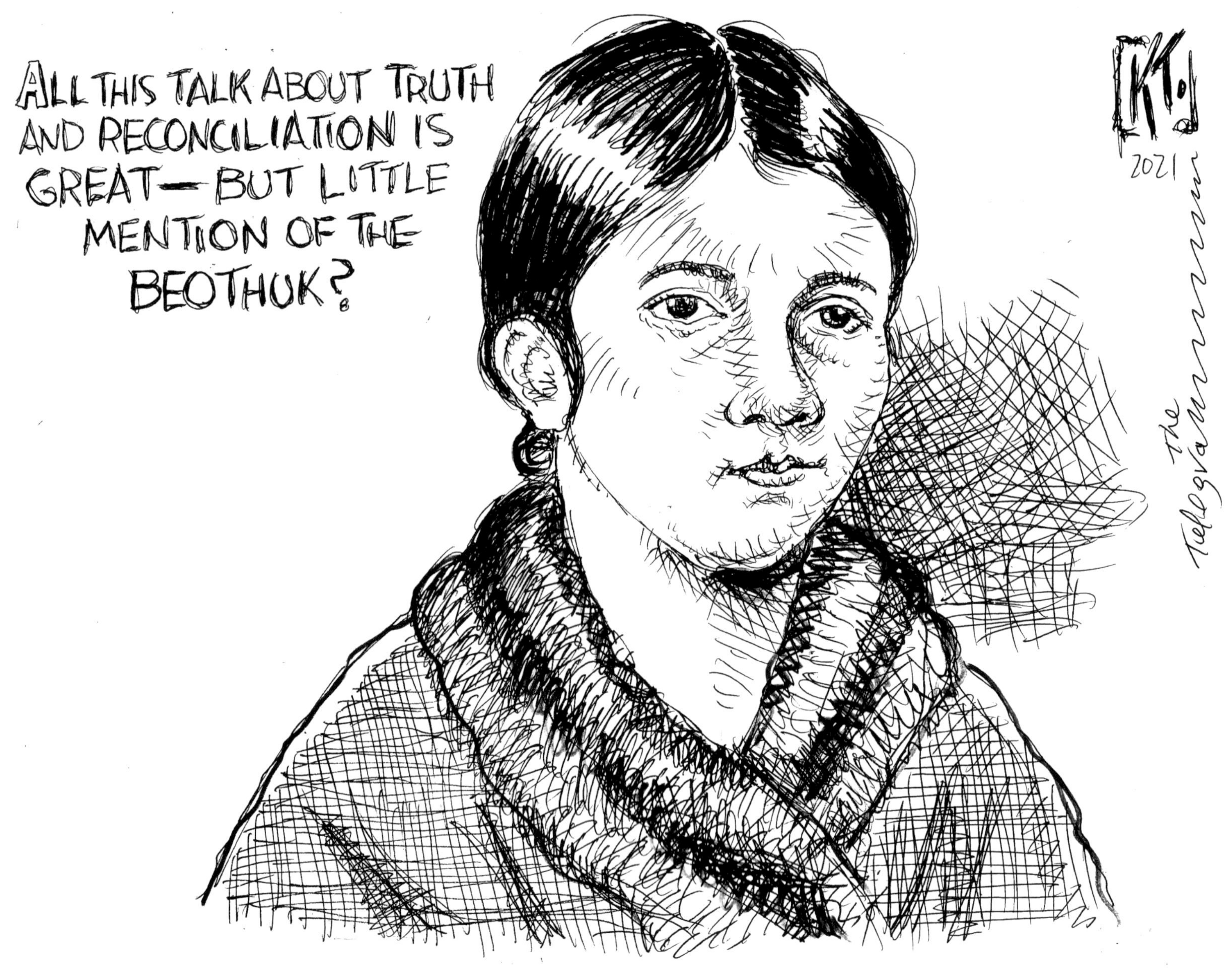

ALL THIS TALK ABOUT TRUTH AND RECONCILIATION IS GREAT—BUT LITTLE MENTION OF THE BEOTHUK?
2021
The Telegram

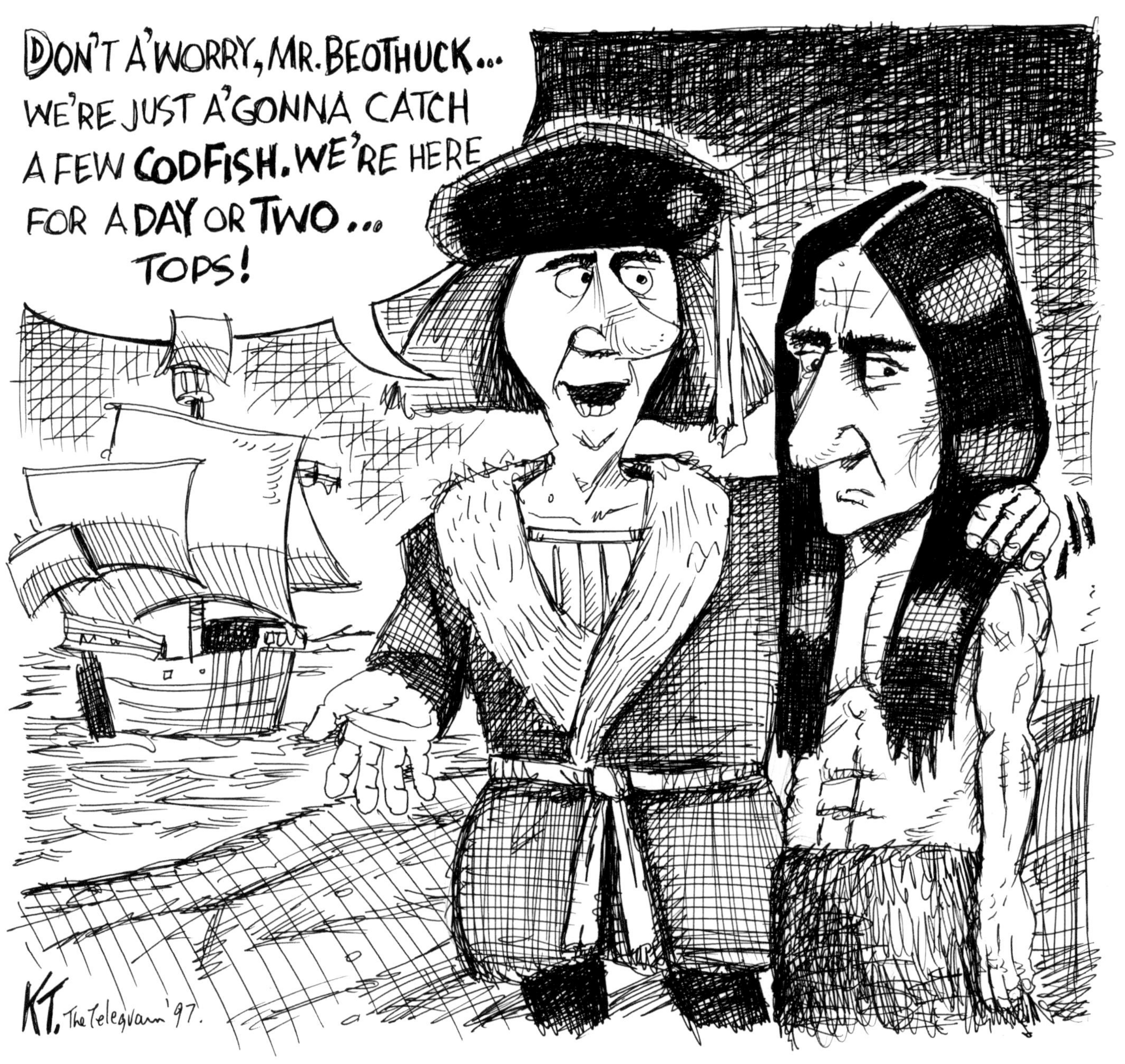

DON'T A'WORRY, MR. BEOTHUCK...
WE'RE JUST A'GONNA CATCH
A FEW CODFISH. WE'RE HERE
FOR A DAY OR TWO...
TOPS!

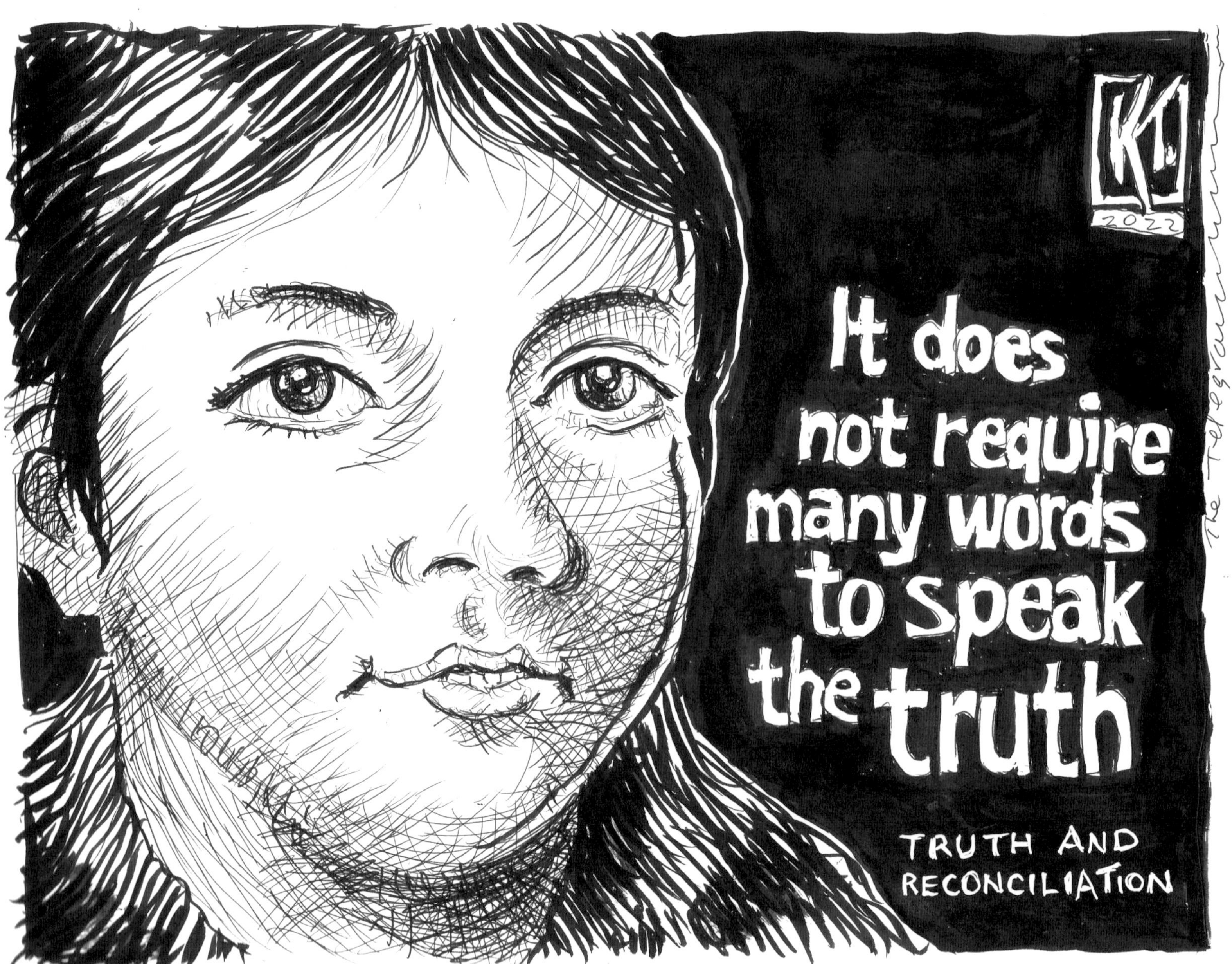

It does not require many words to speak the truth
TRUTH AND RECONCILIATION

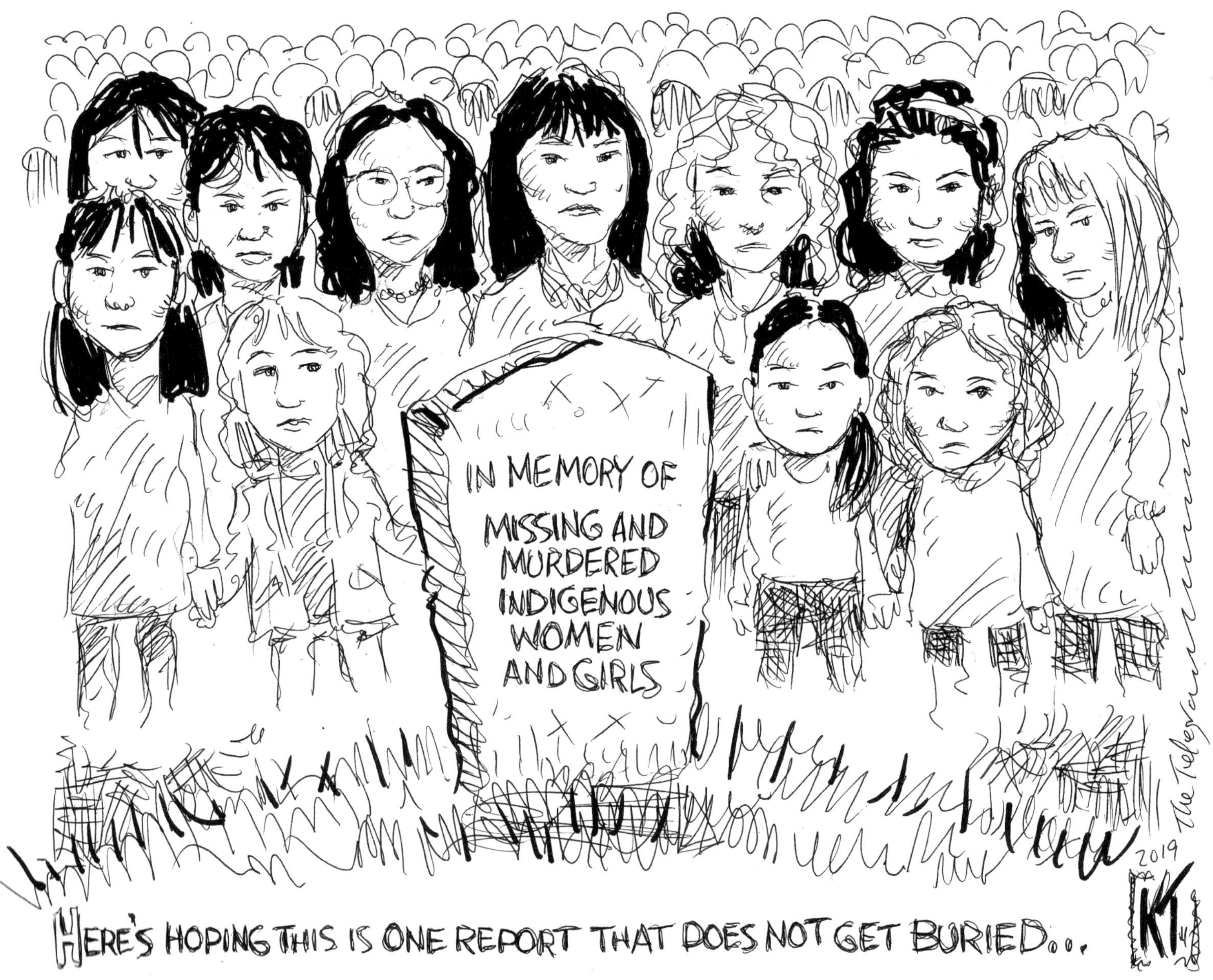
IN MEMORY OF
MISSING AND MURDERED INDIGENOUS WOMEN AND GIRLS
HERE'S HOPING THIS IS ONE REPORT THAT DOES NOT GET BURIED...
2019 The Tele...

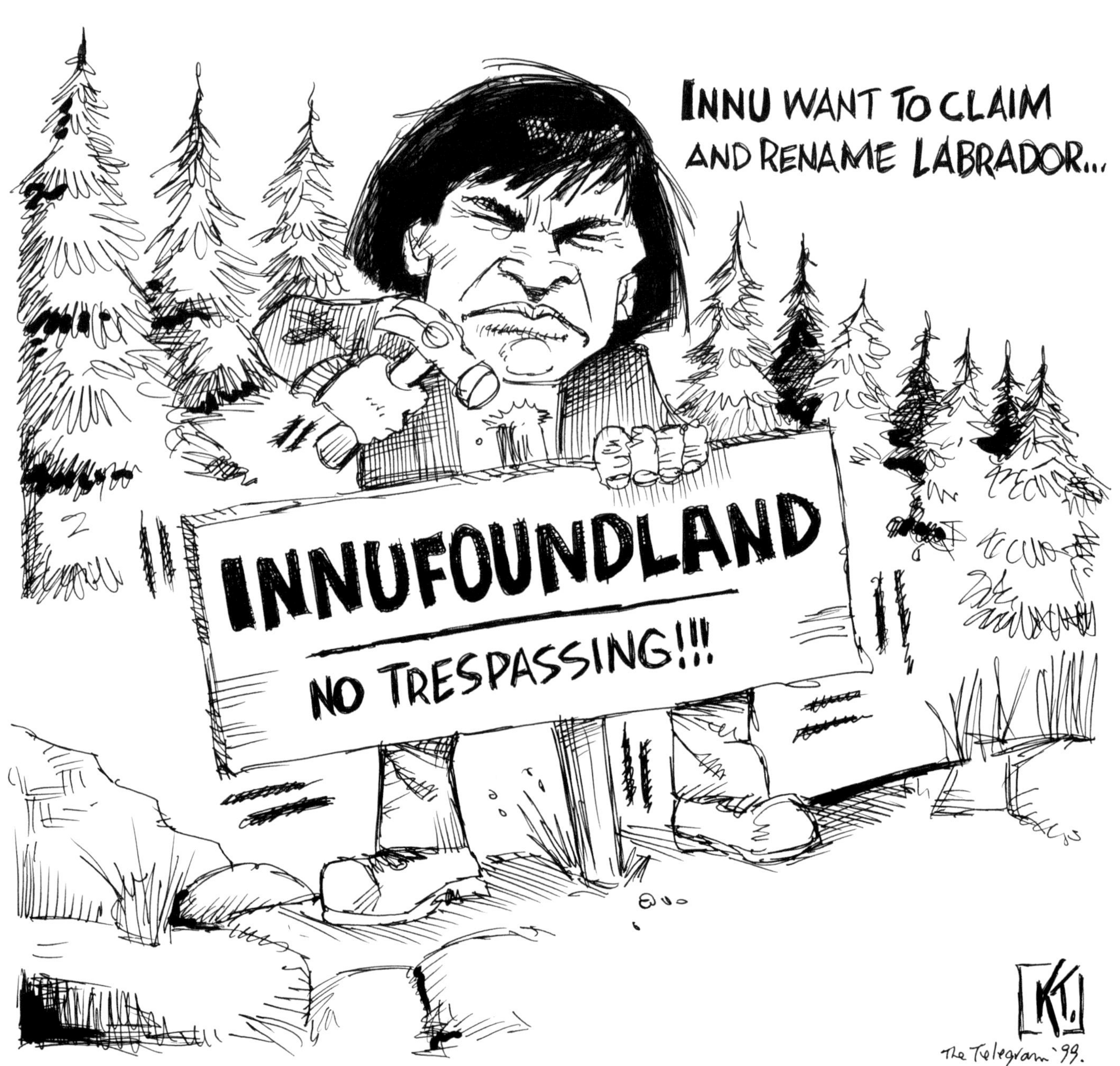

INNU WANT TO CLAIM AND RENAME LABRADOR...
INNUFOUNDLAND
NO TRESPASSING!!!
The Telegram '99.

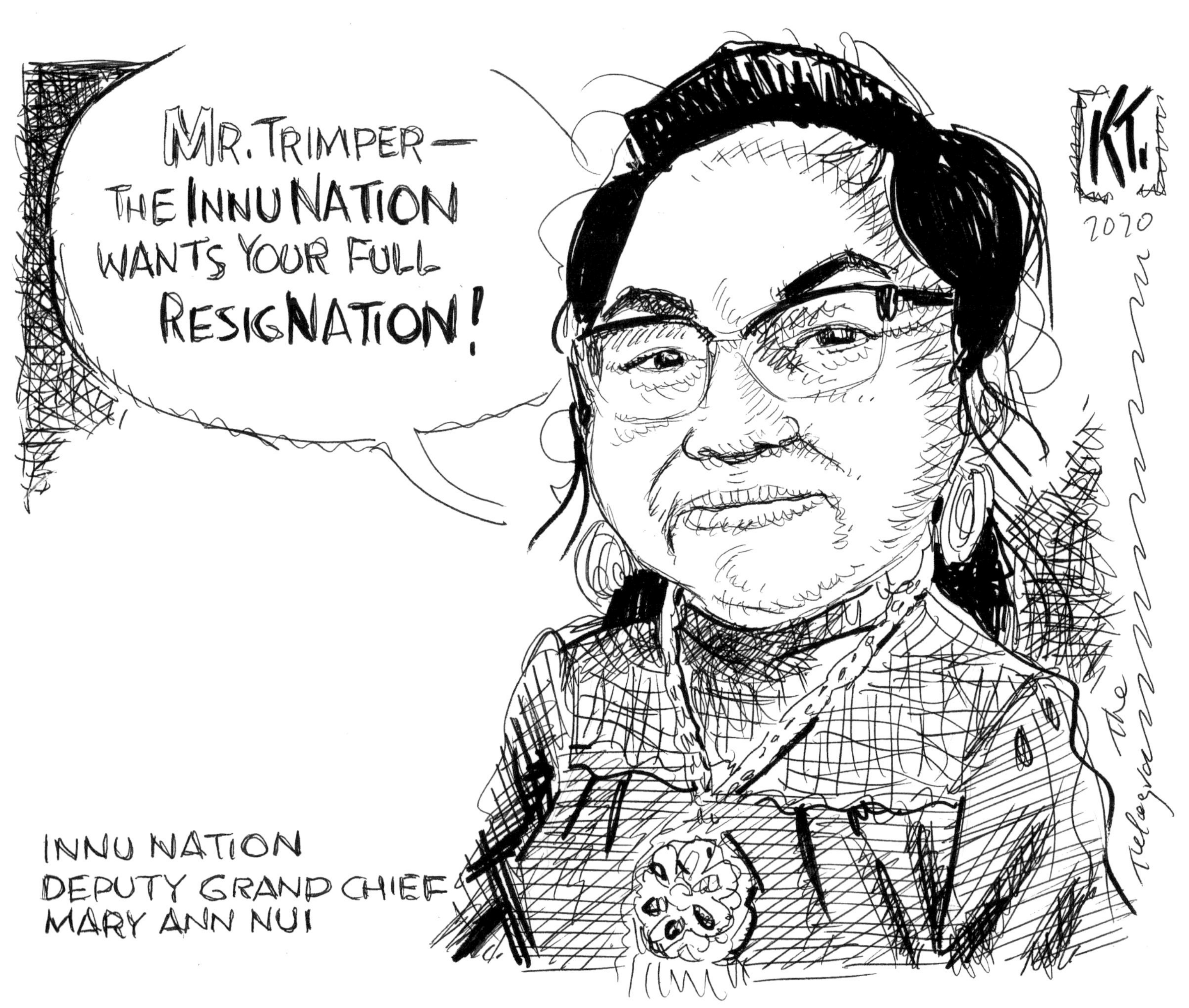

Mr. Trimper—
The Innu Nation
wants your full
Resignation!
2020
INNU NATION
DEPUTY GRAND CHIEF
MARY ANN NUI

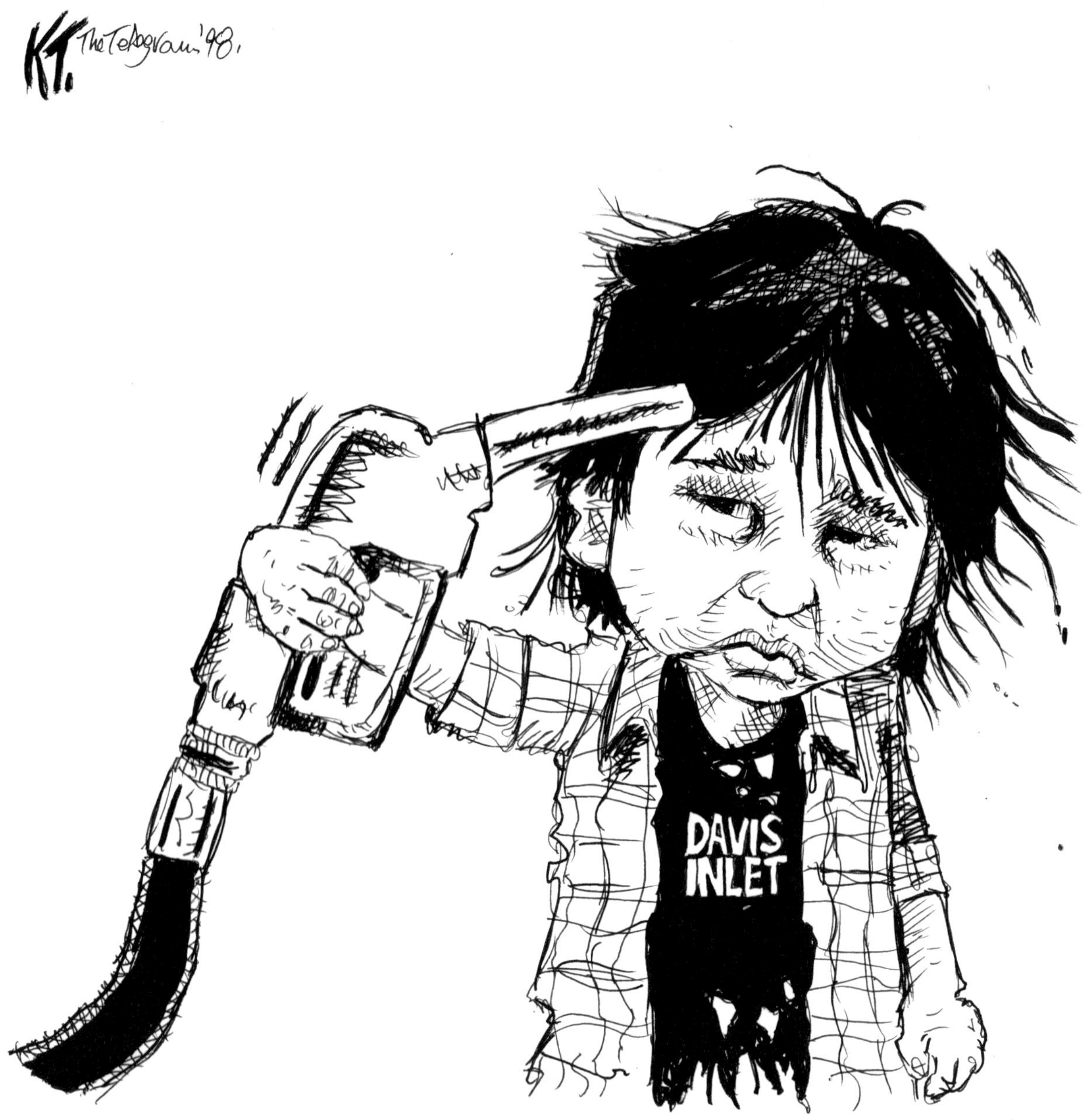

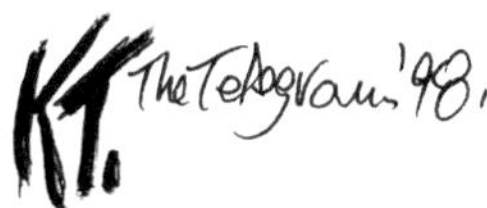

K.T.
The Telegram '98.

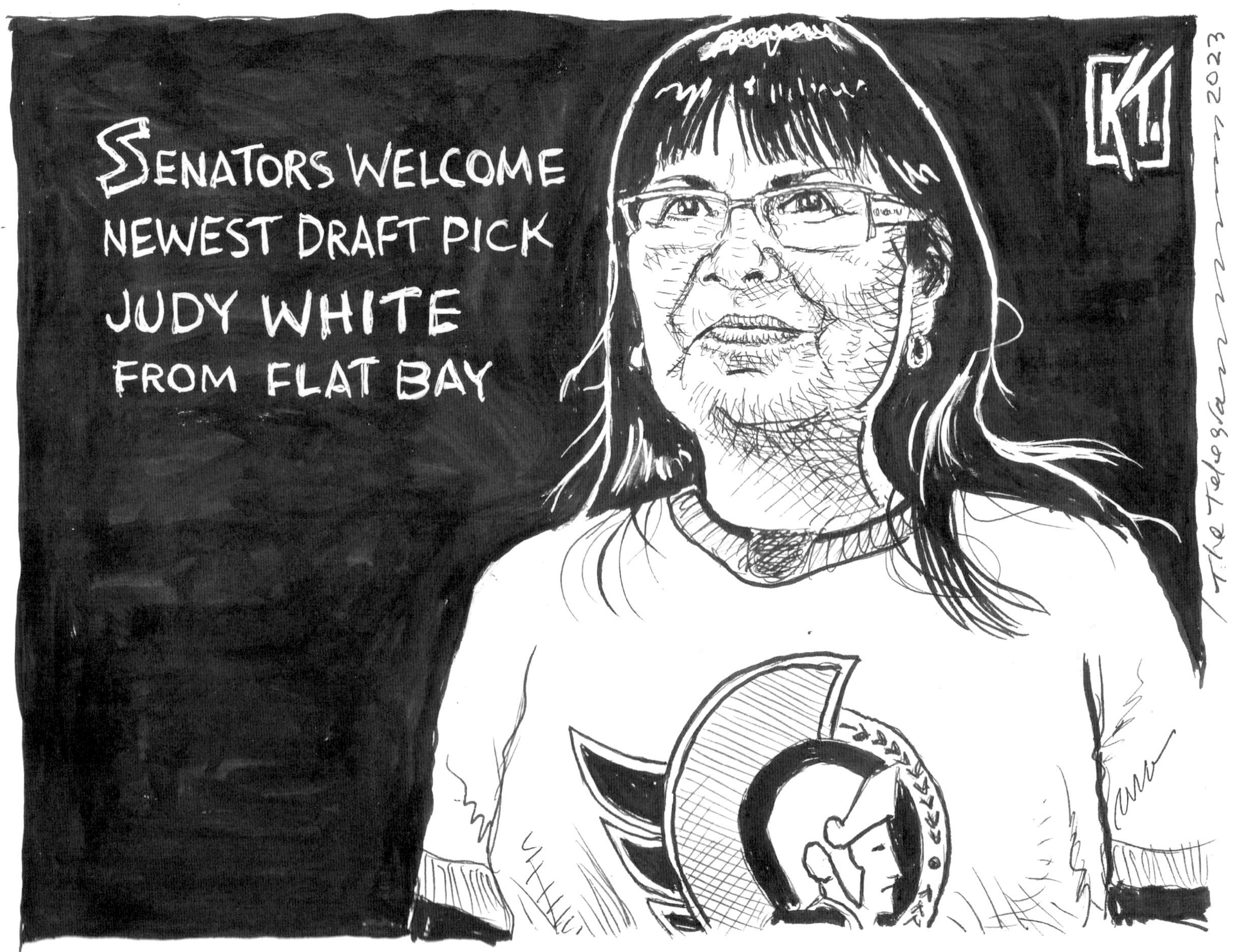

SENATORS WELCOME
NEWEST DRAFT PICK
JUDY WHITE
FROM FLAT BAY
The Telegram 2023

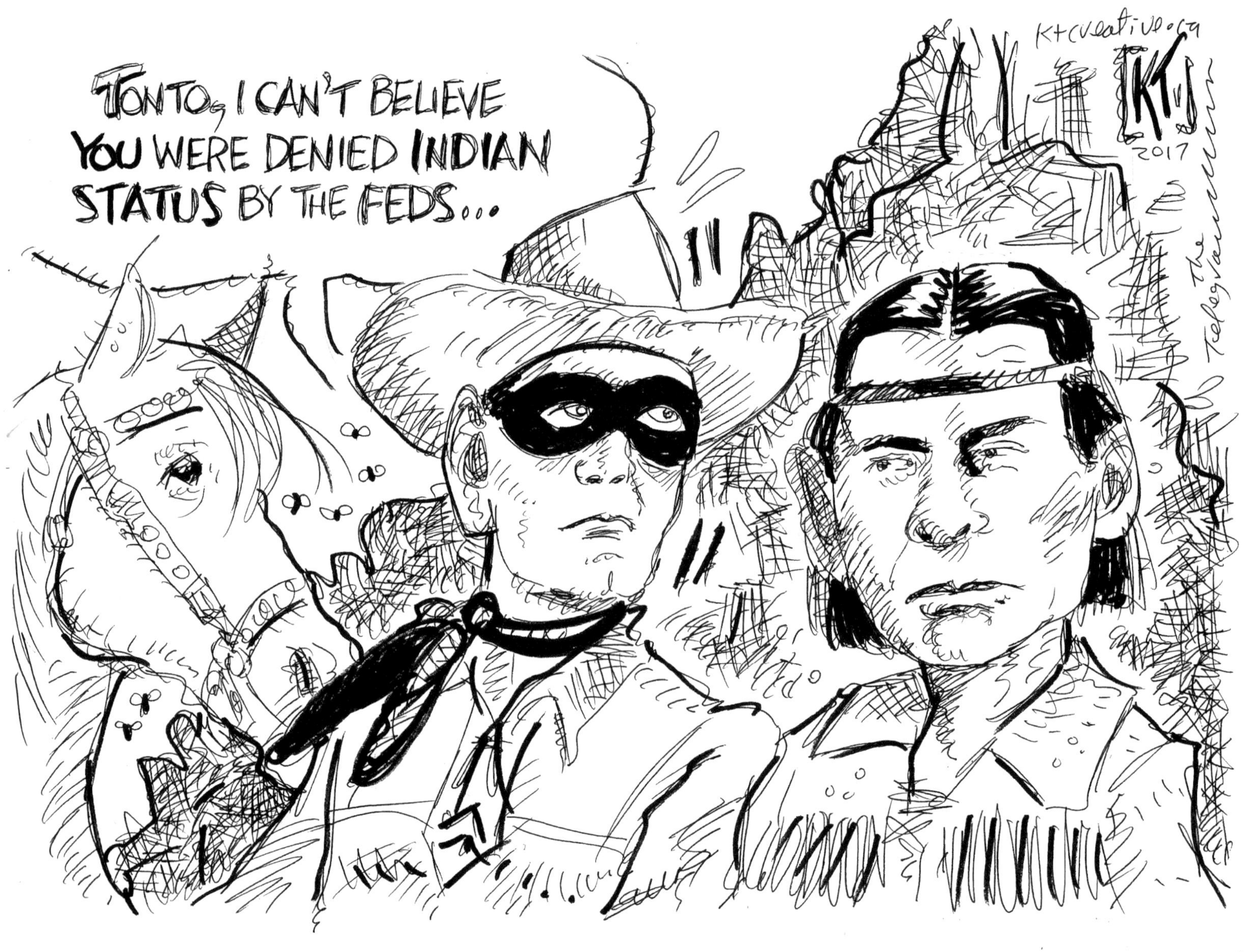

TONTO, I CAN'T BELIEVE YOU WERE DENIED INDIAN STATUS BY THE FEDS...

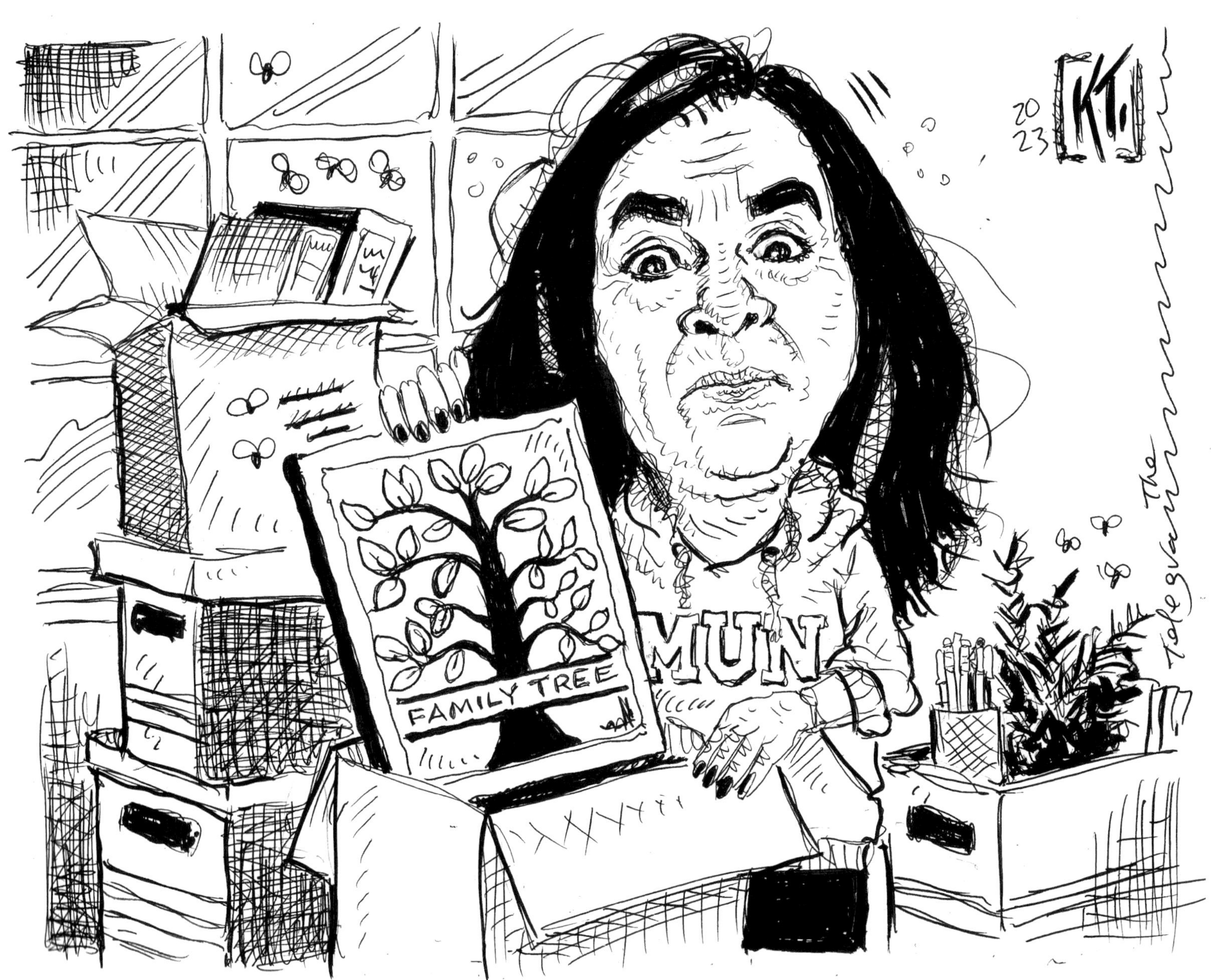

FAMILY TREE
MUN

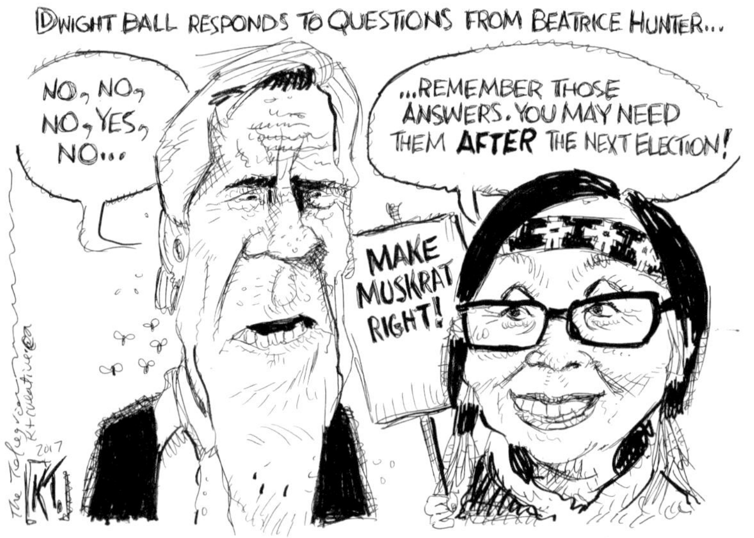

DWIGHT BALL RESPONDS TO QUESTIONS FROM BEATRICE HUNTER...
NO, NO, NO, YES, NO...
...REMEMBER THOSE ANSWERS. YOU MAY NEED THEM AFTER THE NEXT ELECTION!
MAKE MUSKRAT RIGHT!
The Telegram
K+ Tobin
2017


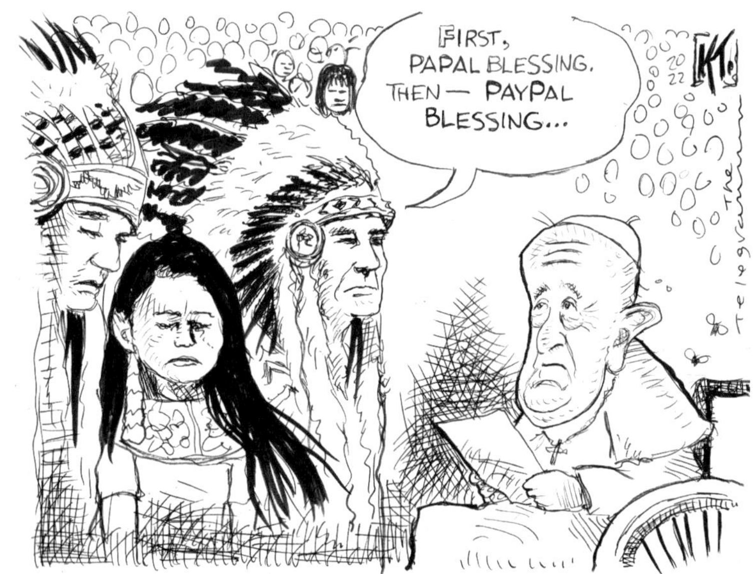

FIRST, PAPAL BLESSING. THEN — PAYPAL BLESSING...
20 22
The Telegram

# POLITICS

*In France, 'poli' means polite or polished. And 'tics' or 'ticks' are small-minded parasites more closely related to spiders than flies. But flies and politics have always been connected. For example, blue-arse fly . . . Tory. Red-arse fly . . . Liberal. Orange-arse fly . . . Trump.*

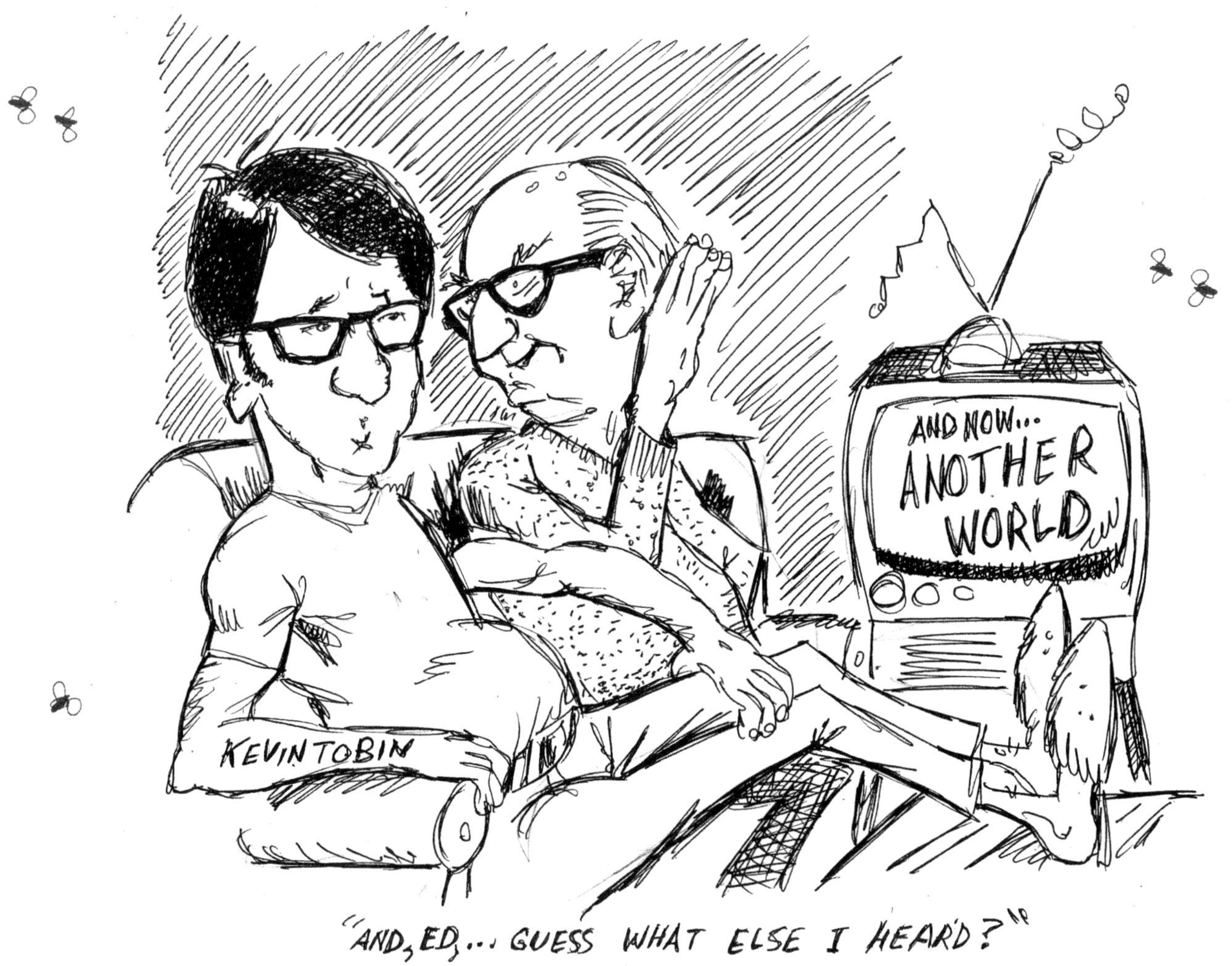


"AND, ED, . . . GUESS WHAT ELSE I HEARD?"

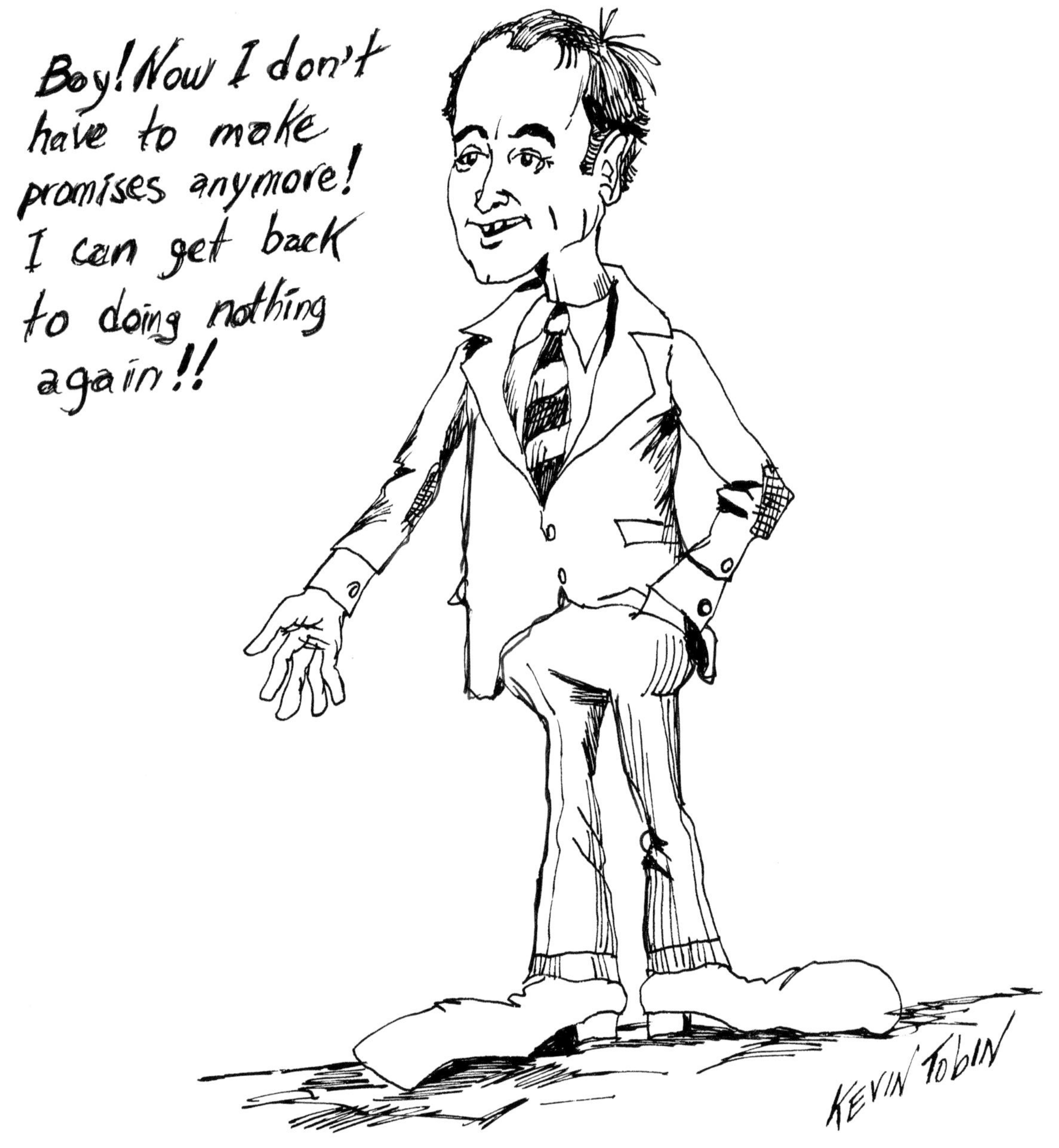

Boy! Now I don't have to make promises anymore! I can get back to doing nothing again!!
KEVIN TOBIN

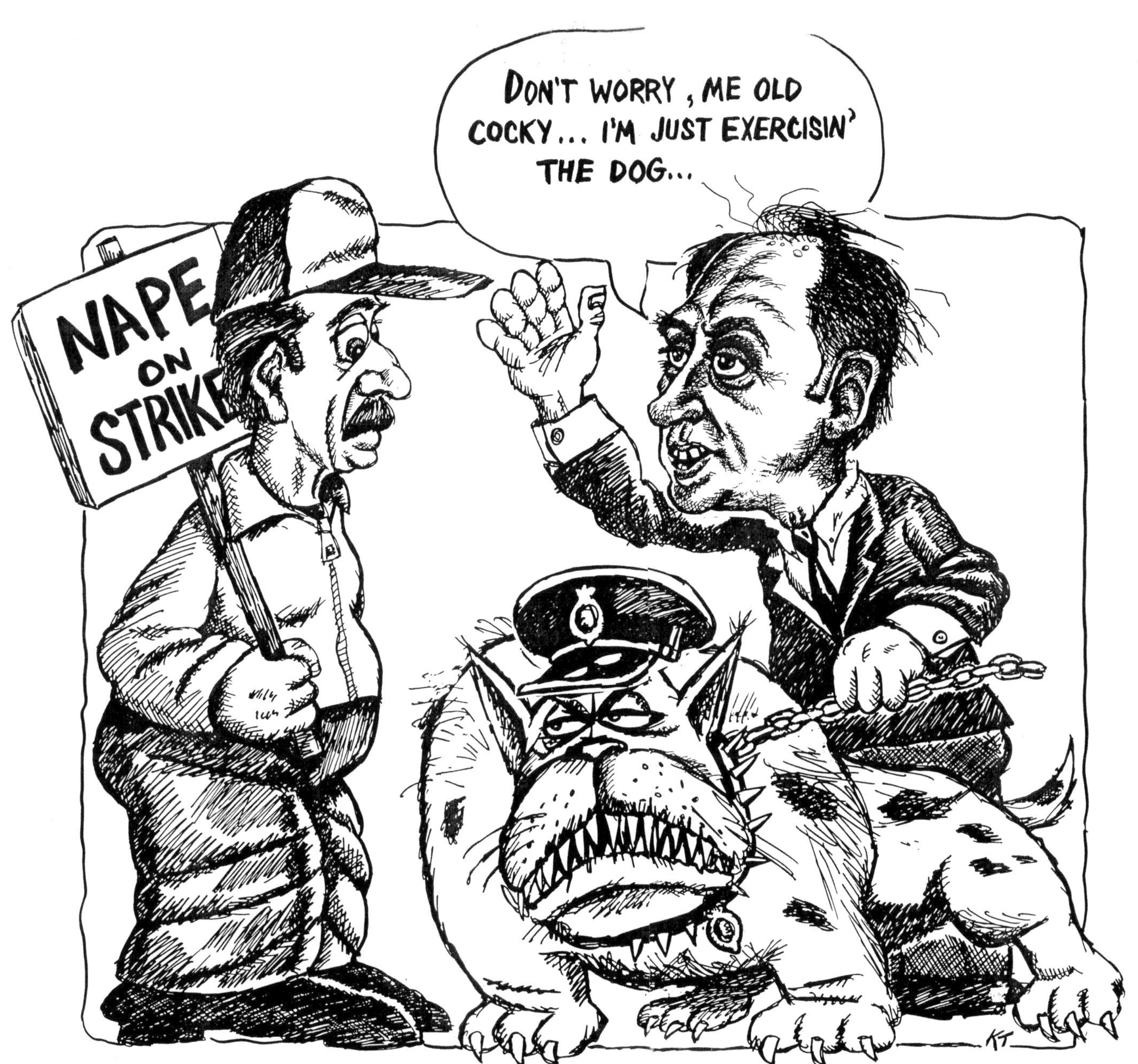

DON'T WORRY, ME OLD COCKY... I'M JUST EXERCISIN' THE DOG...
NAPE ON STRIKE

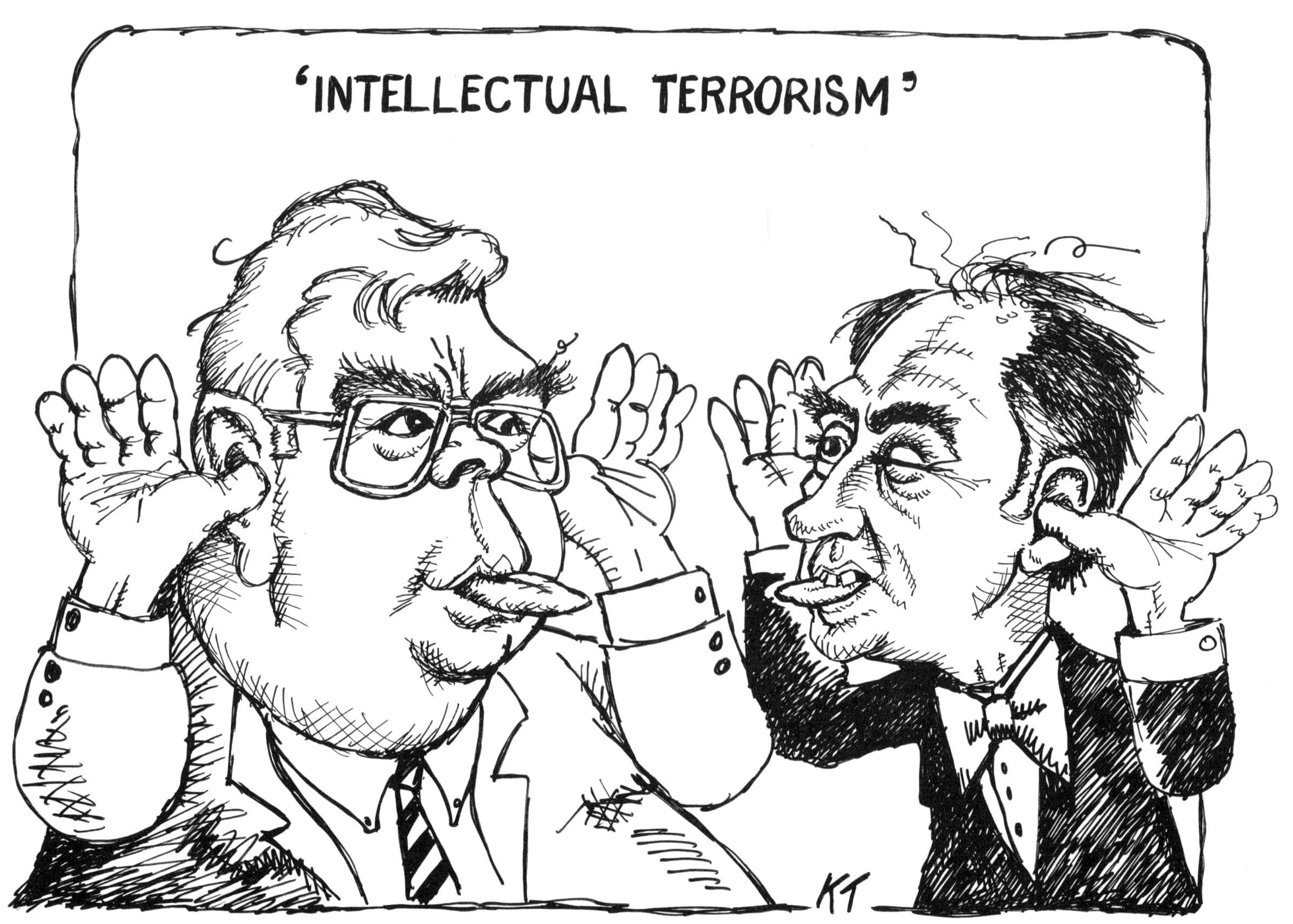

'INTELLECTUAL TERRORISM'
KT

CLYDE TRANSFERRING POWER TO BRIAN...

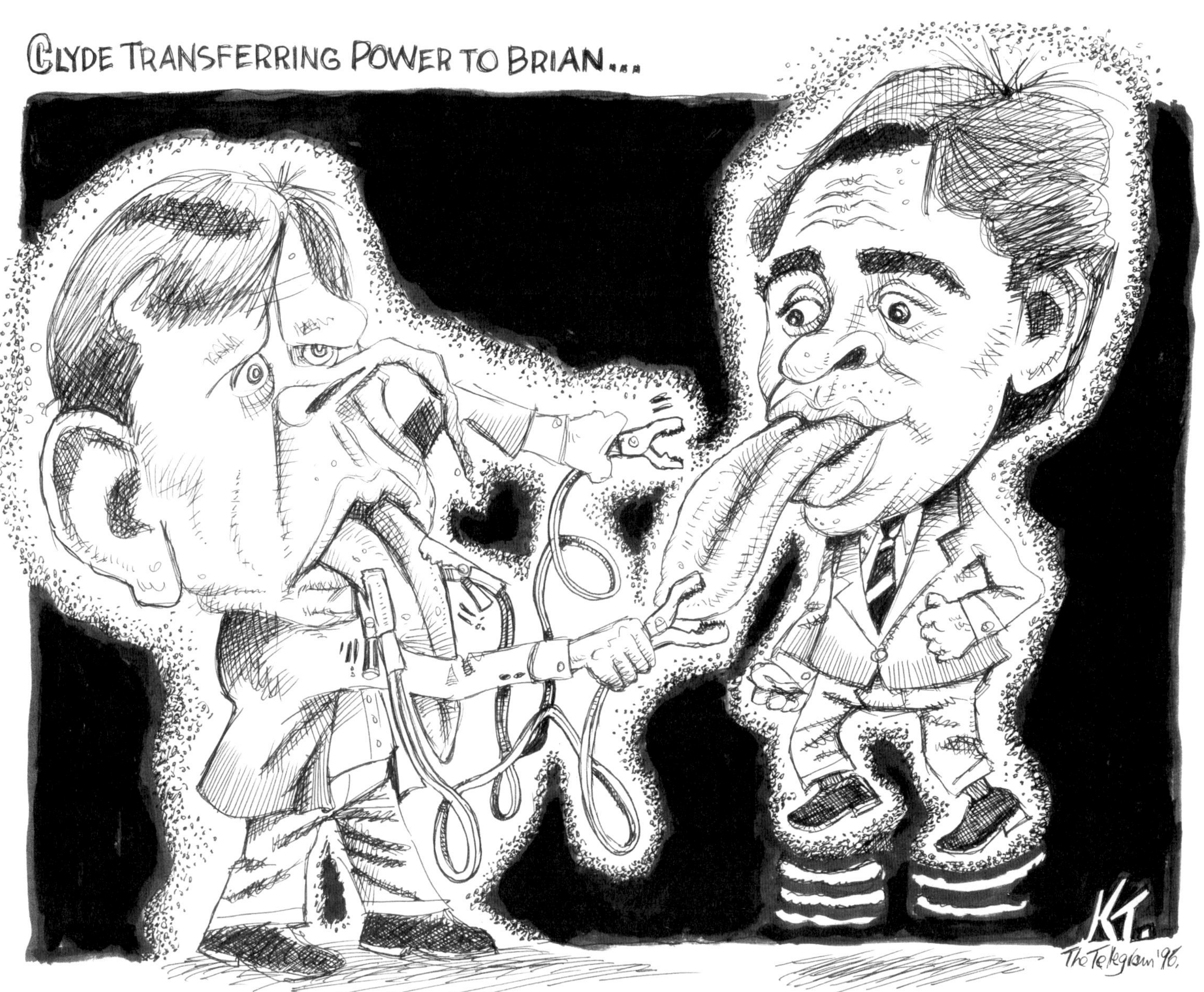

KT.
The Telegram '96.

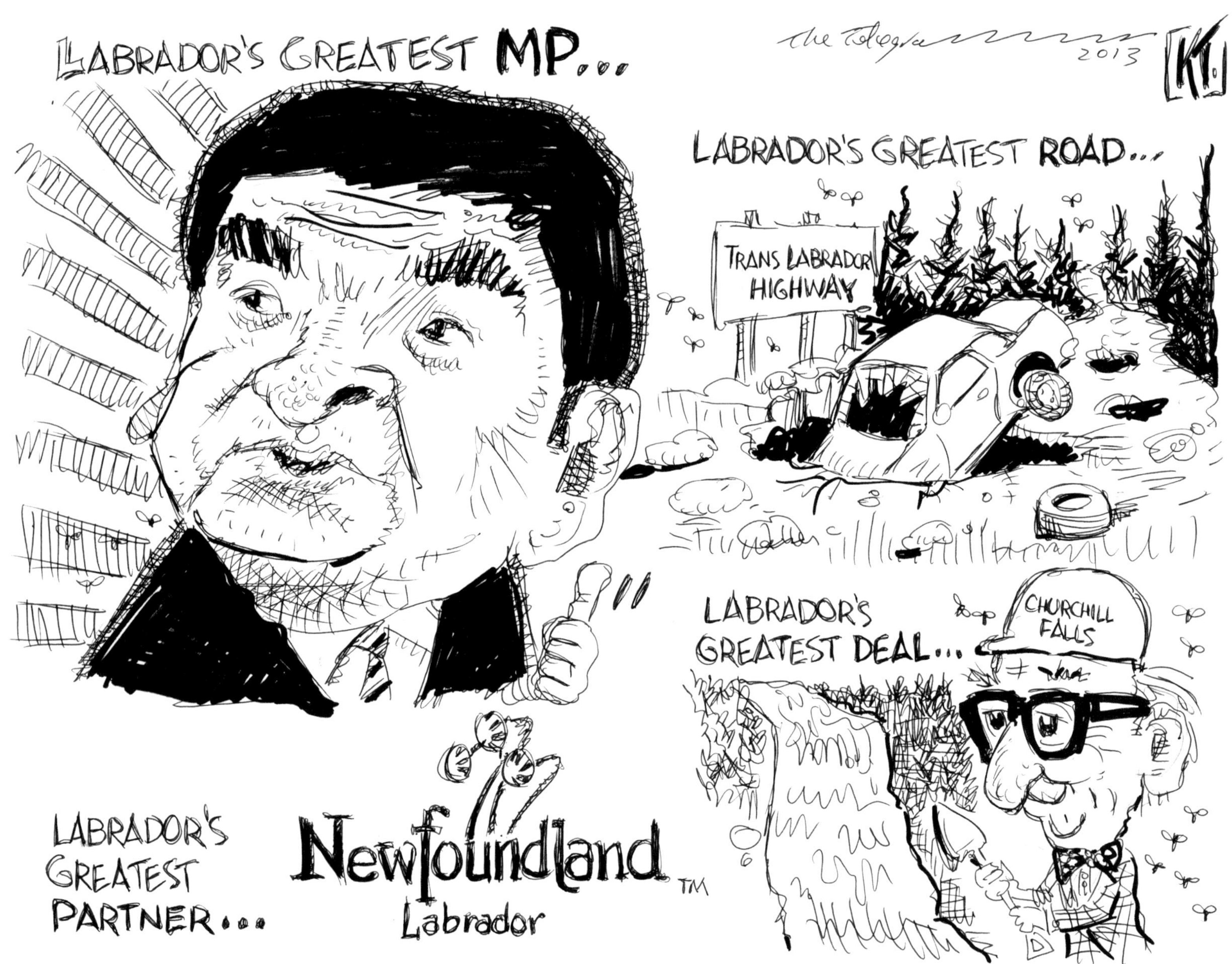

LABRADOR'S GREATEST MP...
the Telegram 2013
LABRADOR'S GREATEST ROAD...
TRANS LABRADOR HIGHWAY
LABRADOR'S GREATEST DEAL...
CHURCHILL FALLS
LABRADOR'S GREATEST PARTNER...
Newfoundland™
Labrador

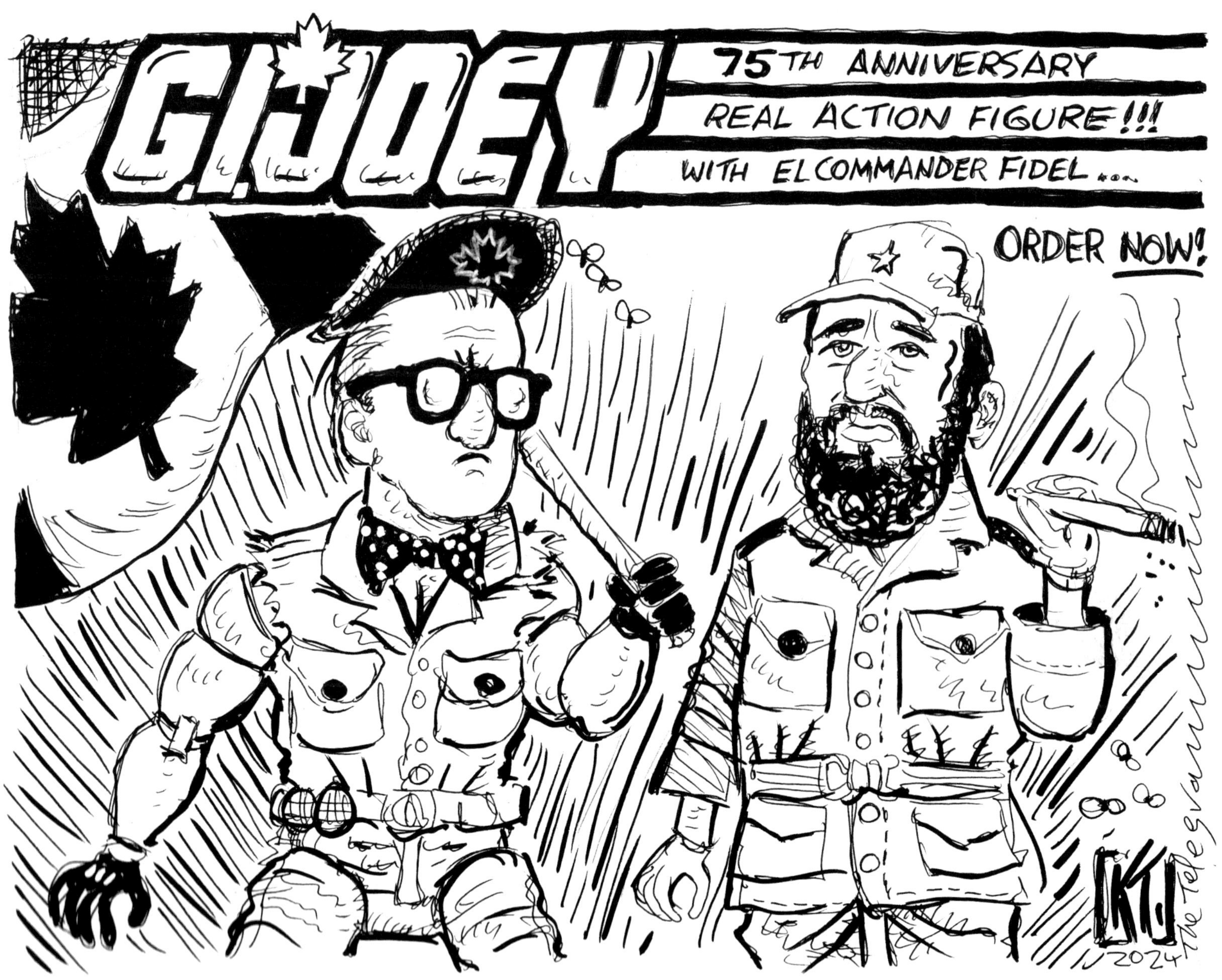

G.I. JOEY
75TH ANNIVERSARY
REAL ACTION FIGURE!!!
WITH EL COMMANDER FIDEL...
ORDER NOW!

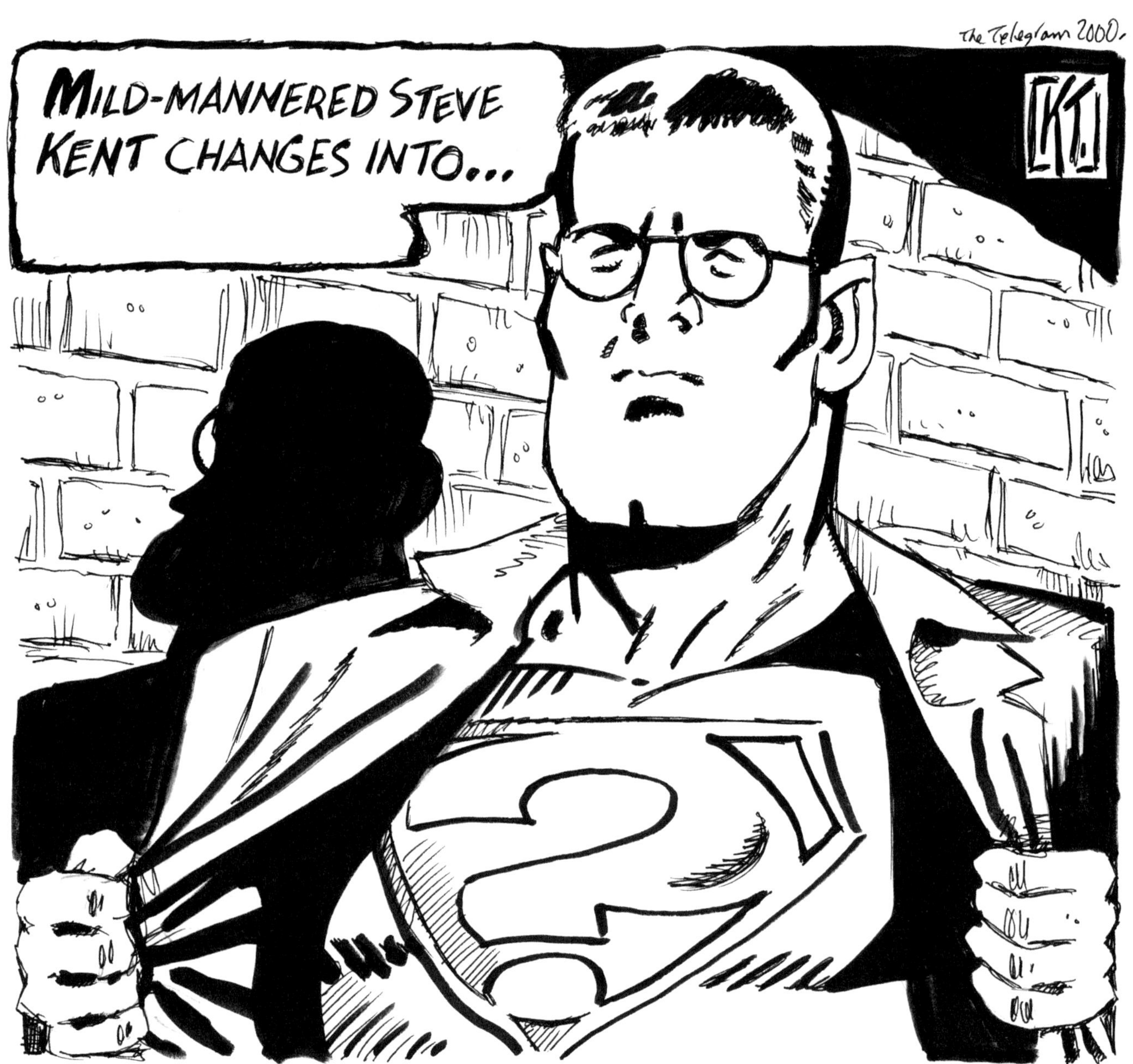
the Telegram 2000.
MILD-MANNERED STEVE KENT CHANGES INTO...

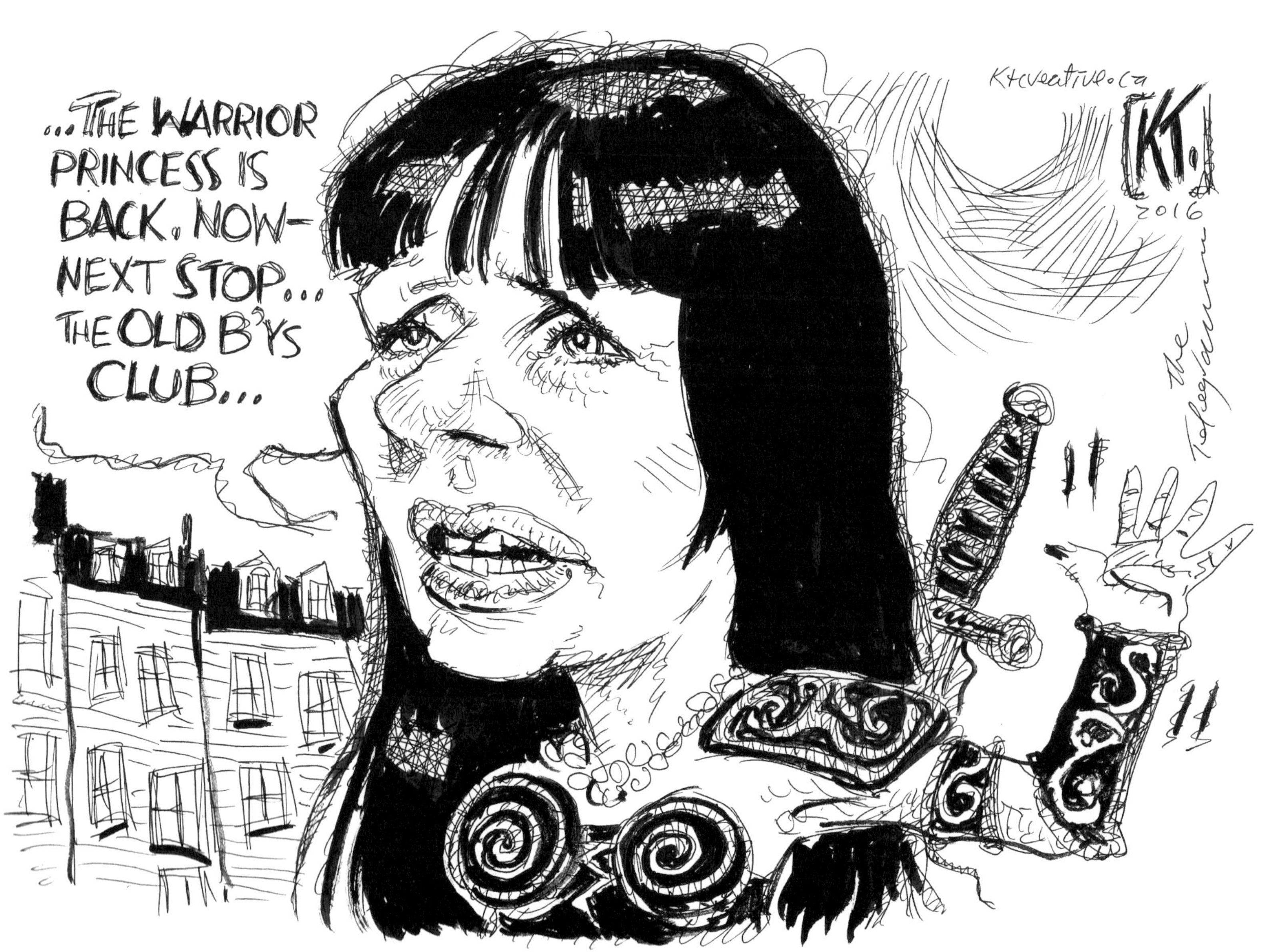
...THE WARRIOR PRINCESS IS BACK. NOW— NEXT STOP... THE OLD B'YS CLUB...
Ktcreative.ca
KT.
2016
The Telegram

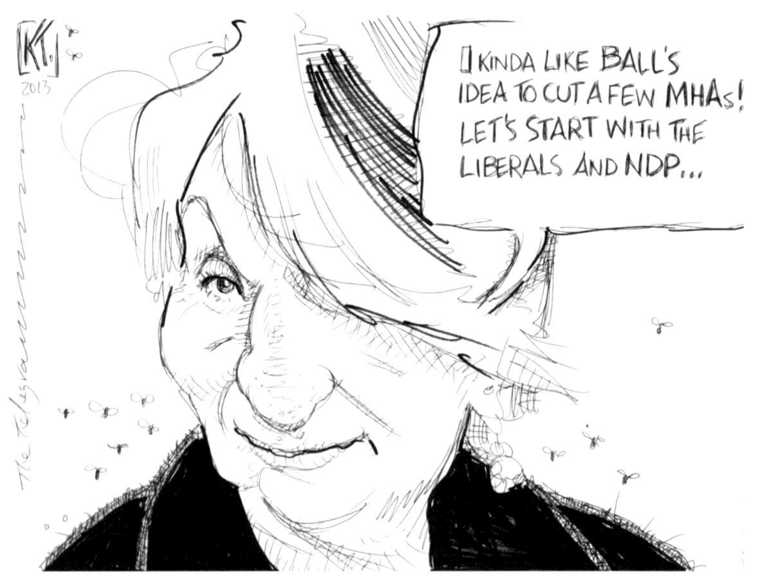
I KINDA LIKE BALL'S IDEA TO CUT A FEW MHAs! LET'S START WITH THE LIBERALS AND NDP...

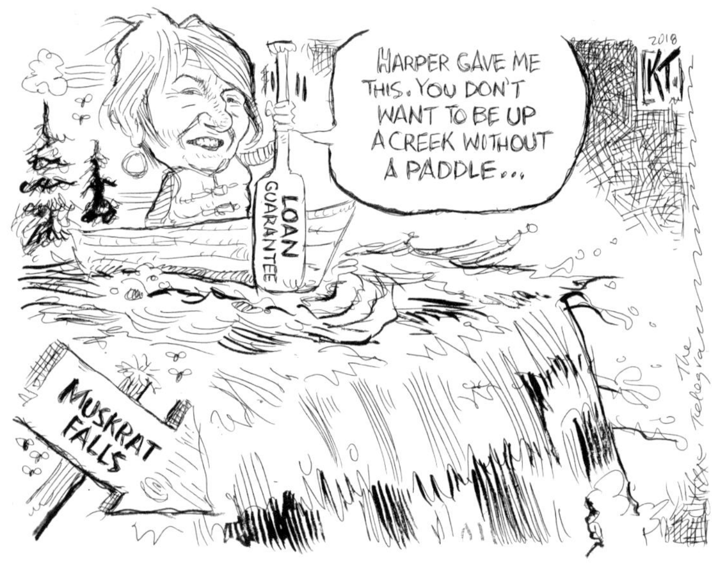
HARPER GAVE ME THIS. YOU DON'T WANT TO BE UP A CREEK WITHOUT A PADDLE...
LOAN GUARANTEE
MUSKRAT FALLS

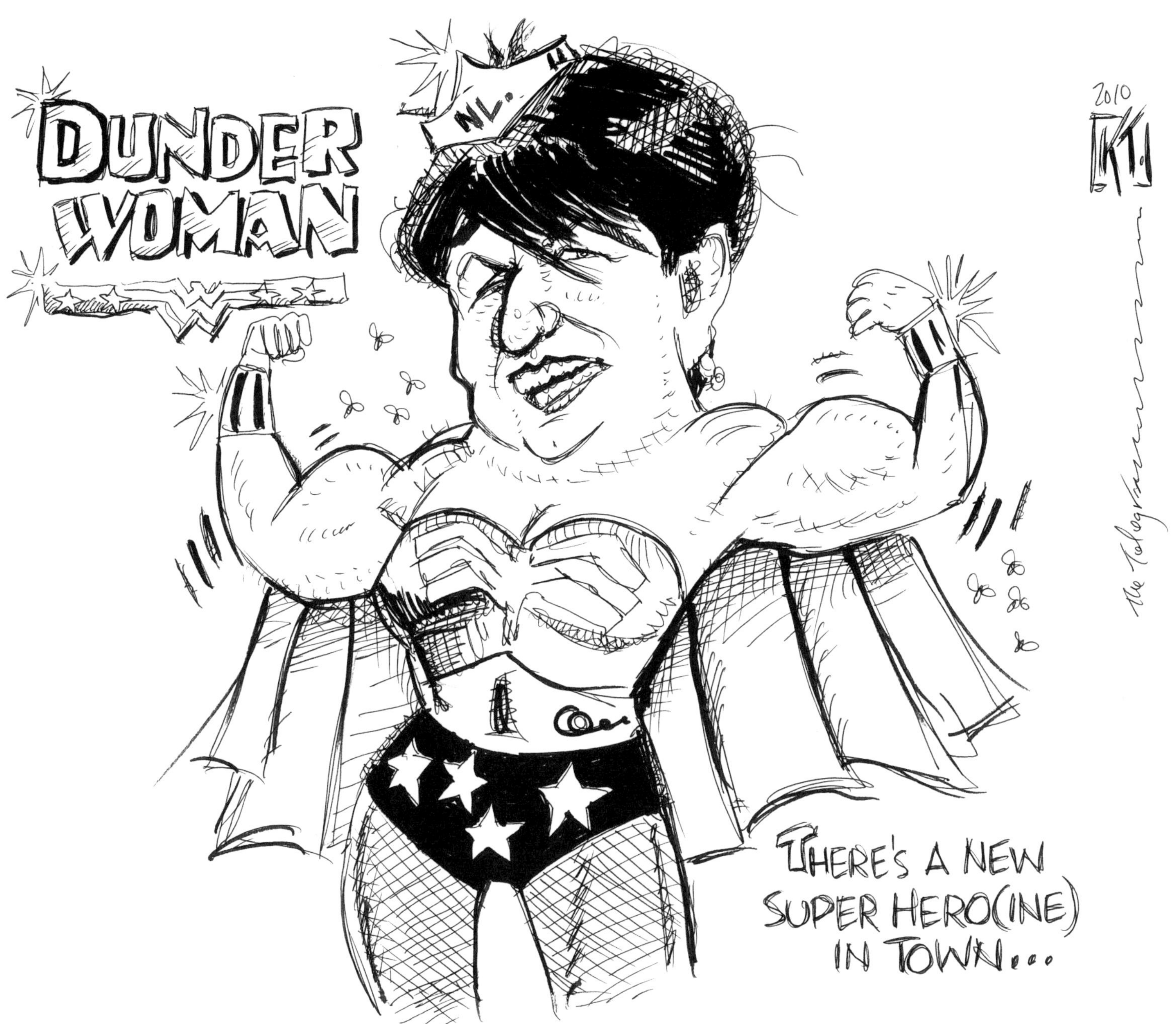
DUNDER WOMAN
NL.
2010
THERE'S A NEW SUPER HERO(INE) IN TOWN...

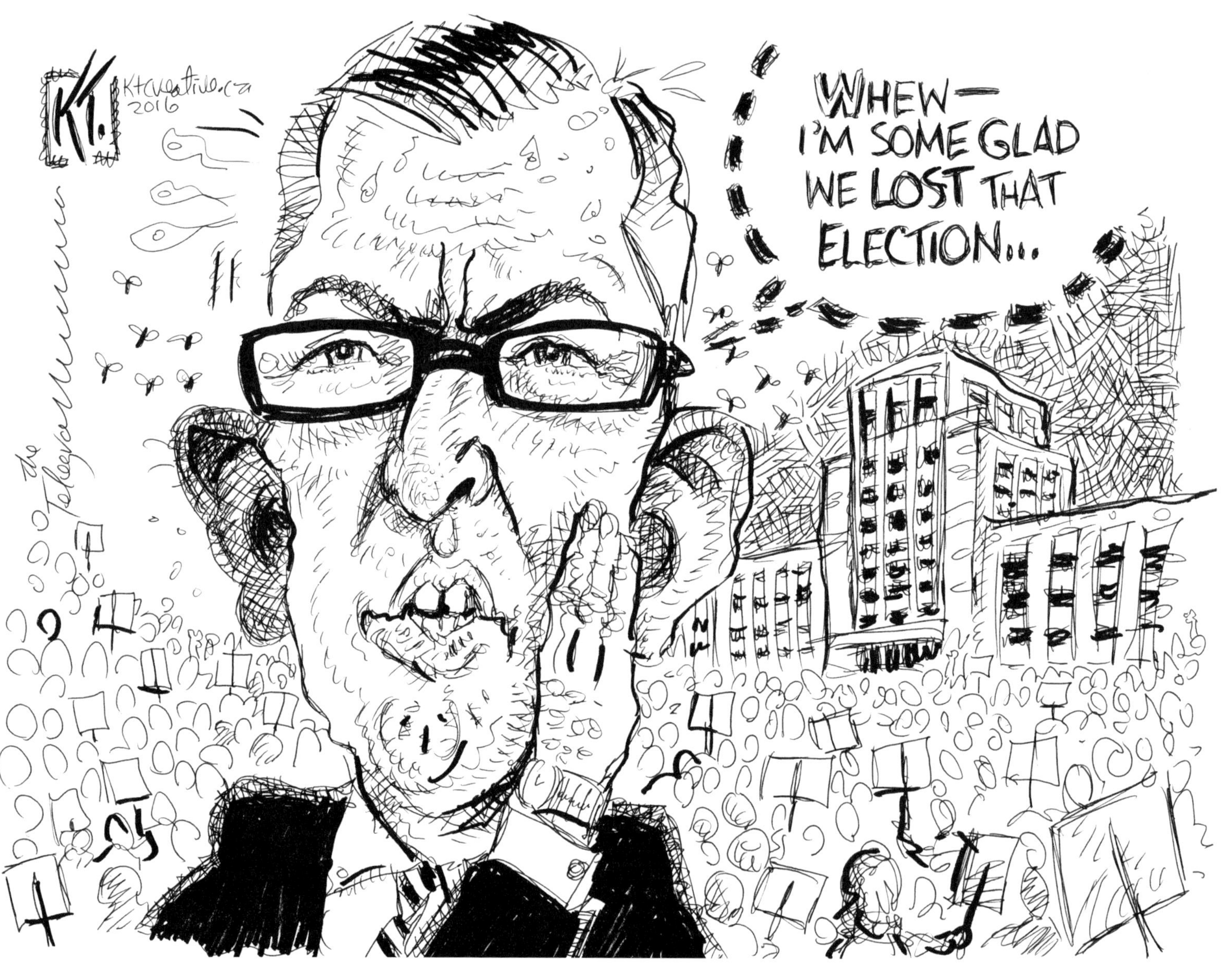

Ktcreative.ca
2016
WHEW—
I'M SOME GLAD
WE LOST THAT
ELECTION...

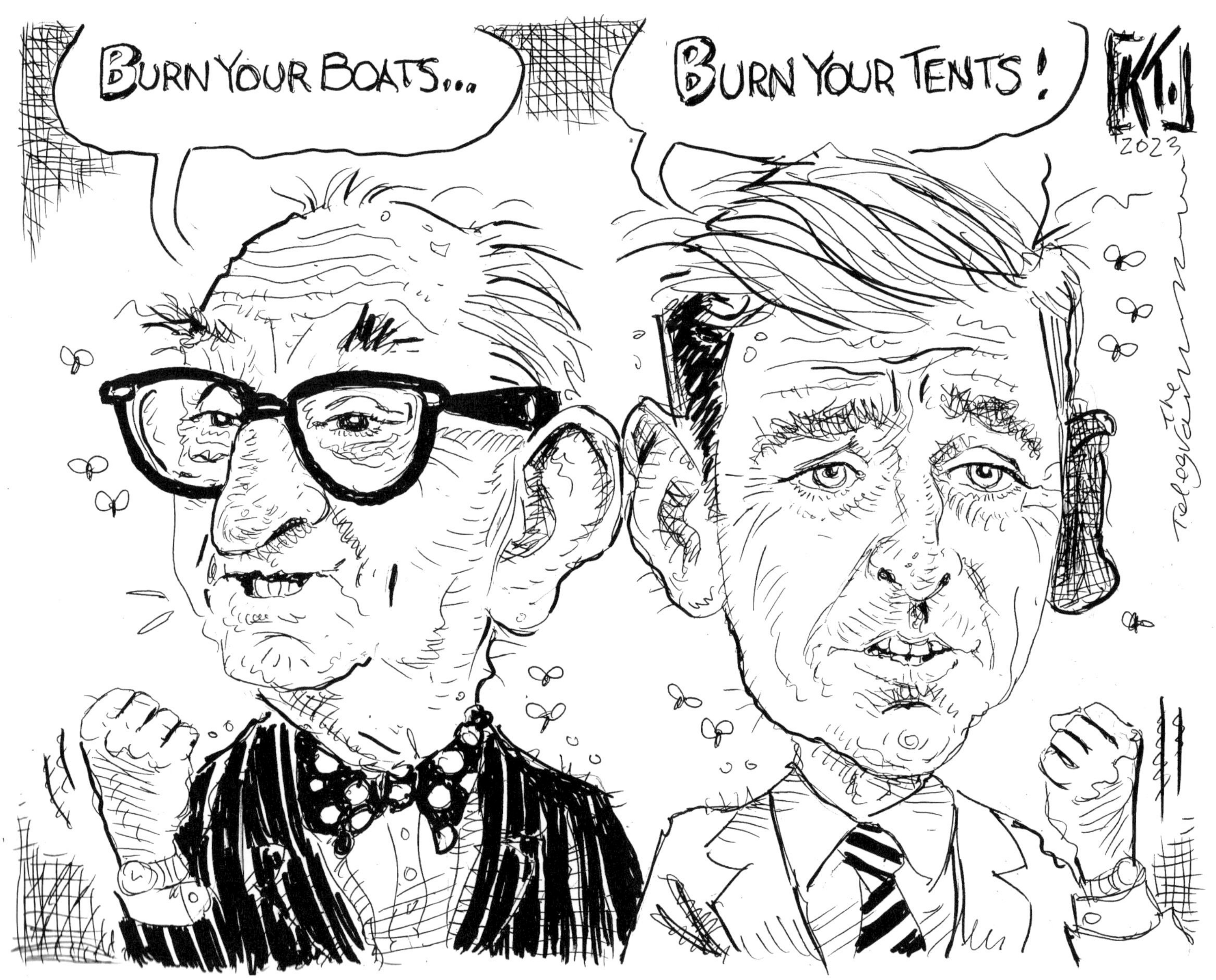

Burn Your Boats...
Burn Your Tents!
2023

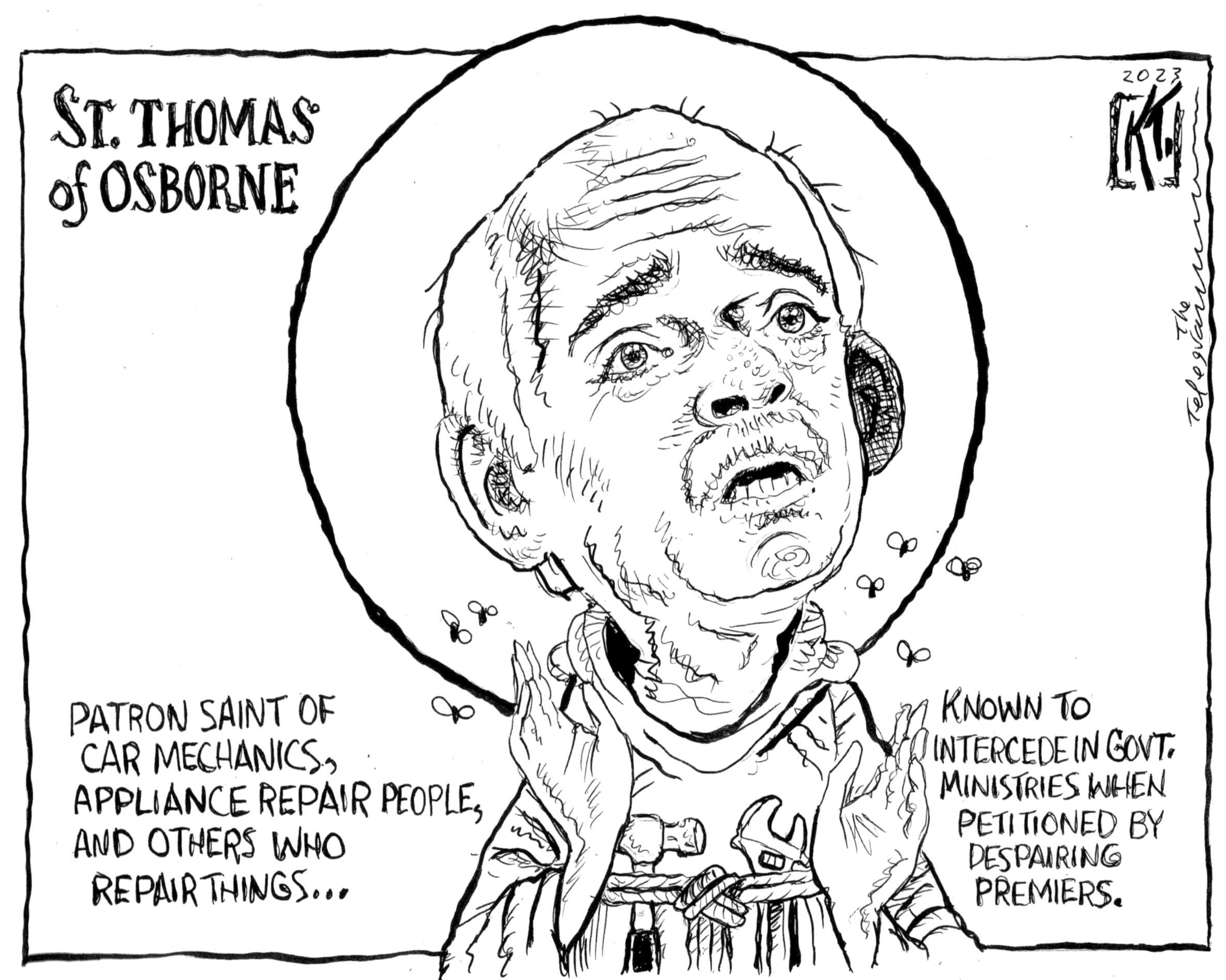

ST. THOMAS of OSBORNE
2023
PATRON SAINT OF CAR MECHANICS, APPLIANCE REPAIR PEOPLE, AND OTHERS WHO REPAIR THINGS...
KNOWN TO INTERCEDE IN GOVT. MINISTRIES WHEN PETITIONED BY DESPAIRING PREMIERS.
The Telegram

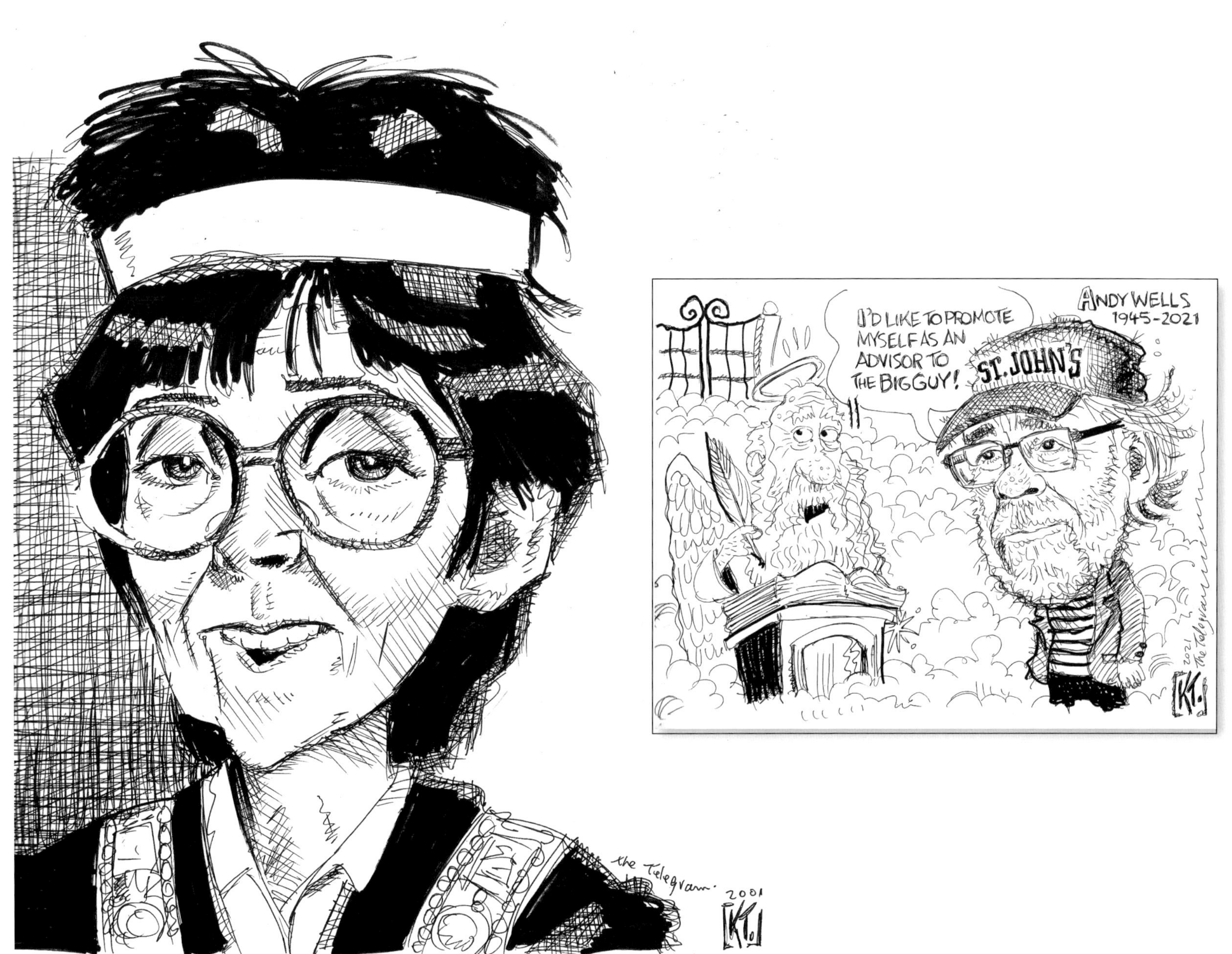

ANDY WELLS
1945-2021
I'D LIKE TO PROMOTE MYSELF AS AN ADVISOR TO THE BIG GUY!
ST. JOHN'S

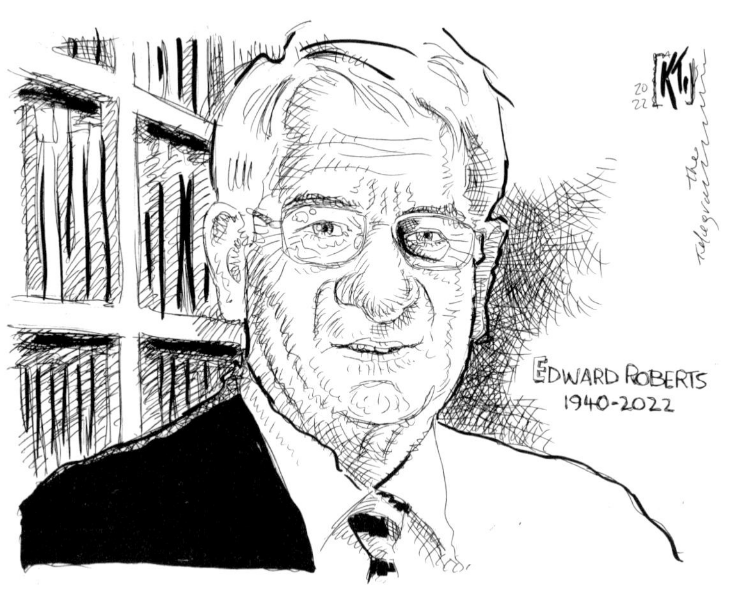

EDWARD ROBERTS
1940-2022


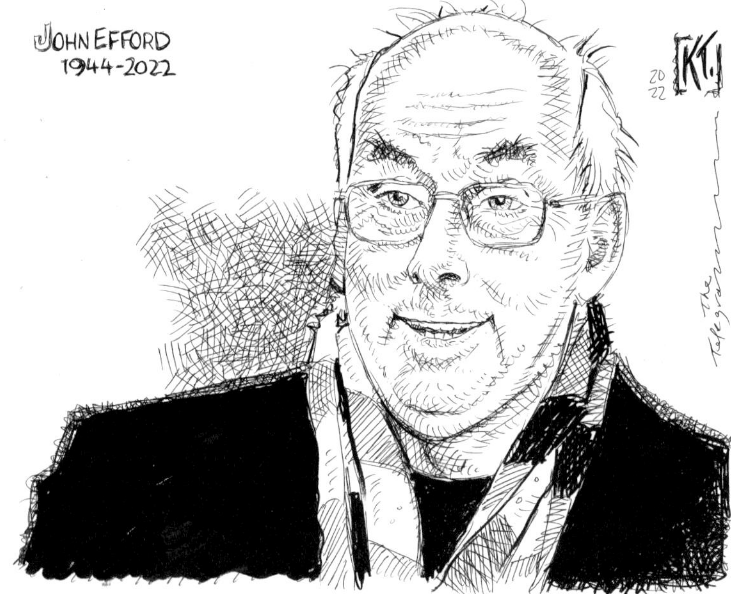

JOHN EFFORD
1944-2022

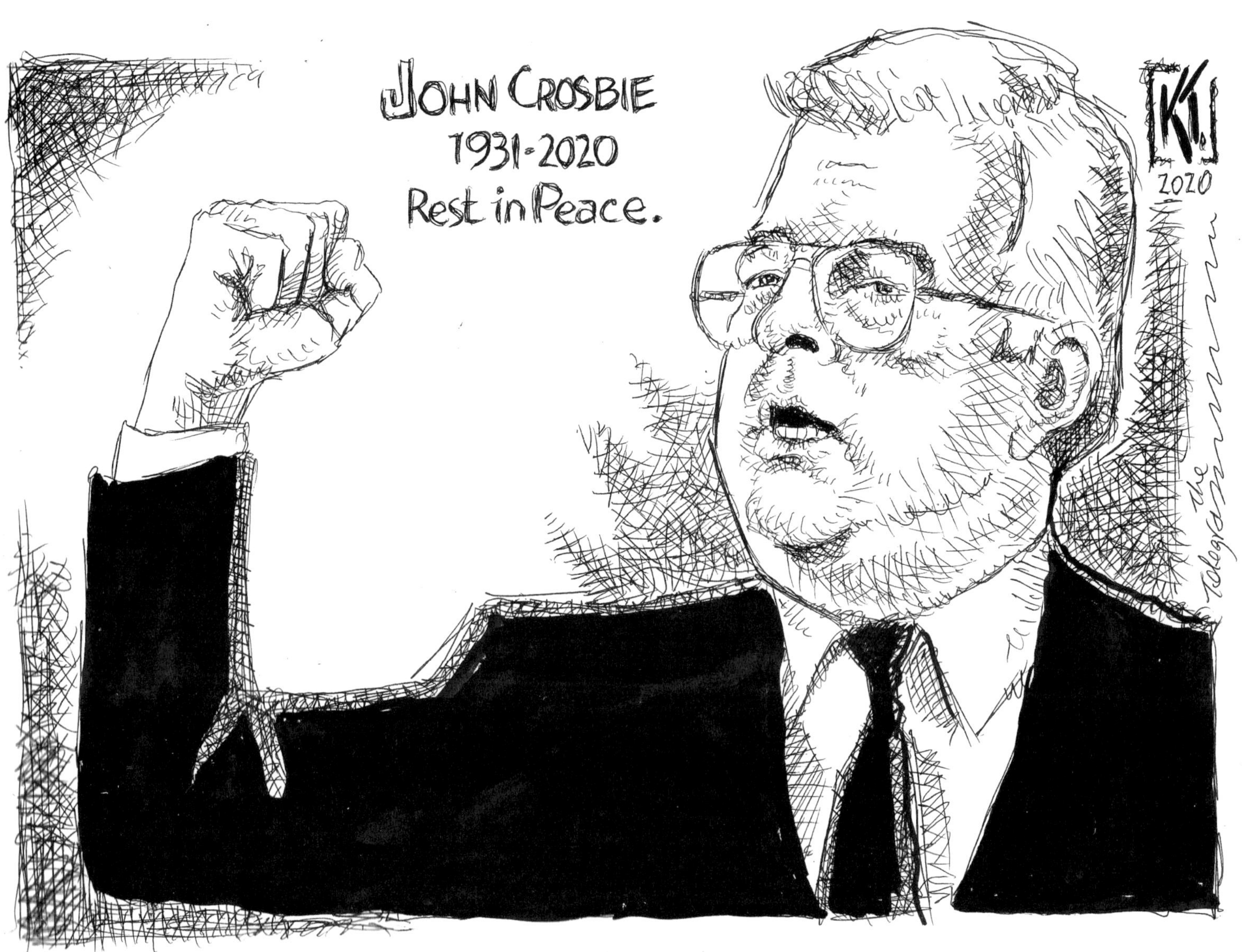
John Crosbie
1931-2020
Rest in Peace.

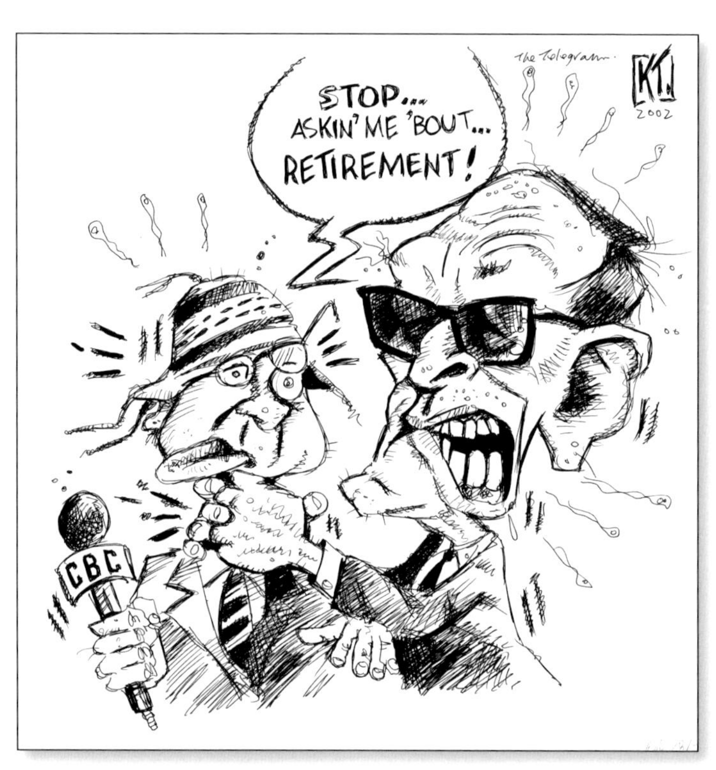

STOP...
ASKIN' ME 'BOUT...
RETIREMENT!
CBC
The Telegram
KT
2002


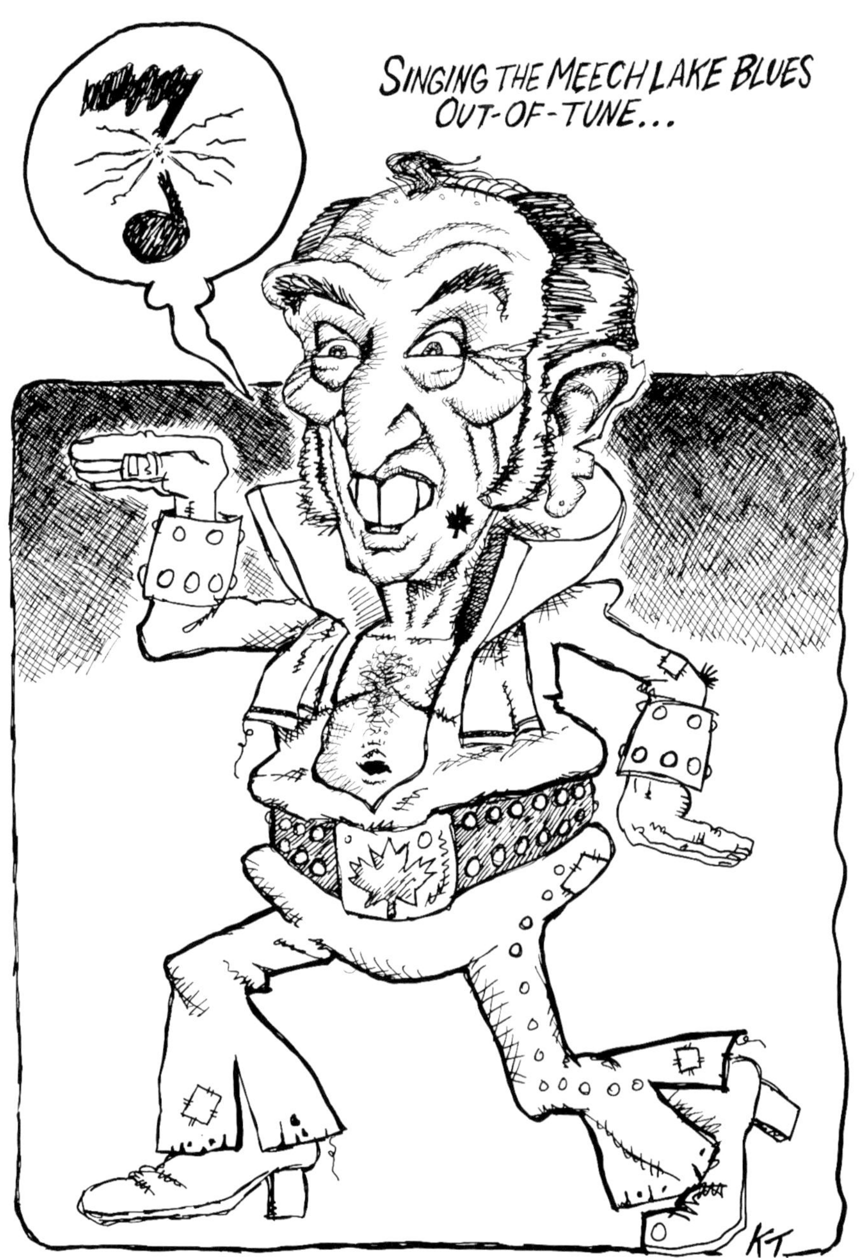

SINGING THE MEECH LAKE BLUES
OUT-OF-TUNE...
KT

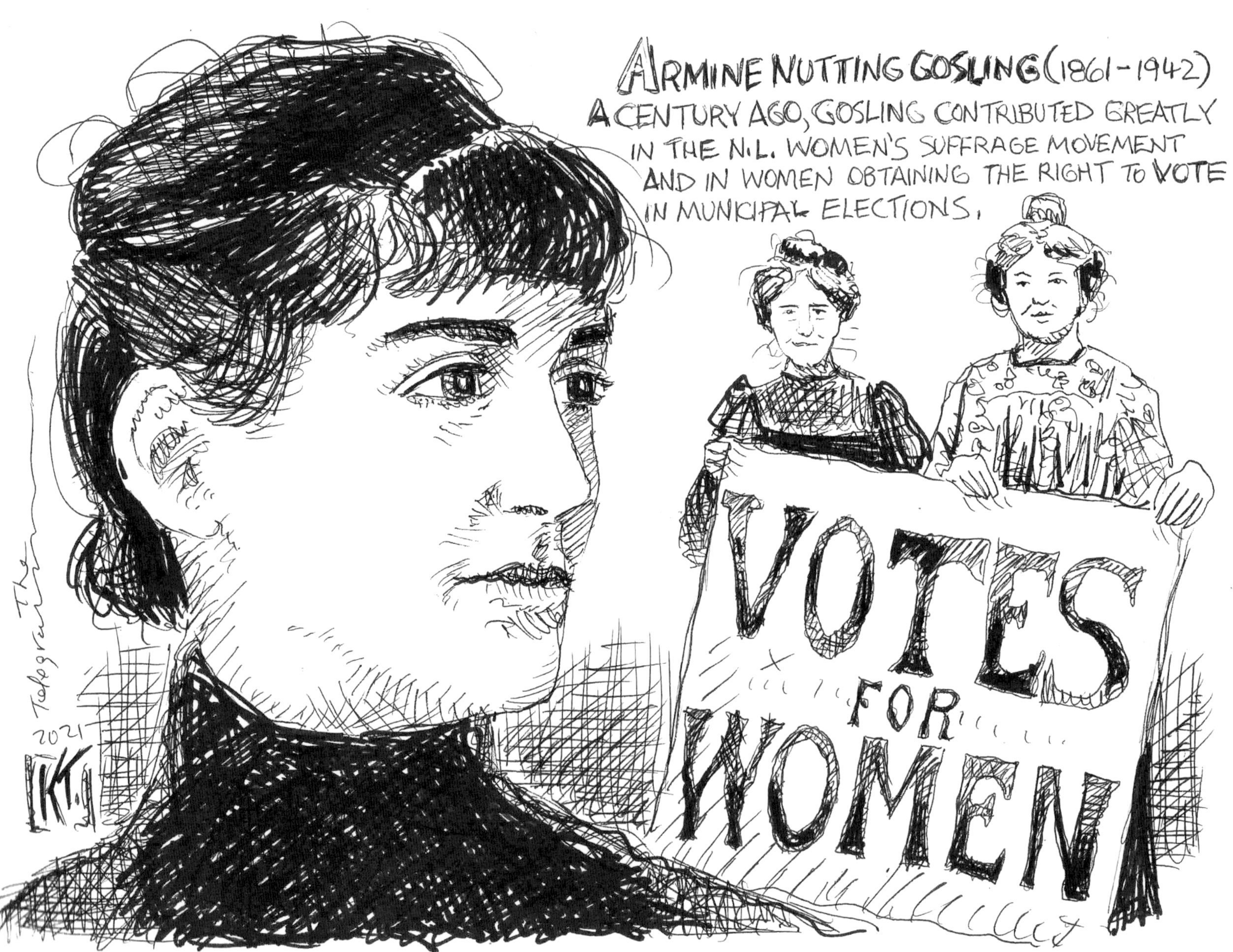

ARMINE NUTTING GOSLING (1861-1942)
A CENTURY AGO, GOSLING CONTRIBUTED GREATLY
IN THE N.L. WOMEN'S SUFFRAGE MOVEMENT
AND IN WOMEN OBTAINING THE RIGHT TO VOTE
IN MUNICIPAL ELECTIONS.
VOTES FOR WOMEN

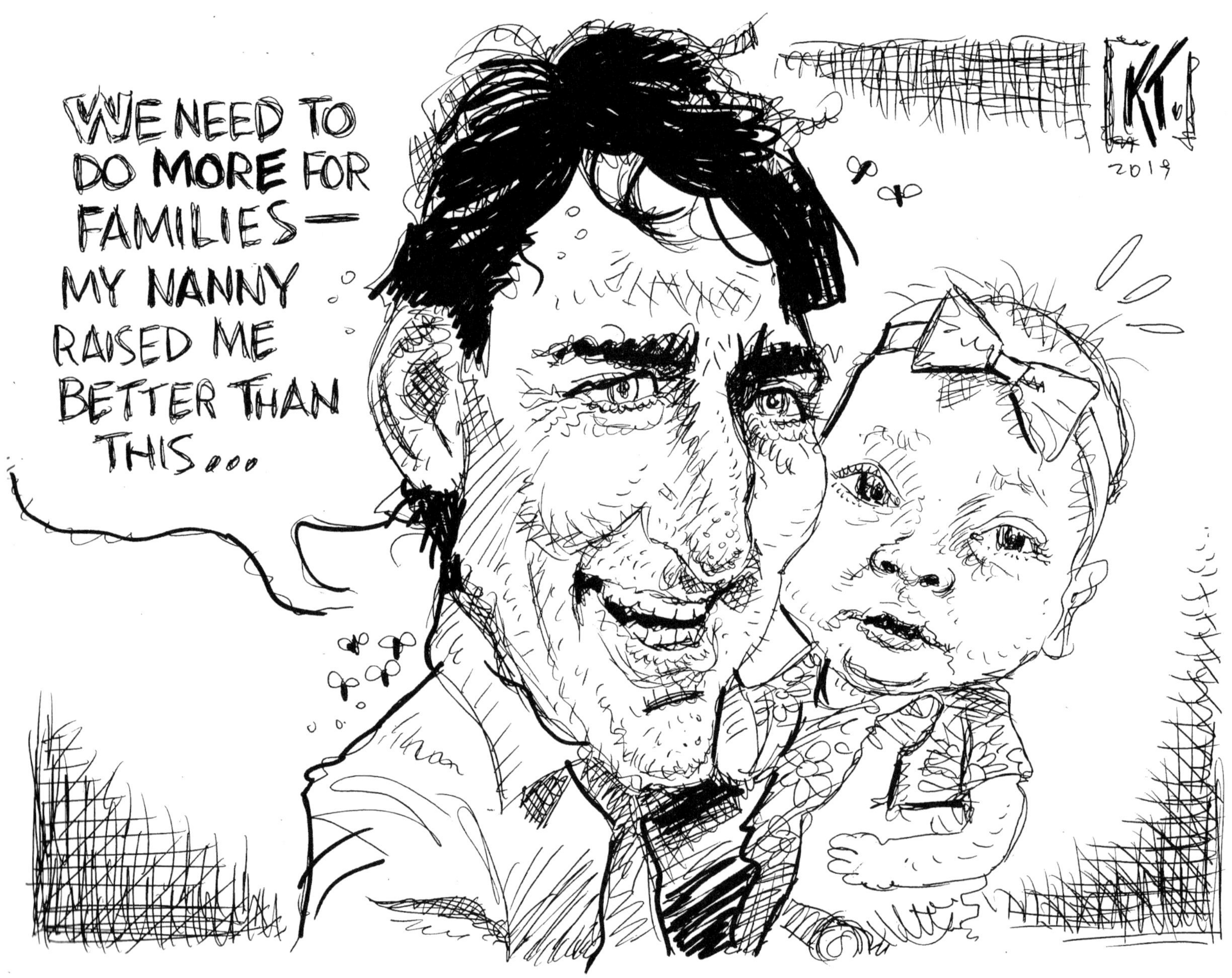

WE NEED TO DO MORE FOR FAMILIES— MY NANNY RAISED ME BETTER THAN THIS...
2019

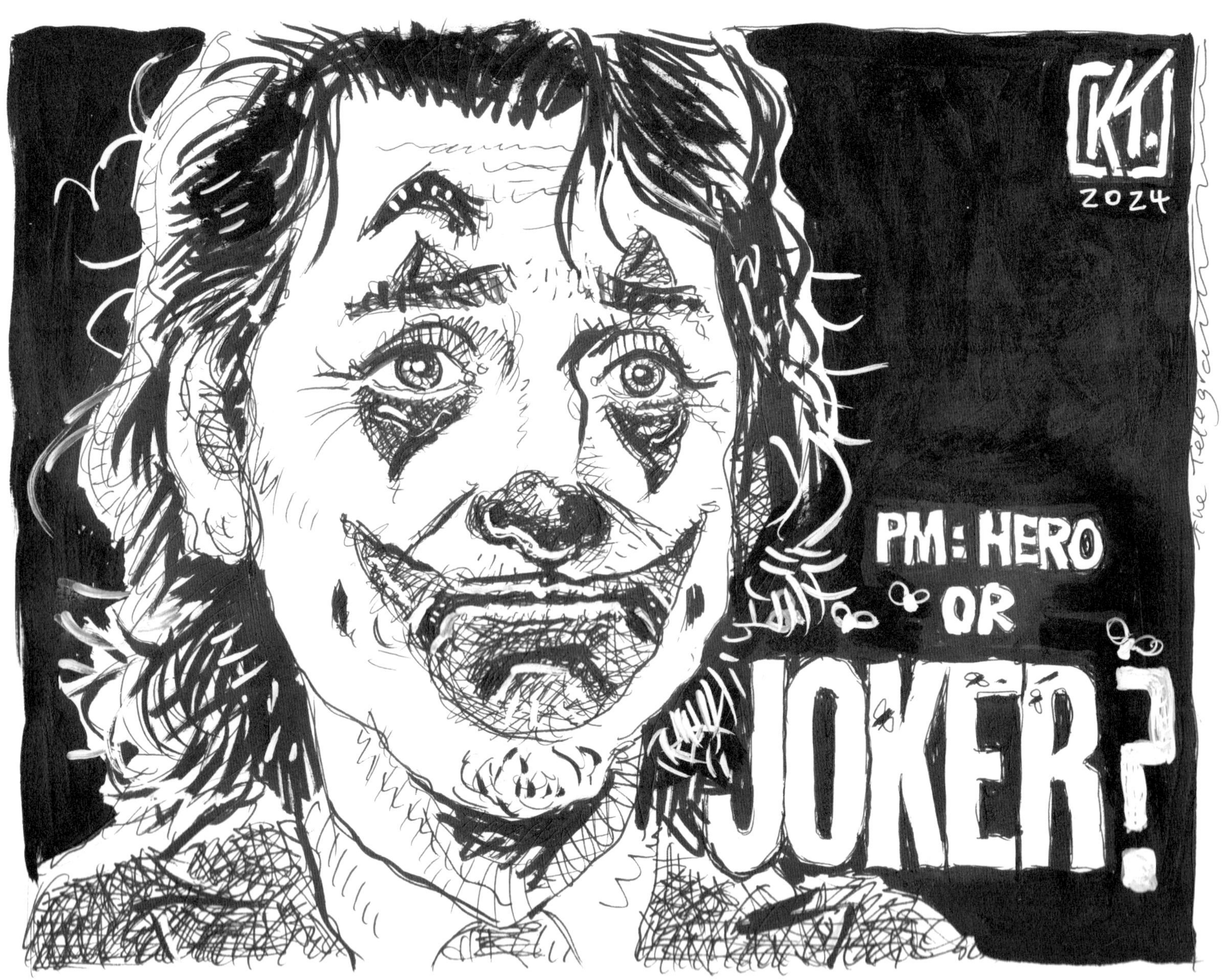

PM: HERO OR JOKER?
2024

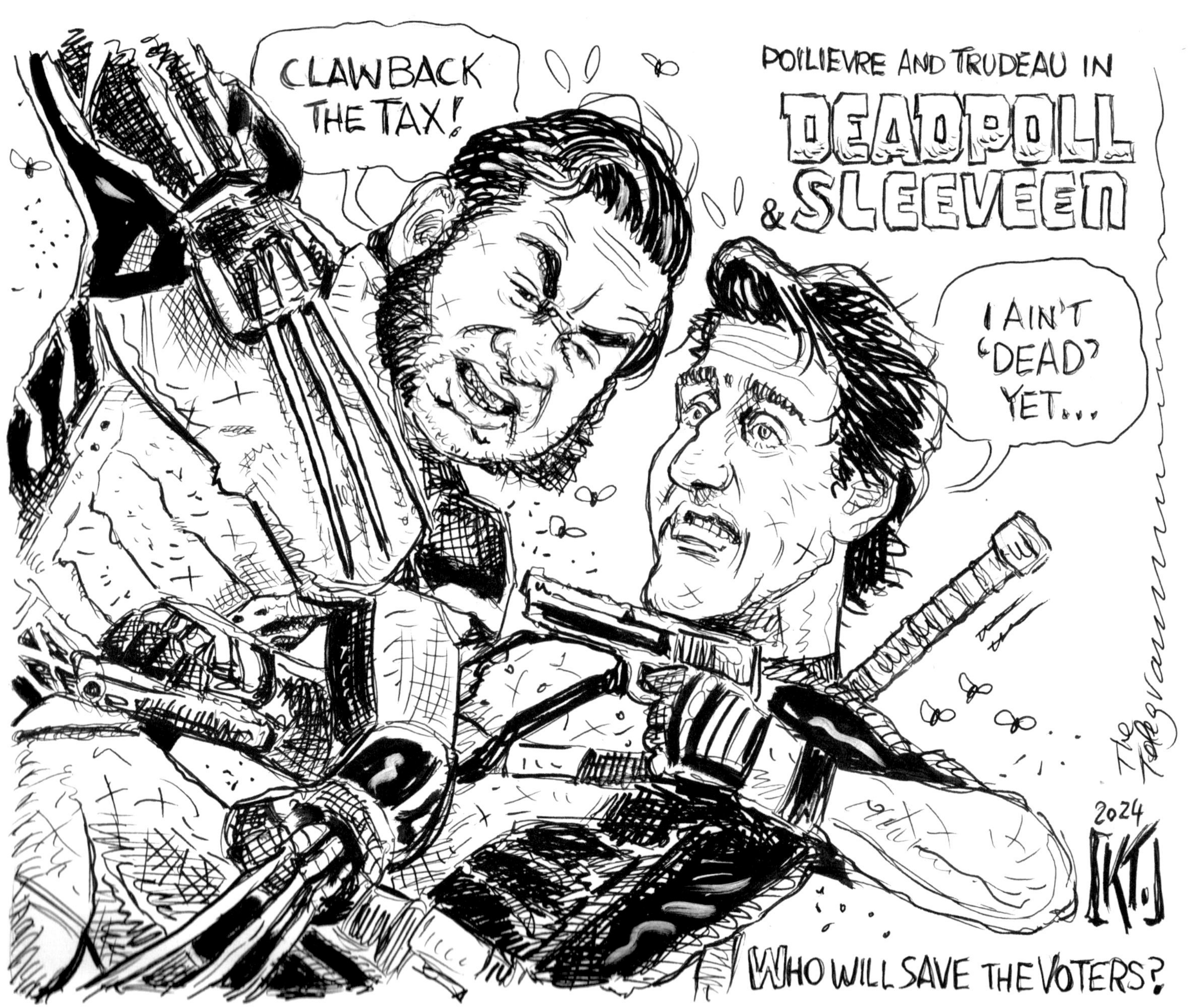

CLAWBACK THE TAX!
POILIEVRE AND TRUDEAU IN
DEADPOLL & SLEEVEEN
I AIN'T "DEAD" YET...
2024
WHO WILL SAVE THE VOTERS?

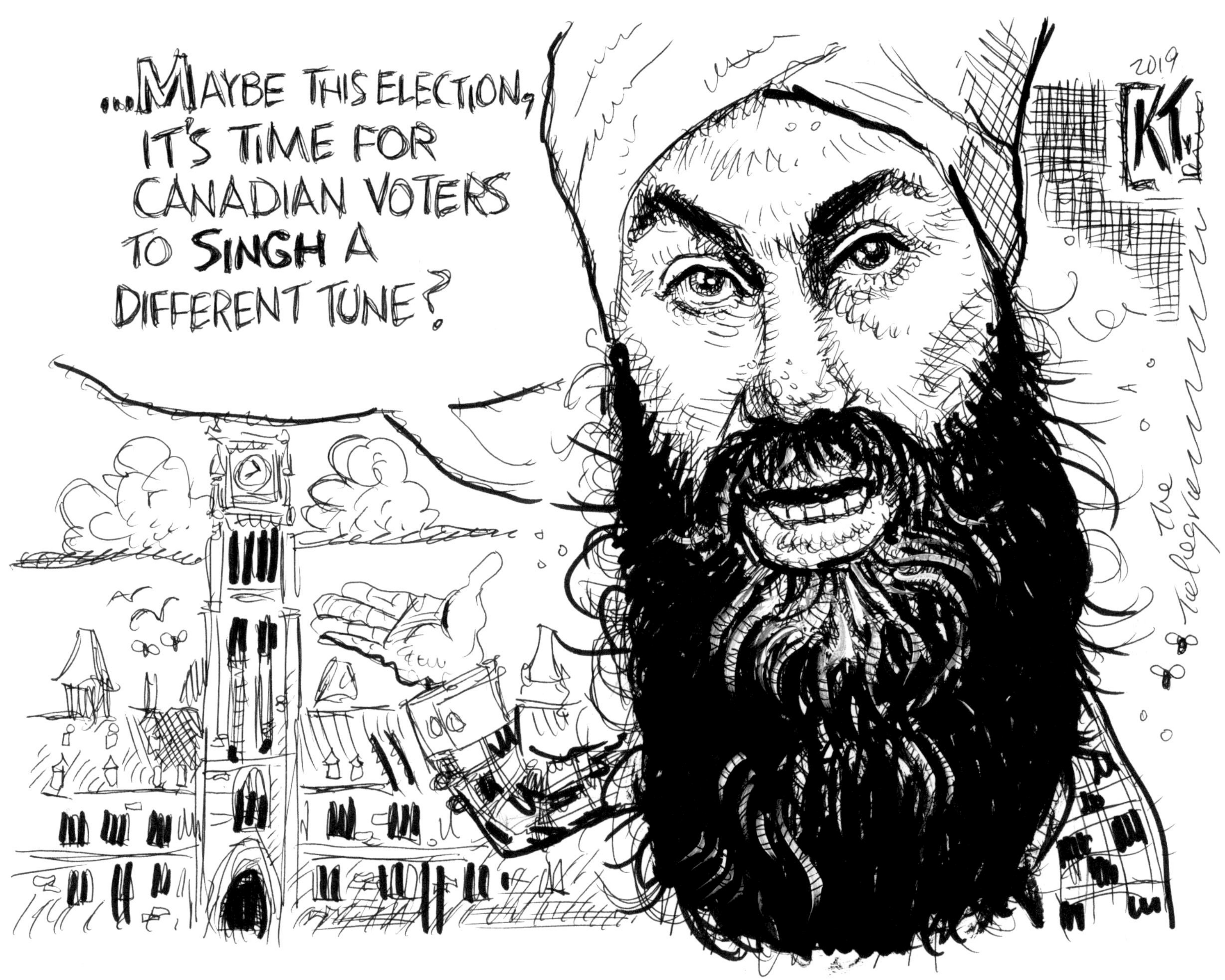

...Maybe this election, it's time for Canadian voters to Singh a different tune?
2019
KT
The Telegram

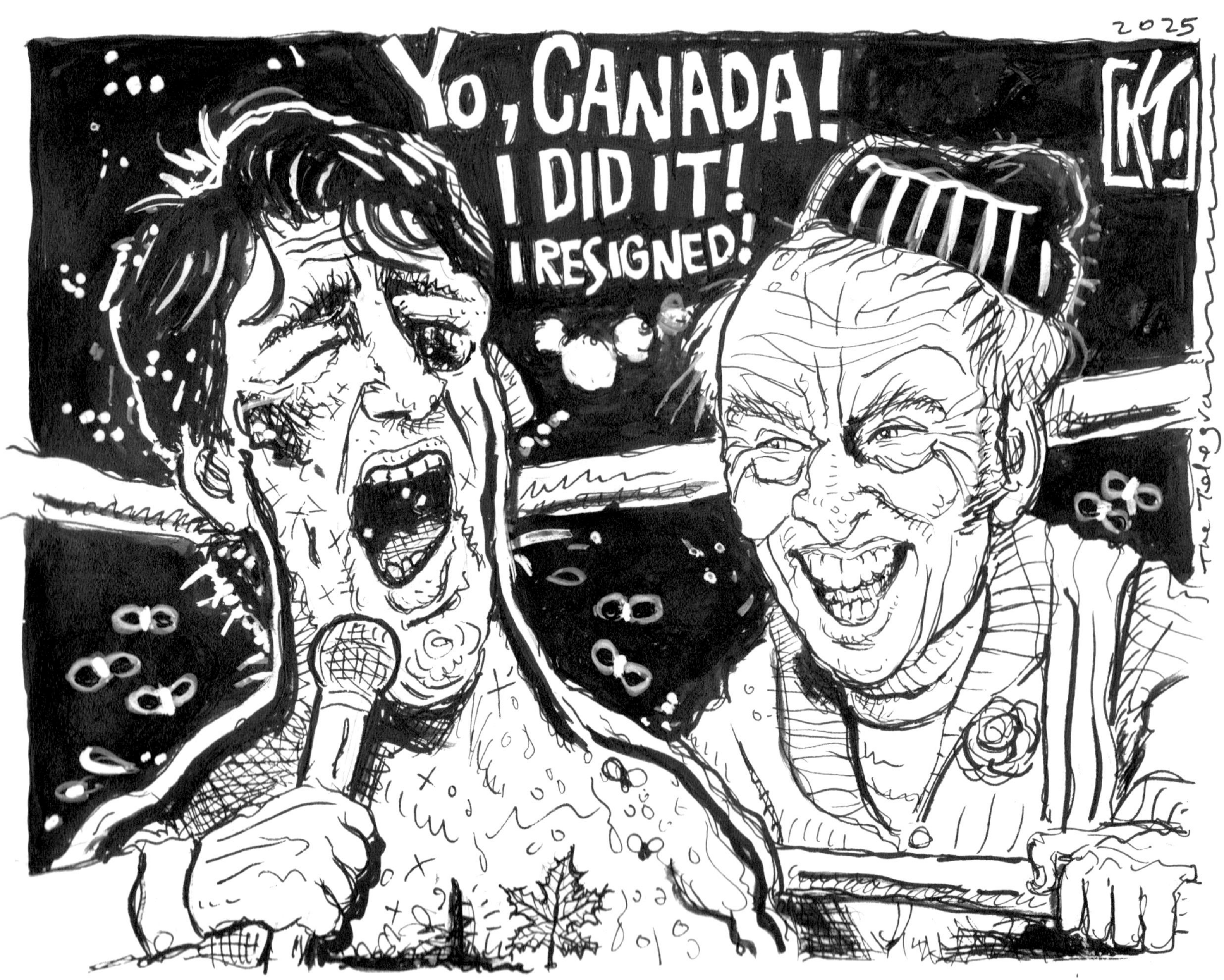
2025
Yo, CANADA!
I DID IT!
I RESIGNED!

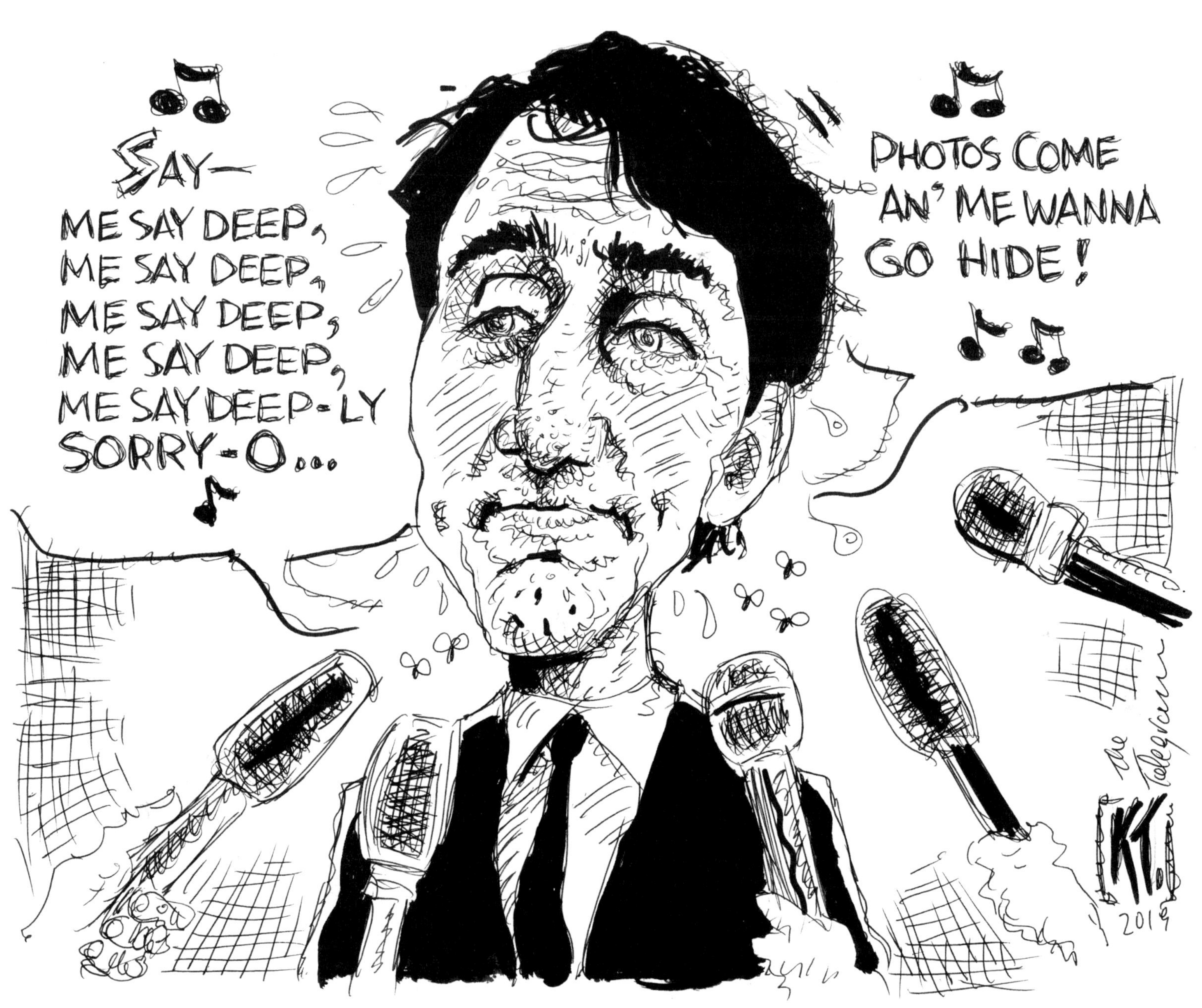

SAY—
ME SAY DEEP,
ME SAY DEEP,
ME SAY DEEP,
ME SAY DEEP,
ME SAY DEEP-LY
SORRY-O...

PHOTOS COME
AN' ME WANNA
GO HIDE!

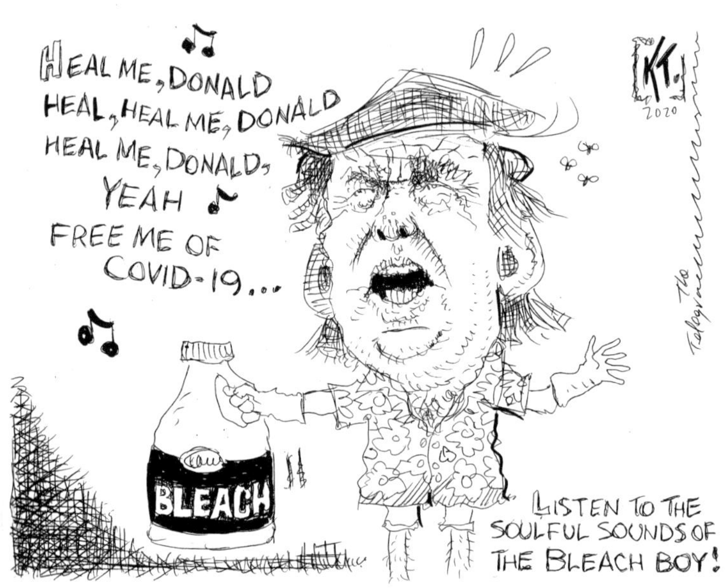

HEAL ME, DONALD
HEAL, HEAL ME, DONALD
HEAL ME, DONALD,
YEAH
FREE ME OF
COVID-19...
BLEACH
LISTEN TO THE
SOULFUL SOUNDS OF
THE BLEACH BOY!


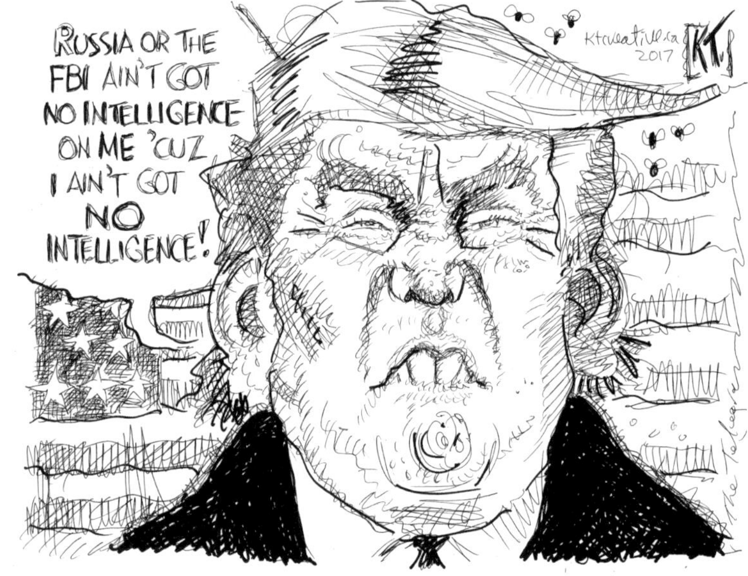

RUSSIA OR THE
FBI AIN'T GOT
NO INTELLIGENCE
ON ME 'CUZ
I AIN'T GOT
NO
INTELLIGENCE!

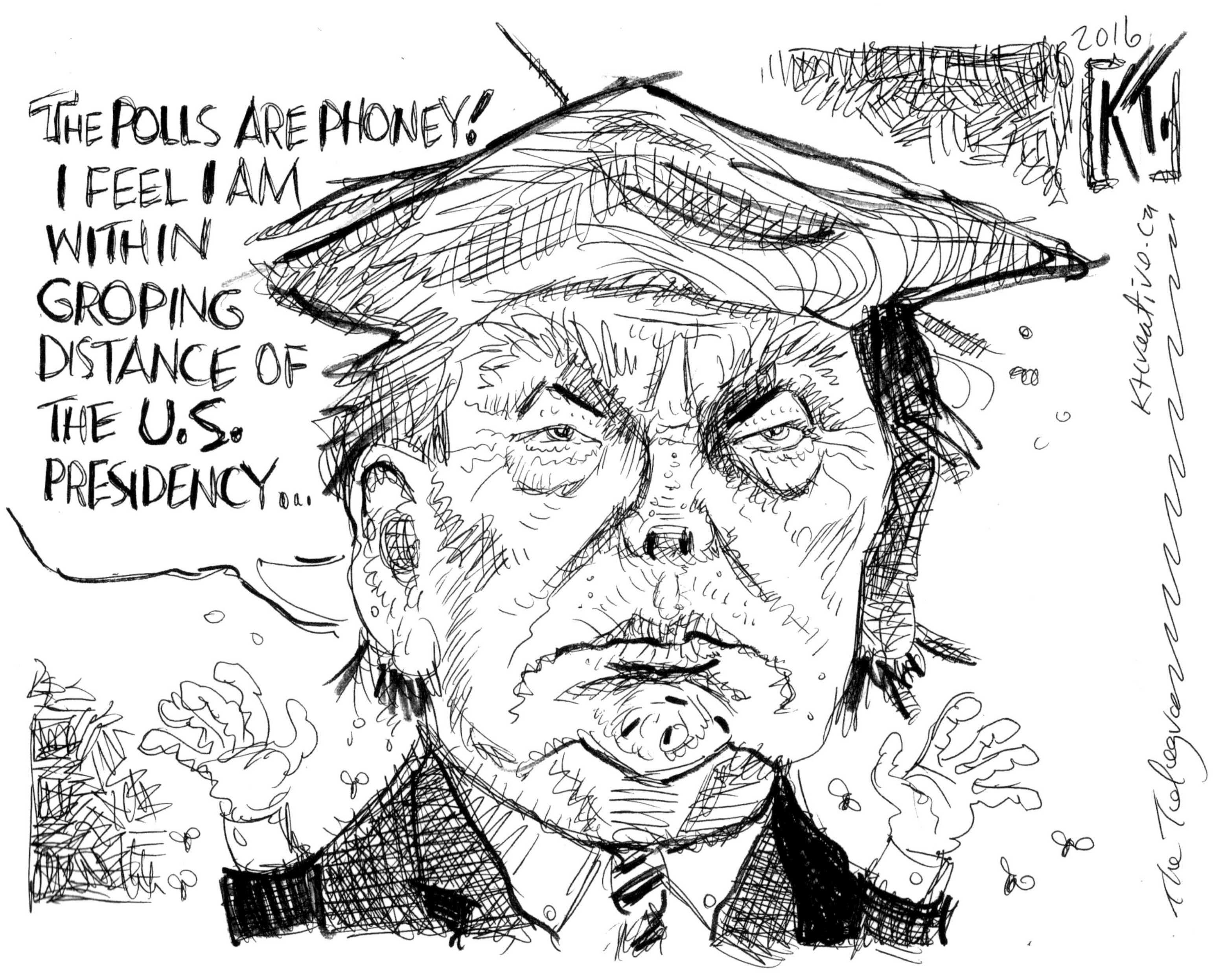

THE POLLS ARE PHONEY!
I FEEL I AM
WITHIN
GROPING
DISTANCE OF
THE U.S.
PRESIDENCY...
2016
KTkreativ.ca
The Telegram

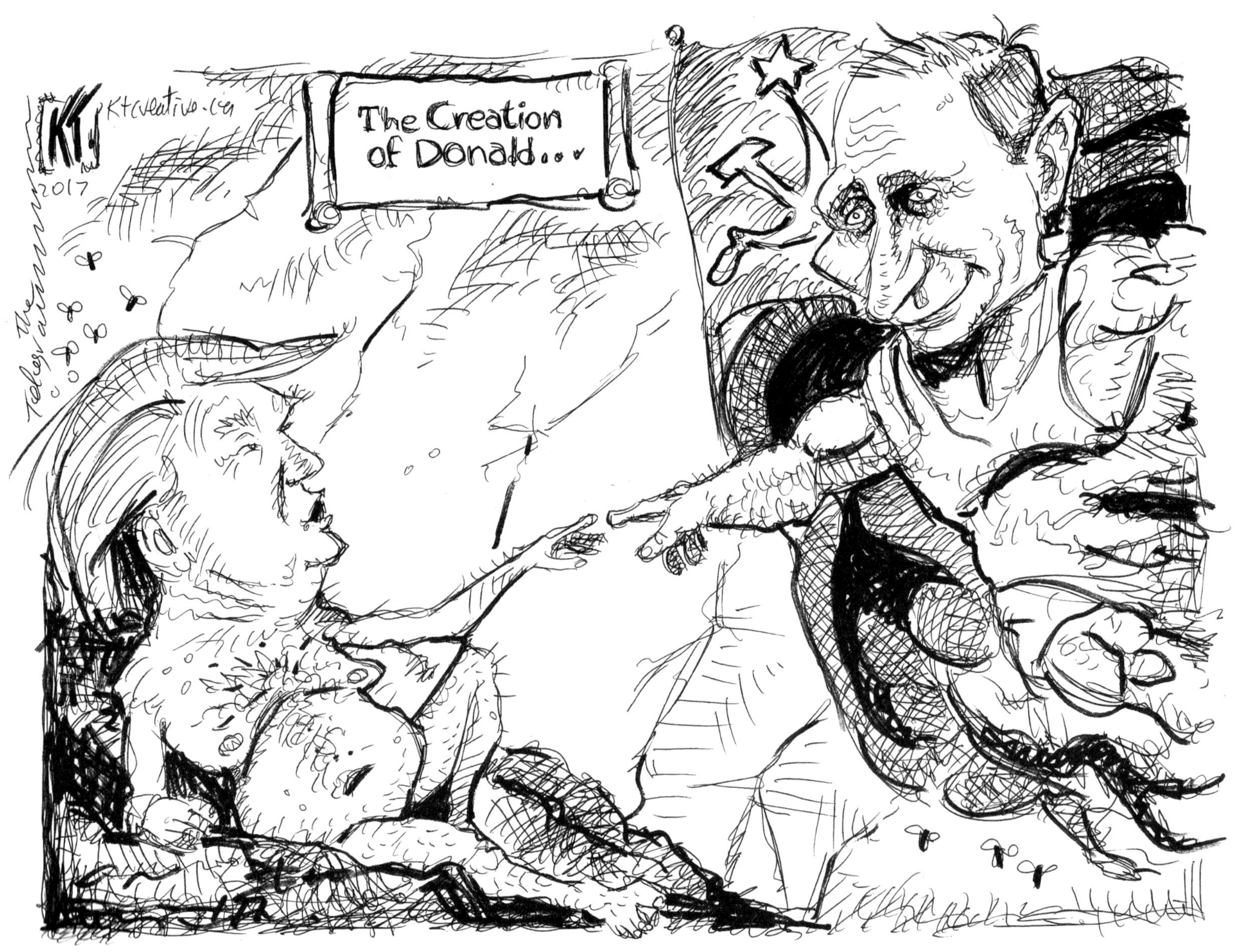

KTcreative.com
2017
The Creation
of Donald...

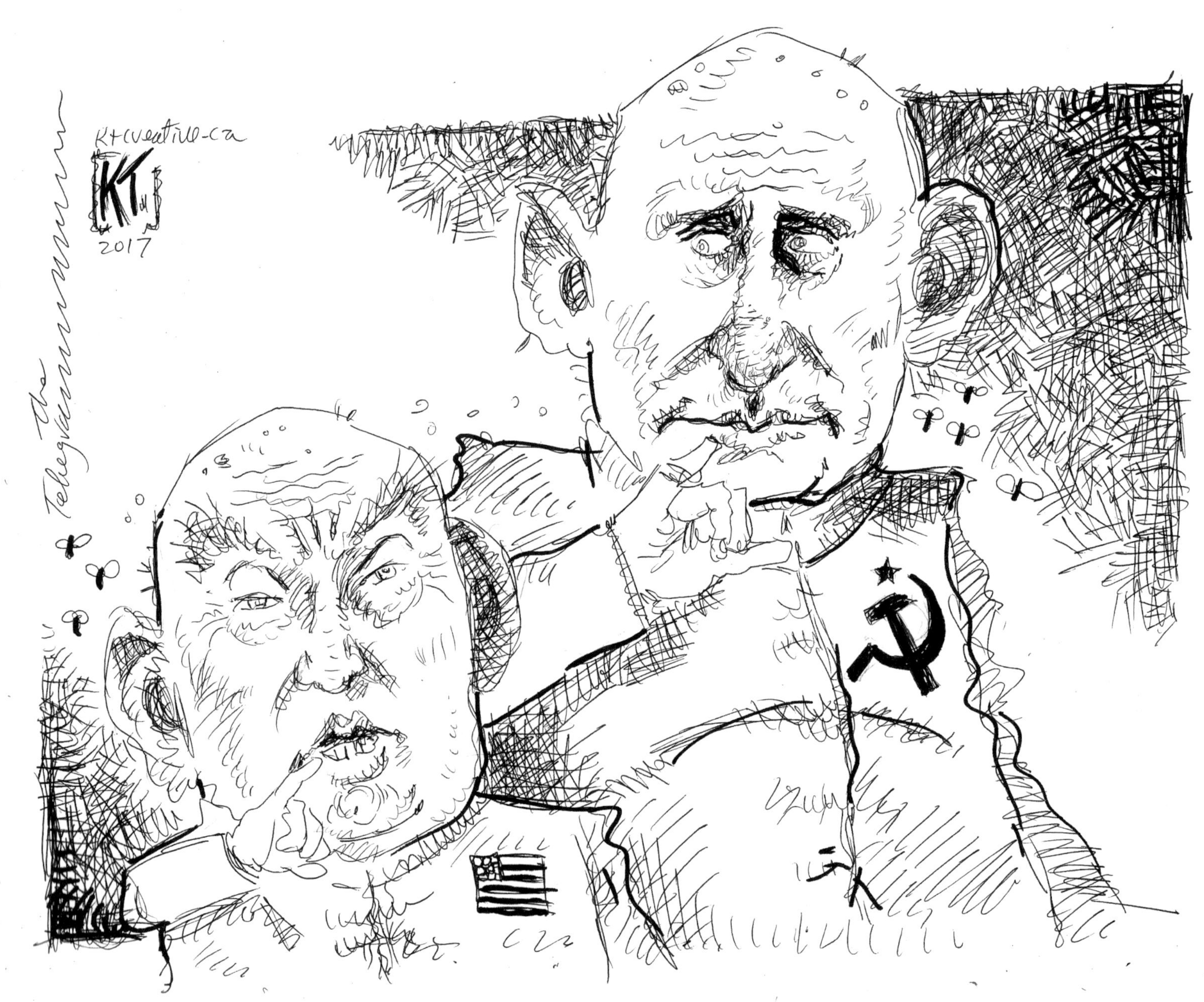

ktcreative.ca
KT
2017
The Telegram

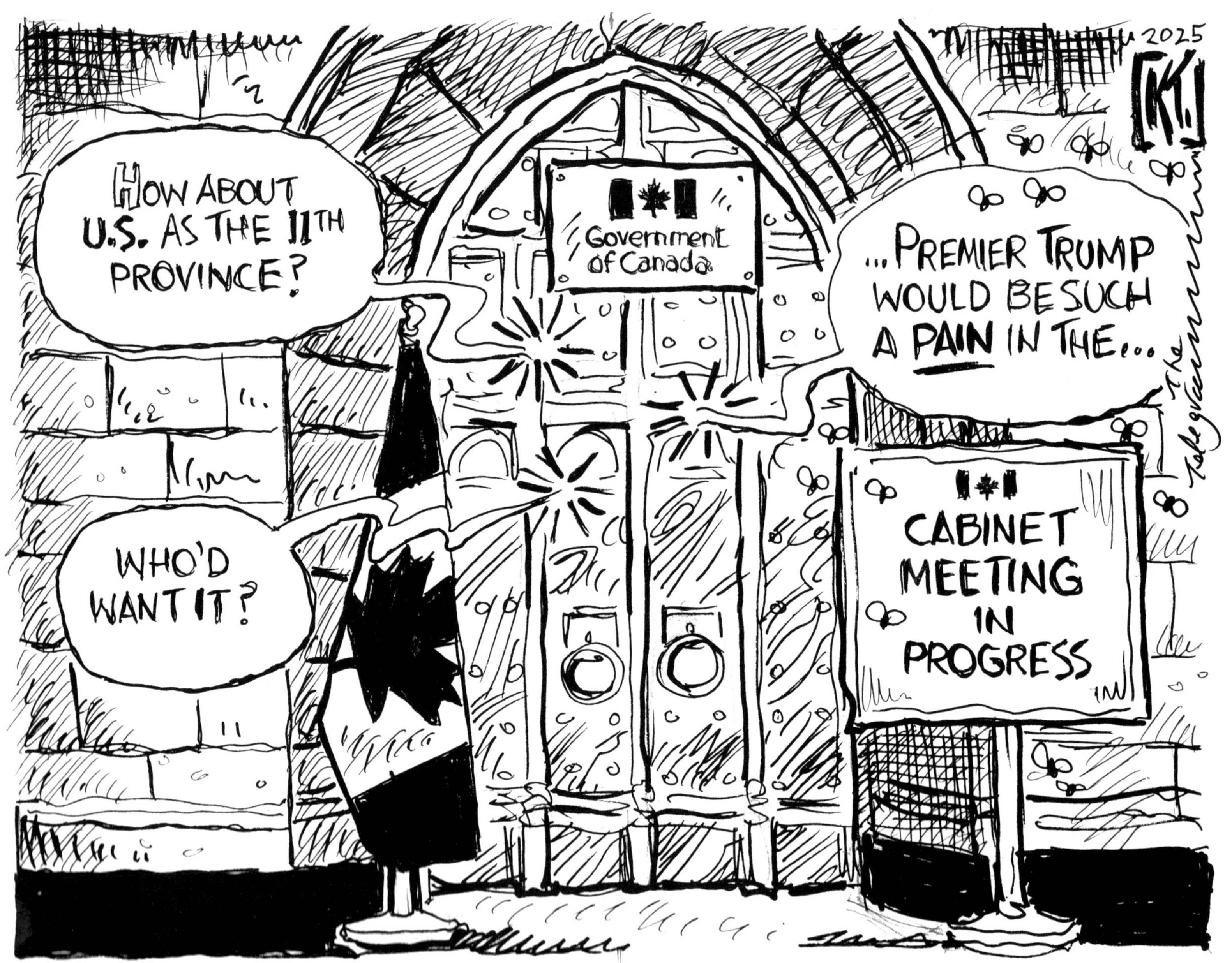

HOW ABOUT U.S. AS THE 11TH PROVINCE?
WHO'D WANT IT?
Government of Canada
...PREMIER TRUMP WOULD BE SUCH A PAIN IN THE...
CABINET MEETING IN PROGRESS
2025

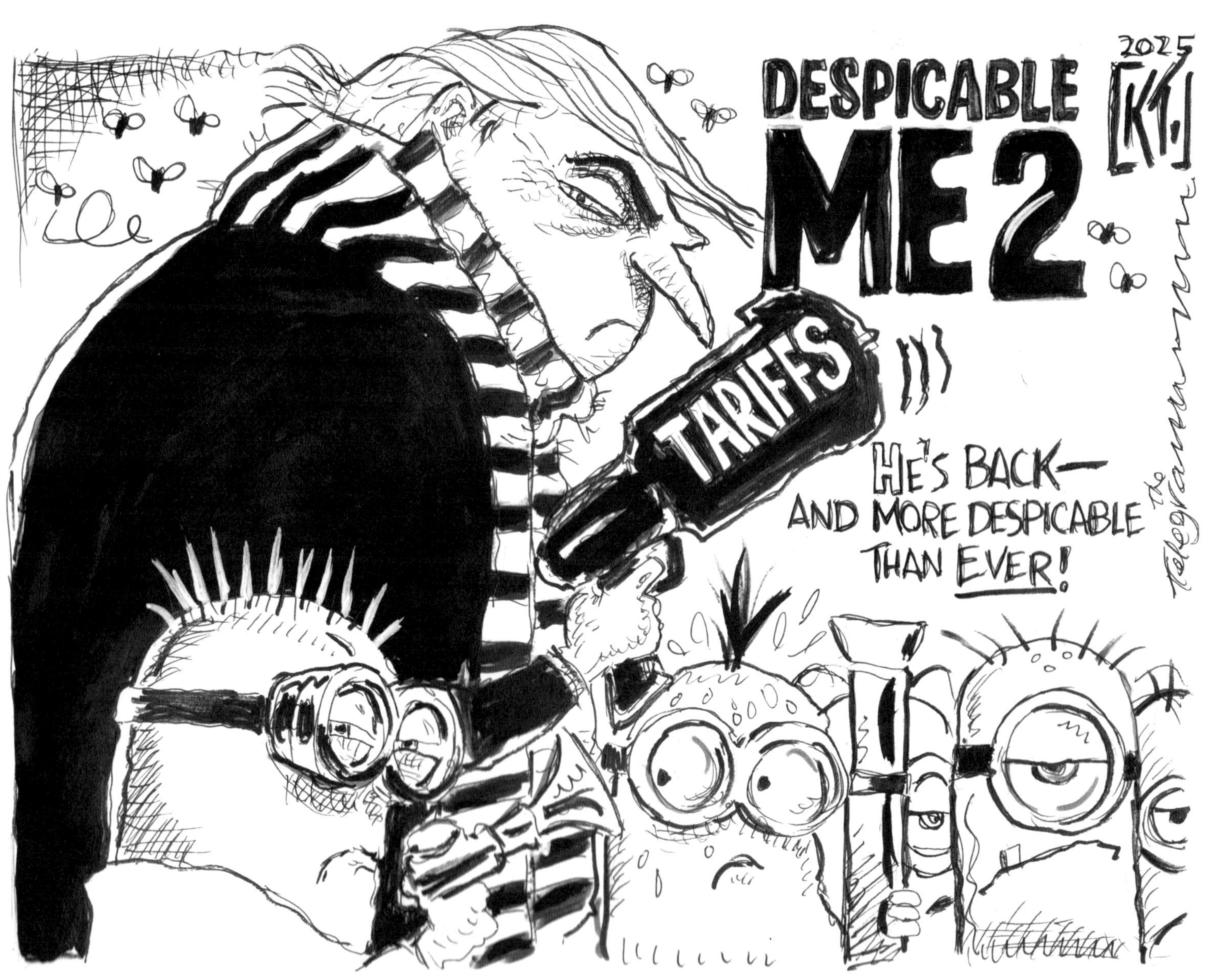

DESPICABLE
ME 2
2025
[K.T.]
TARIFFS
HE'S BACK—
AND MORE DESPICABLE
THAN EVER!

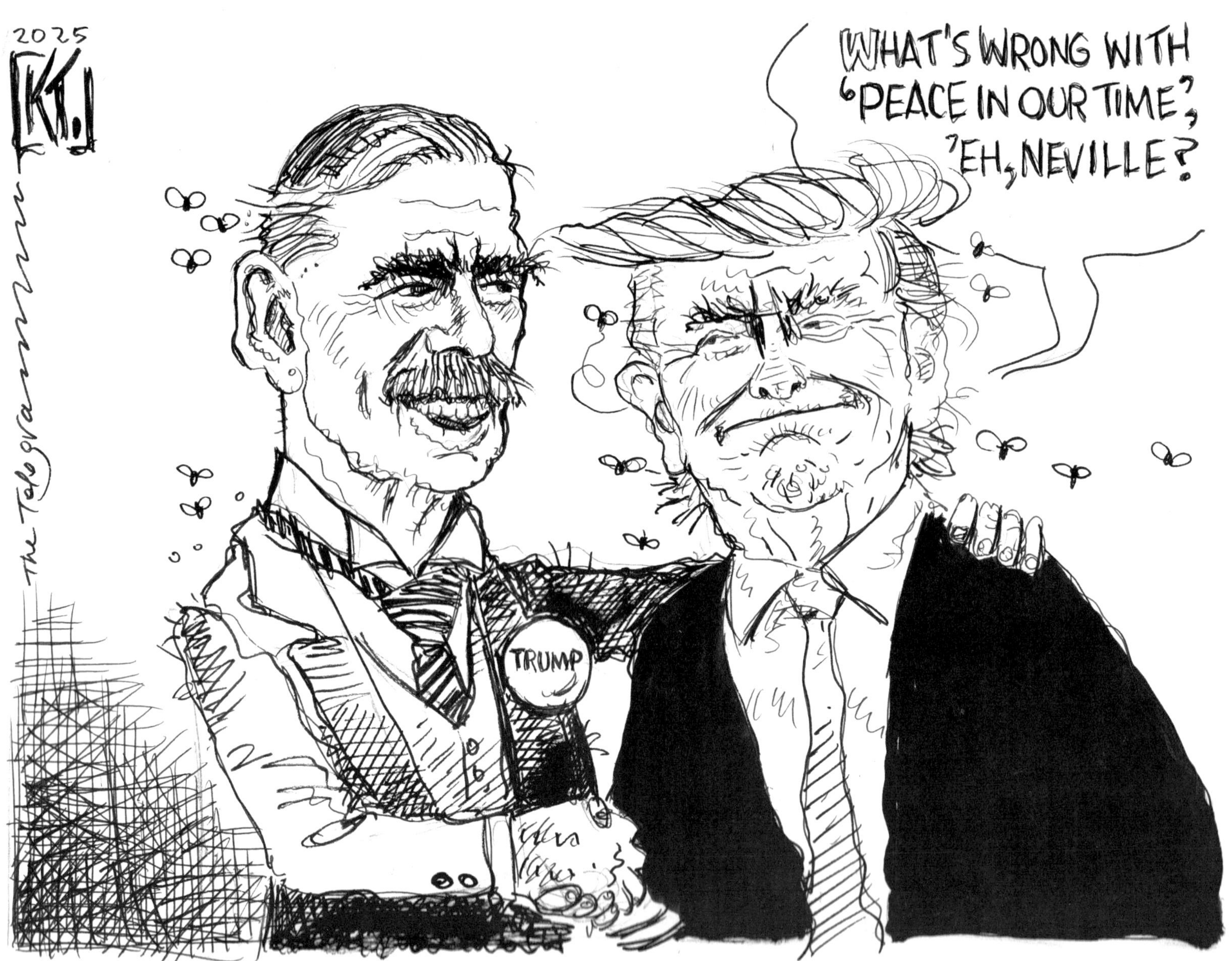

2025
The Telegram
WHAT'S WRONG WITH 'PEACE IN OUR TIME', 'EH, NEVILLE?
TRUMP

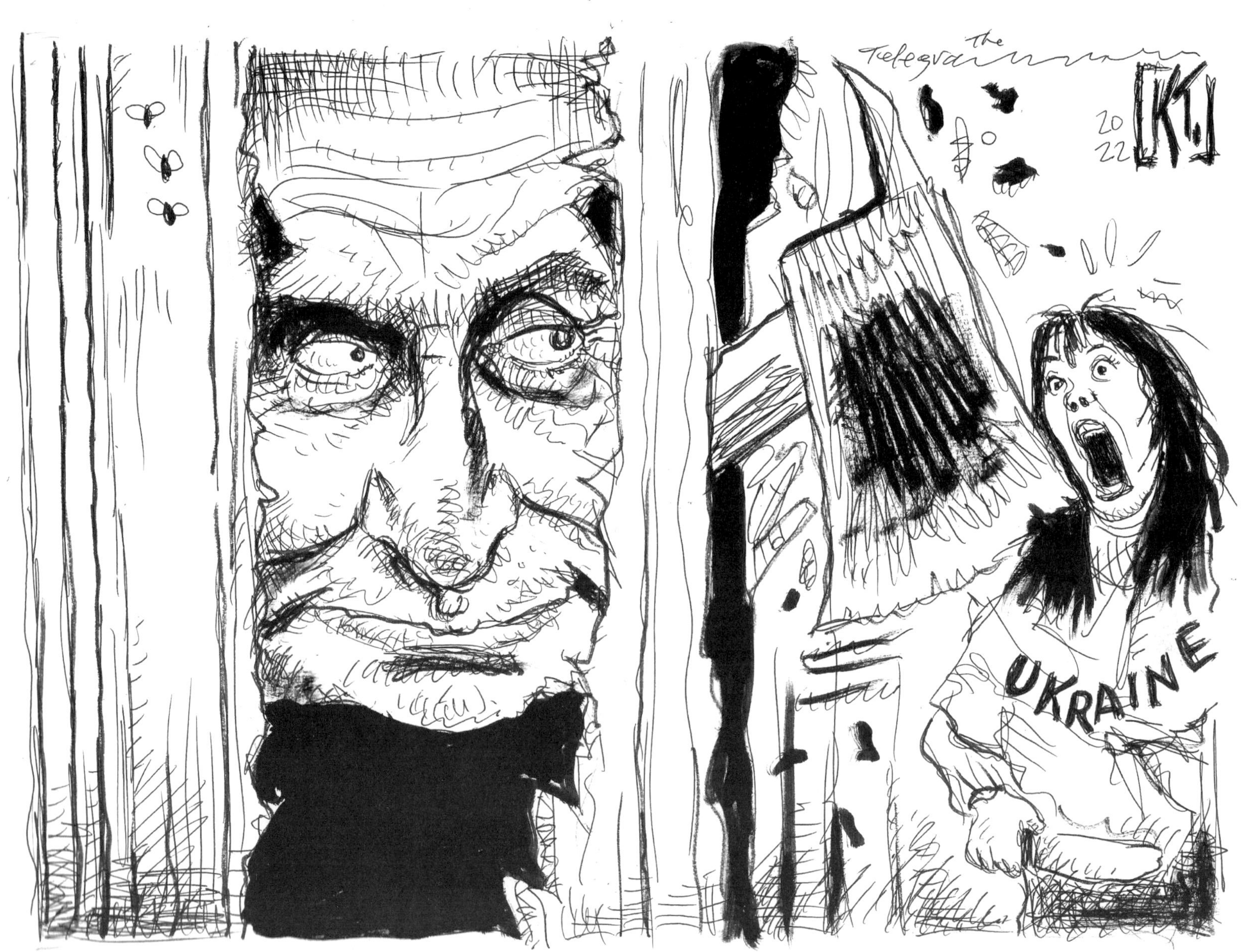
the
Telegraph
20
22
[KT]
UKRAINE

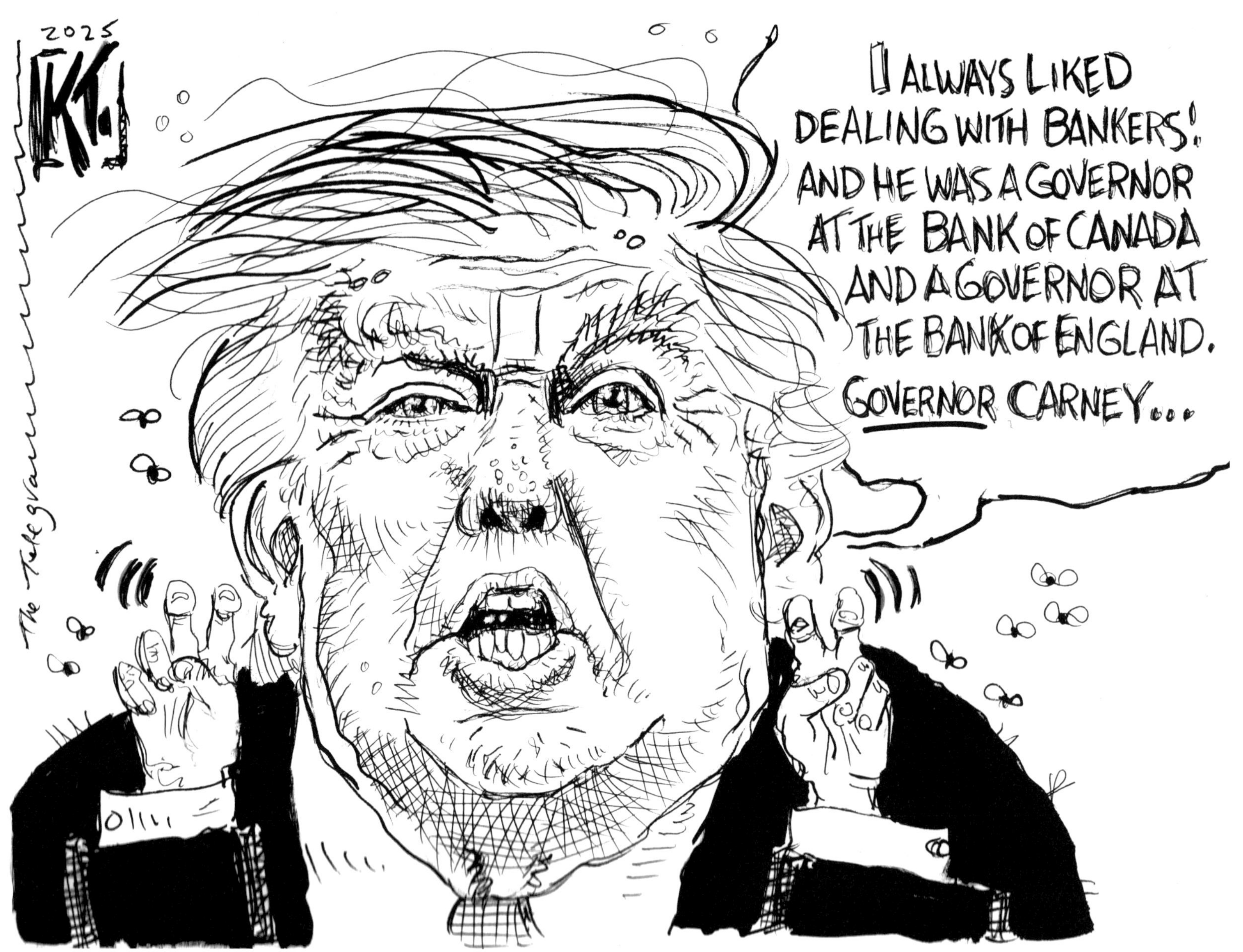
2025
The Telegram
I ALWAYS LIKED DEALING WITH BANKERS!
AND HE WAS A GOVERNOR AT THE BANK OF CANADA AND A GOVERNOR AT THE BANK OF ENGLAND.
GOVERNOR CARNEY...

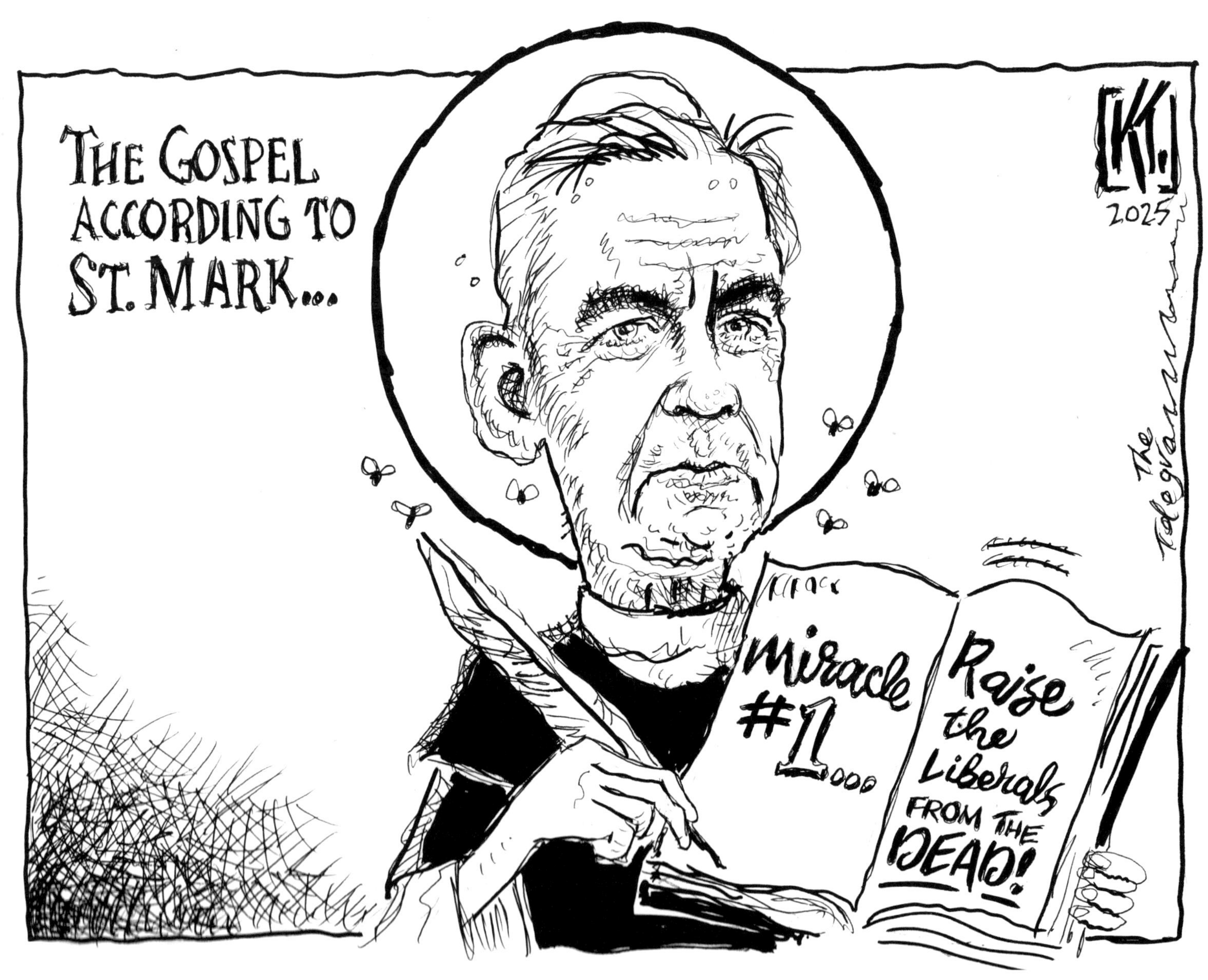

THE GOSPEL ACCORDING TO ST. MARK...
KT
2025
The Telegram
Miracle #1...
Raise the Liberals FROM THE DEAD!

# KT's NEWSMAKER OF THE YEAR

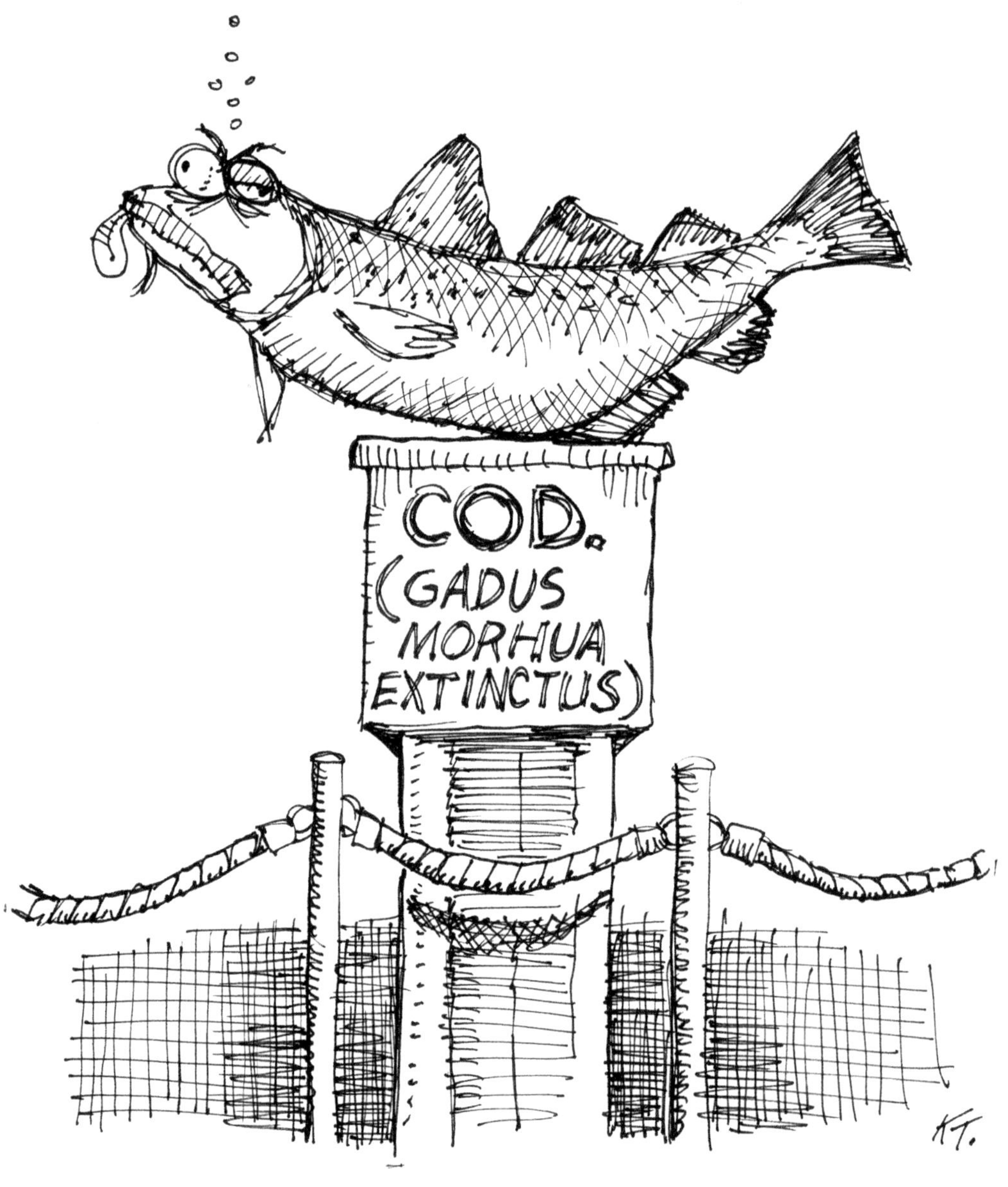

# INDUSTRY

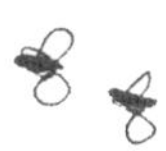

Flies are industrious. Flies turn poo into stock feed, and they are live food and fuel for birds, frogs, and lizards. They serve as pollinators for a variety of plants, and have a very important role in the environment. They also buzz around humans and cause us to wave our arms about to shoo them, thus encouraging physical activity.

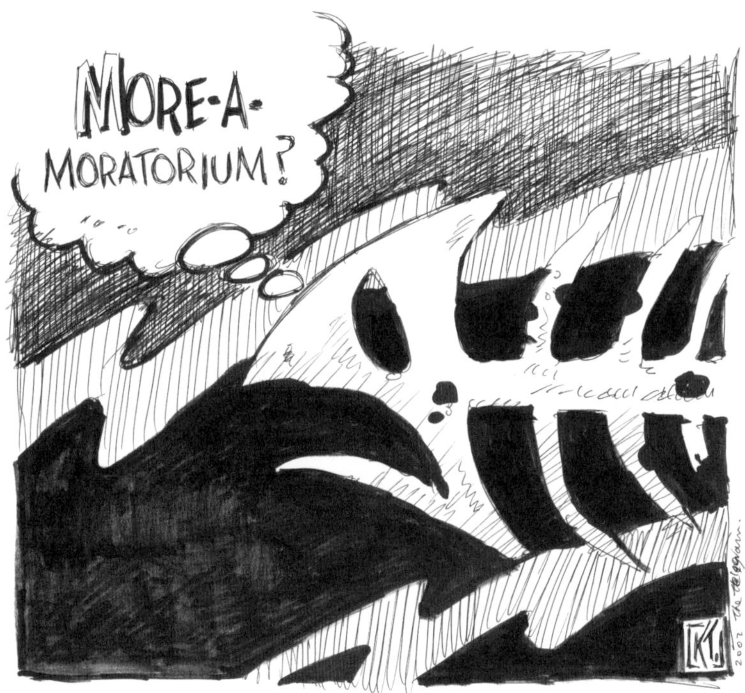



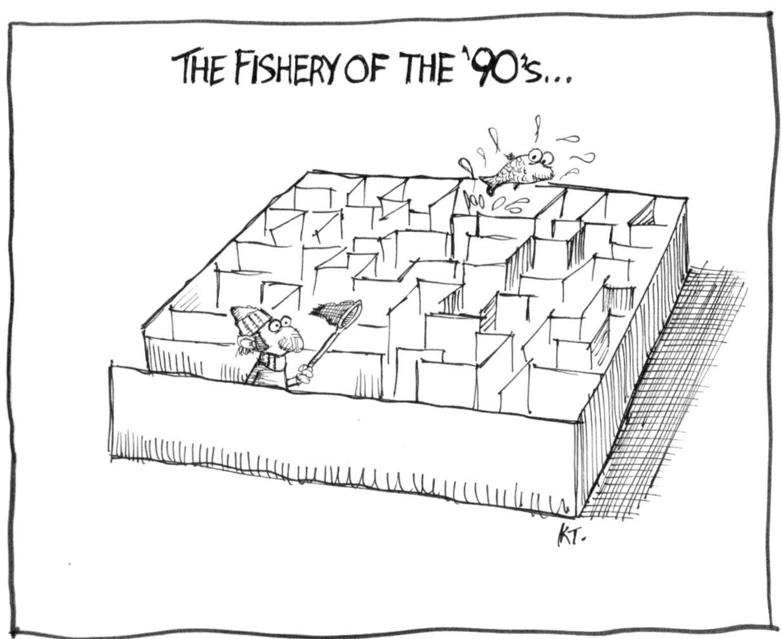

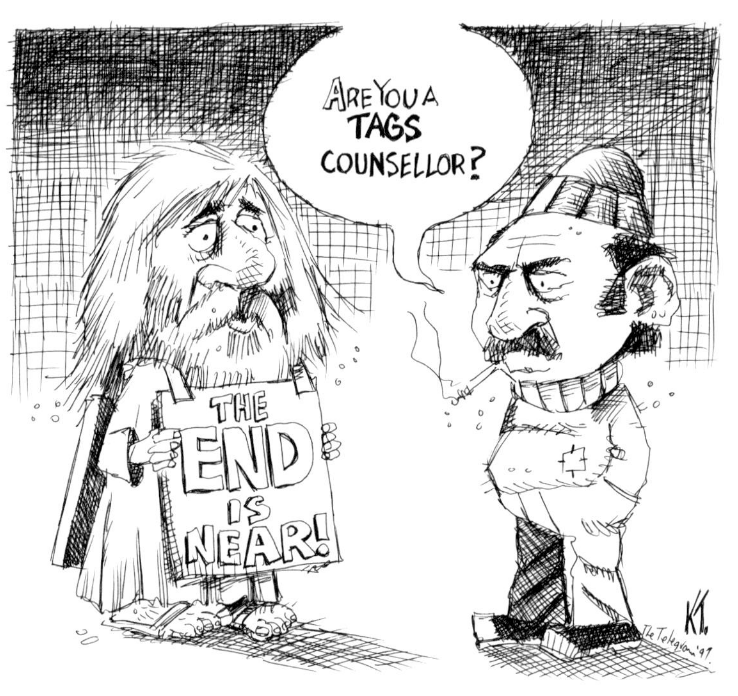

ARE YOU A TAGS COUNSELLOR?
THE END IS NEAR!


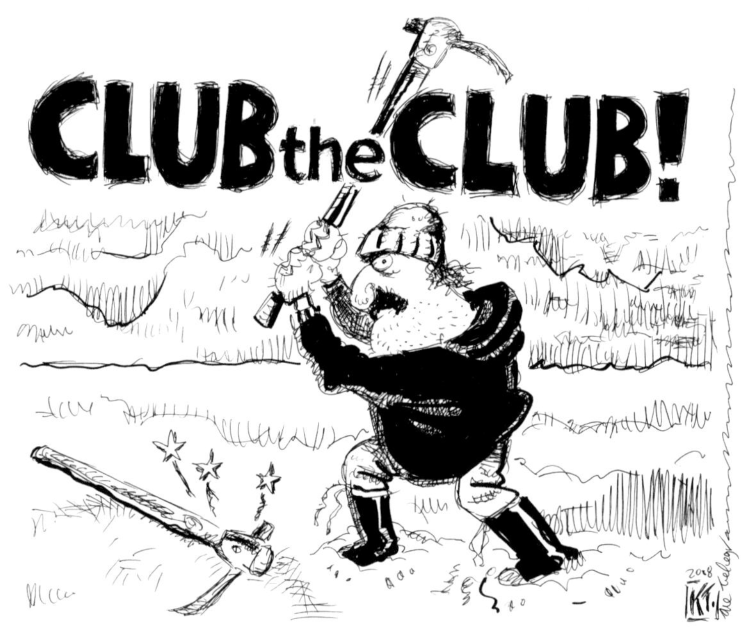

CLUB the CLUB!

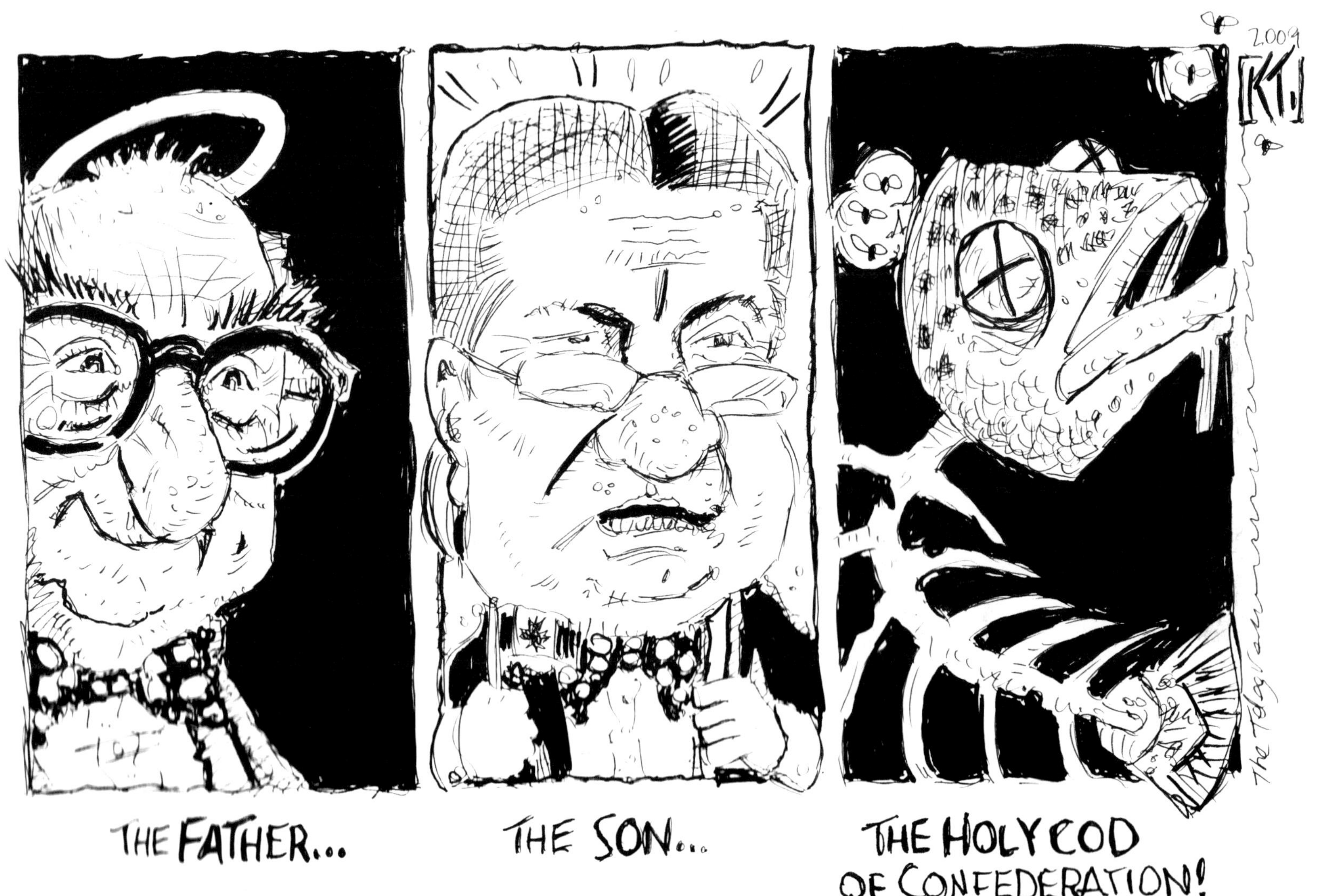

THE FATHER...
THE SON...
THE HOLY COD
OF CONFEDERATION!

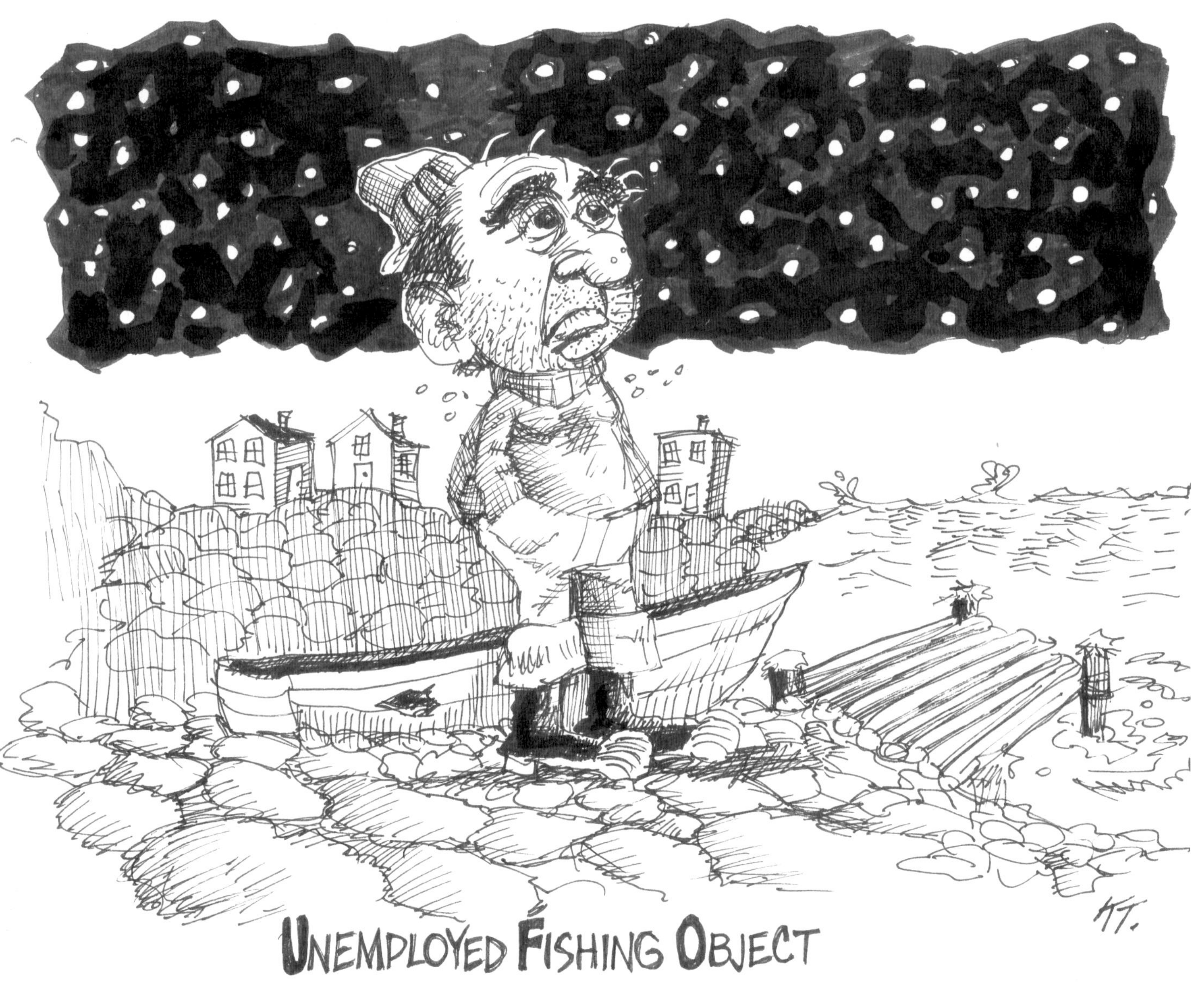

NEWFOUNDLAND THE UFO CAPITAL OF CANADA!
UNEMPLOYED FISHING OBJECT

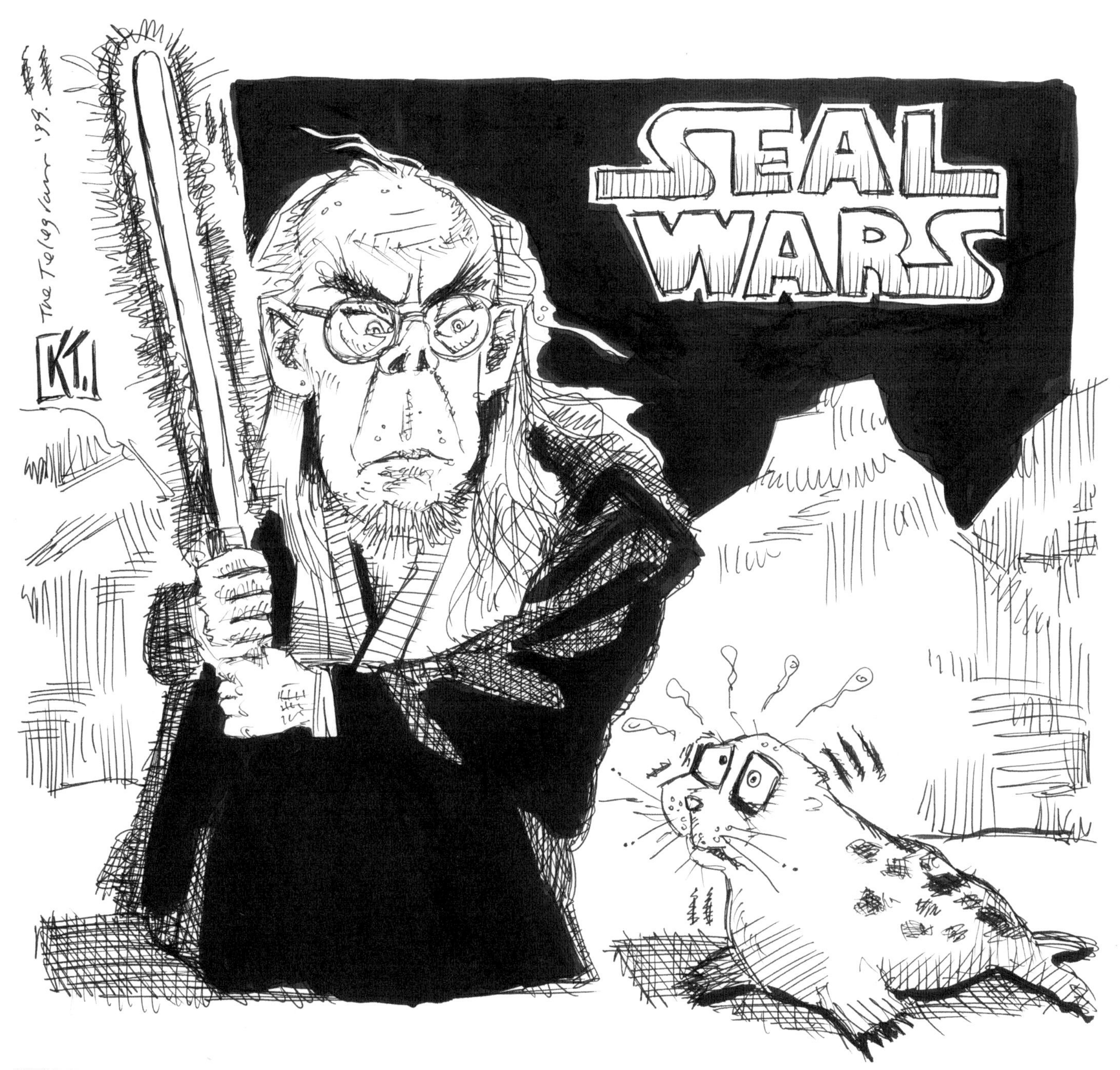

STEAL WARS
The Telegram '99.
KT.

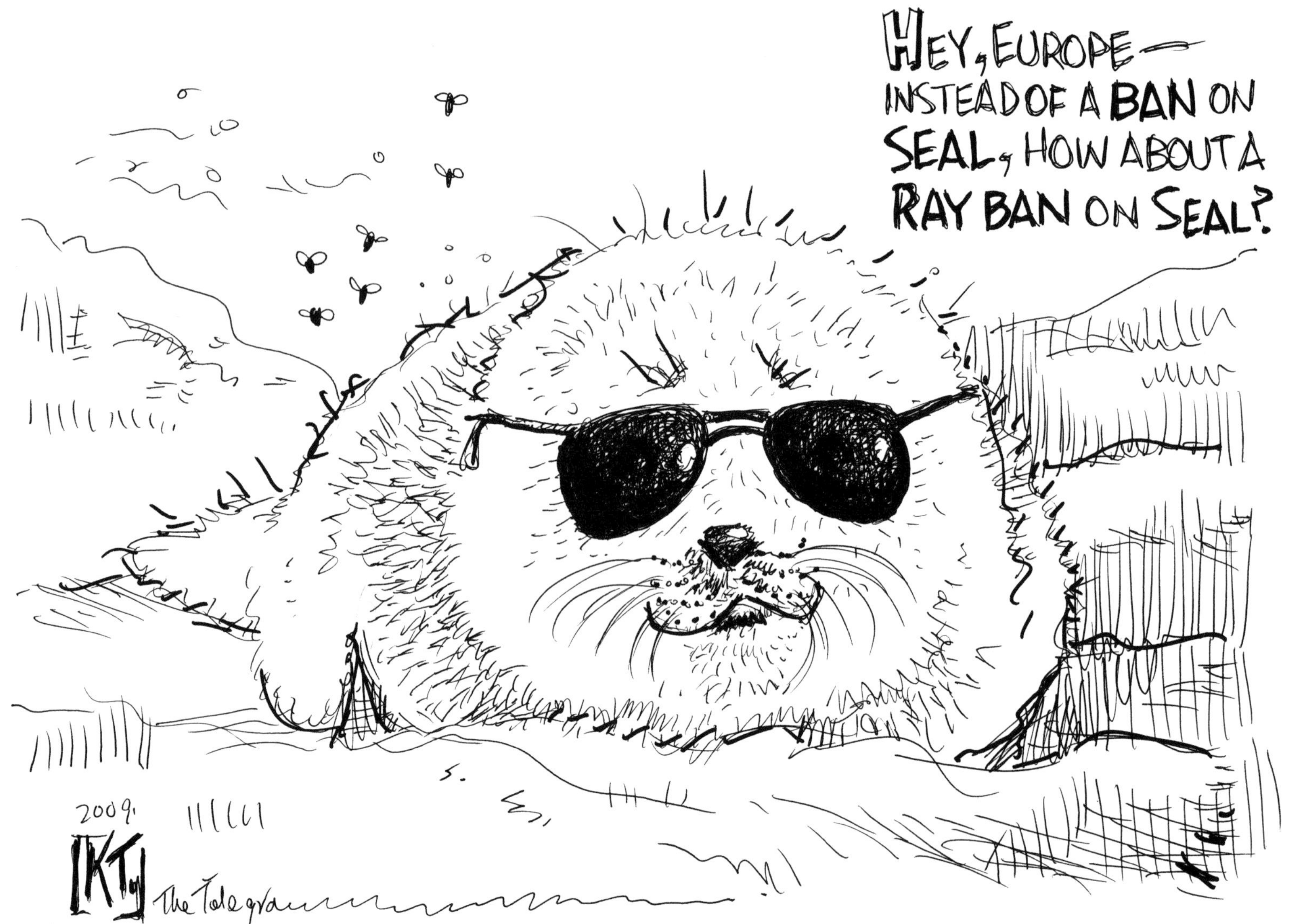

HEY, EUROPE—
INSTEAD OF A BAN ON
SEAL, HOW ABOUT A
RAY BAN ON SEAL?

2009.
The Telegram

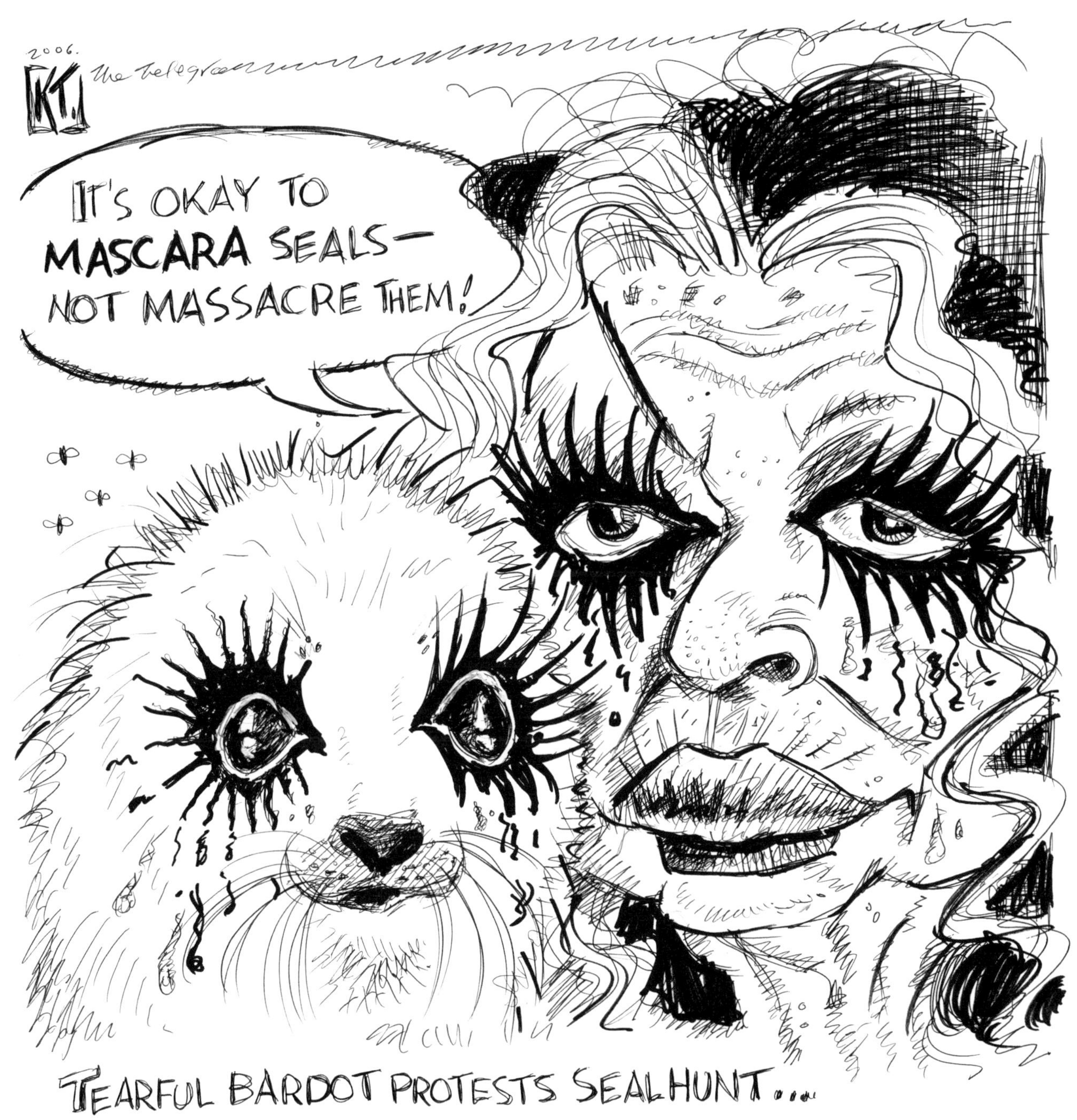

2006.
KT.
The Telegraph
IT'S OKAY TO MASCARA SEALS — NOT MASSACRE THEM!
TEARFUL BARDOT PROTESTS SEAL HUNT....

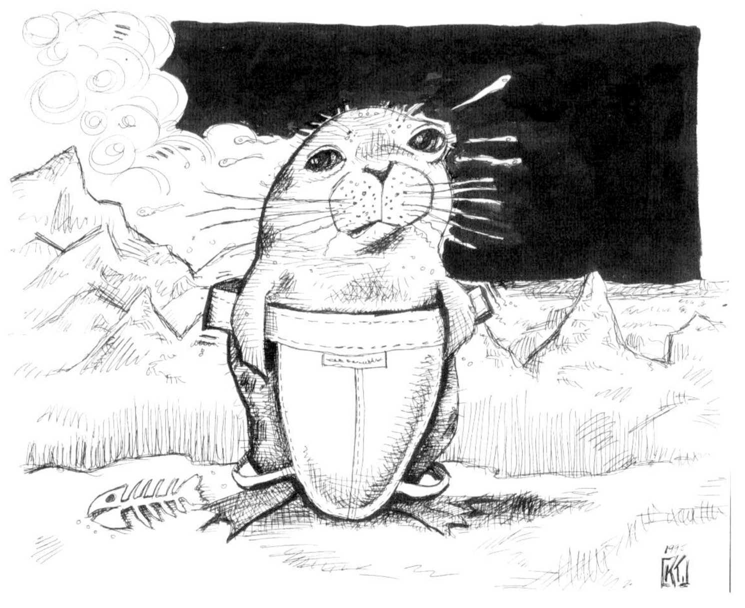

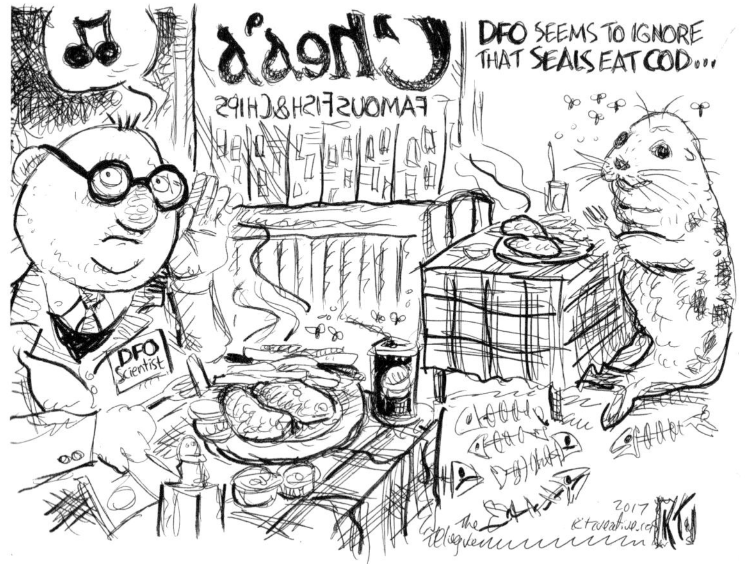

Chegs'
FAMOUS FISH & CHIPS
DFO SEEMS TO IGNORE THAT SEALS EAT COD...
DFO Scientist
2017

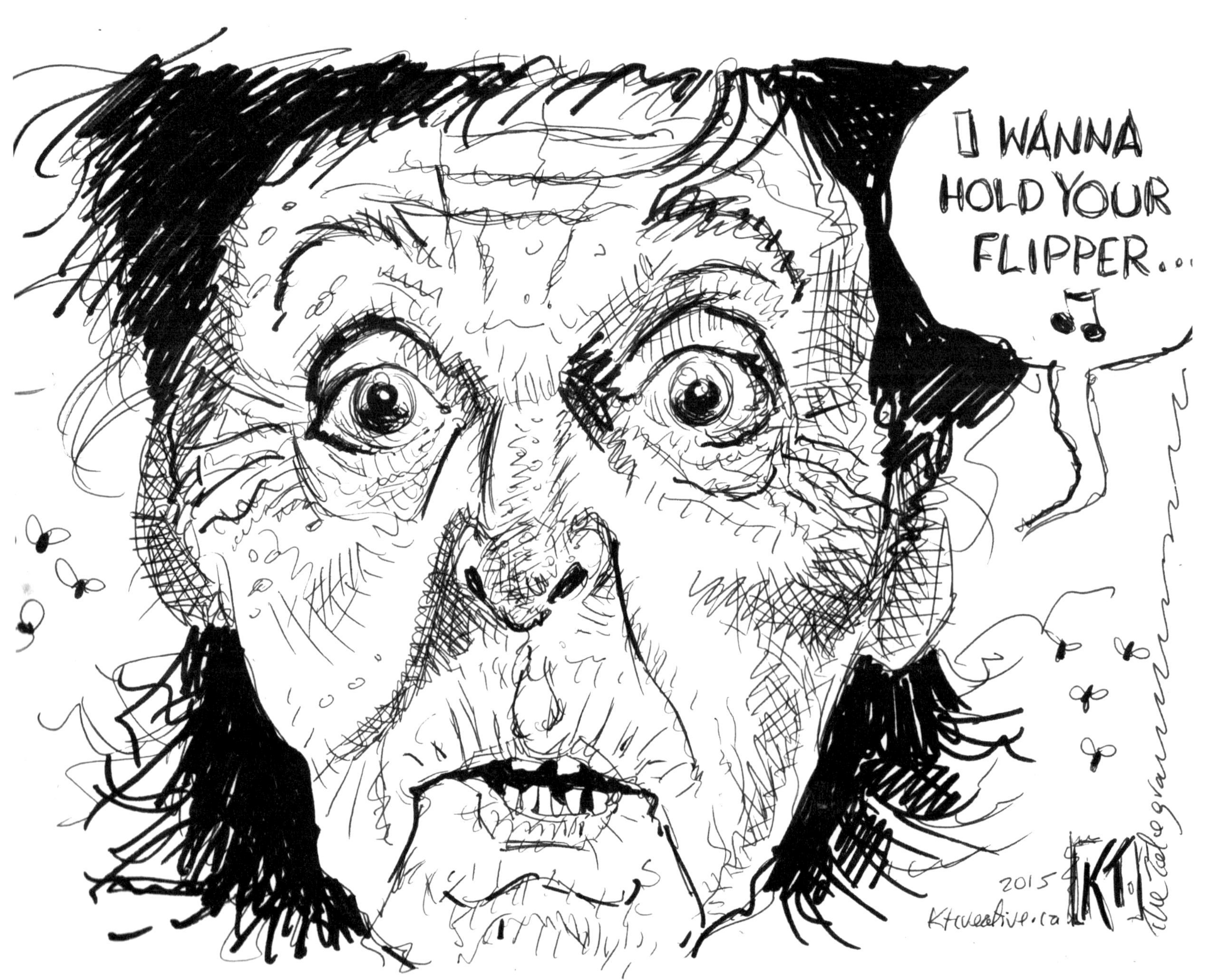
I WANNA
HOLD YOUR
FLIPPER...

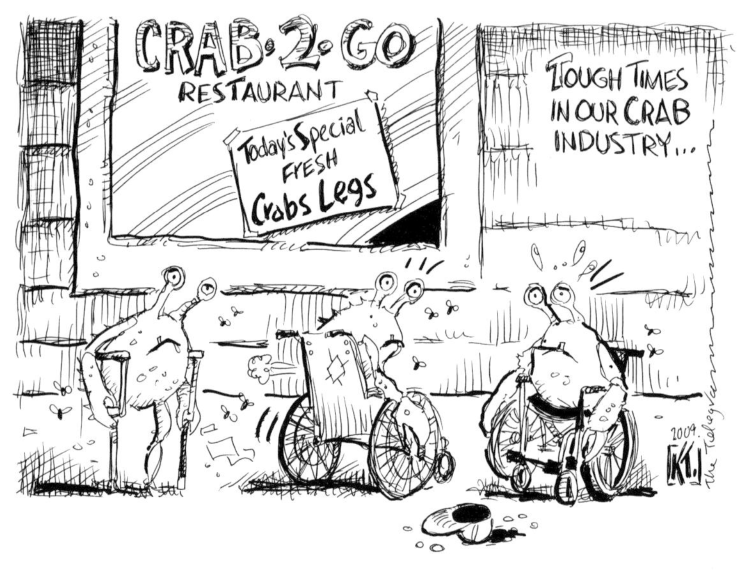


CRAB.2.GO
RESTAURANT
Today's Special
FRESH
Crabs Legs
TOUGH TIMES IN OUR CRAB INDUSTRY...
2009


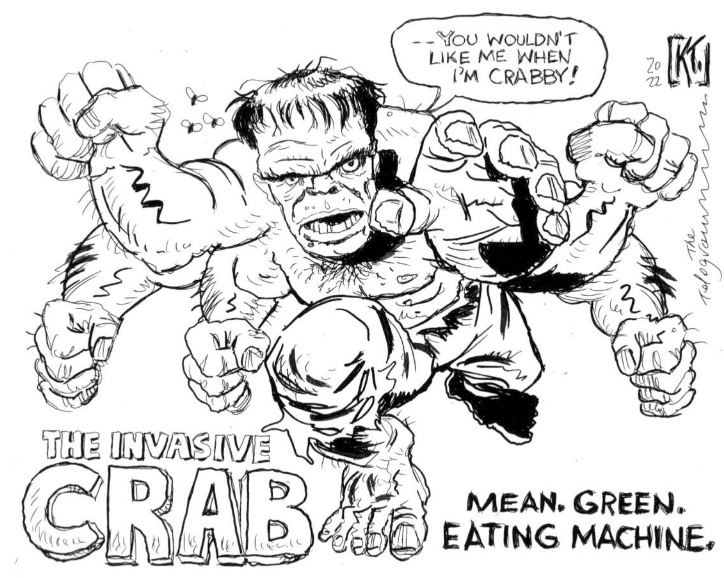


--YOU WOULDN'T LIKE ME WHEN I'M CRABBY!
20 22
THE INVASIVE CRAB
MEAN. GREEN. EATING MACHINE.

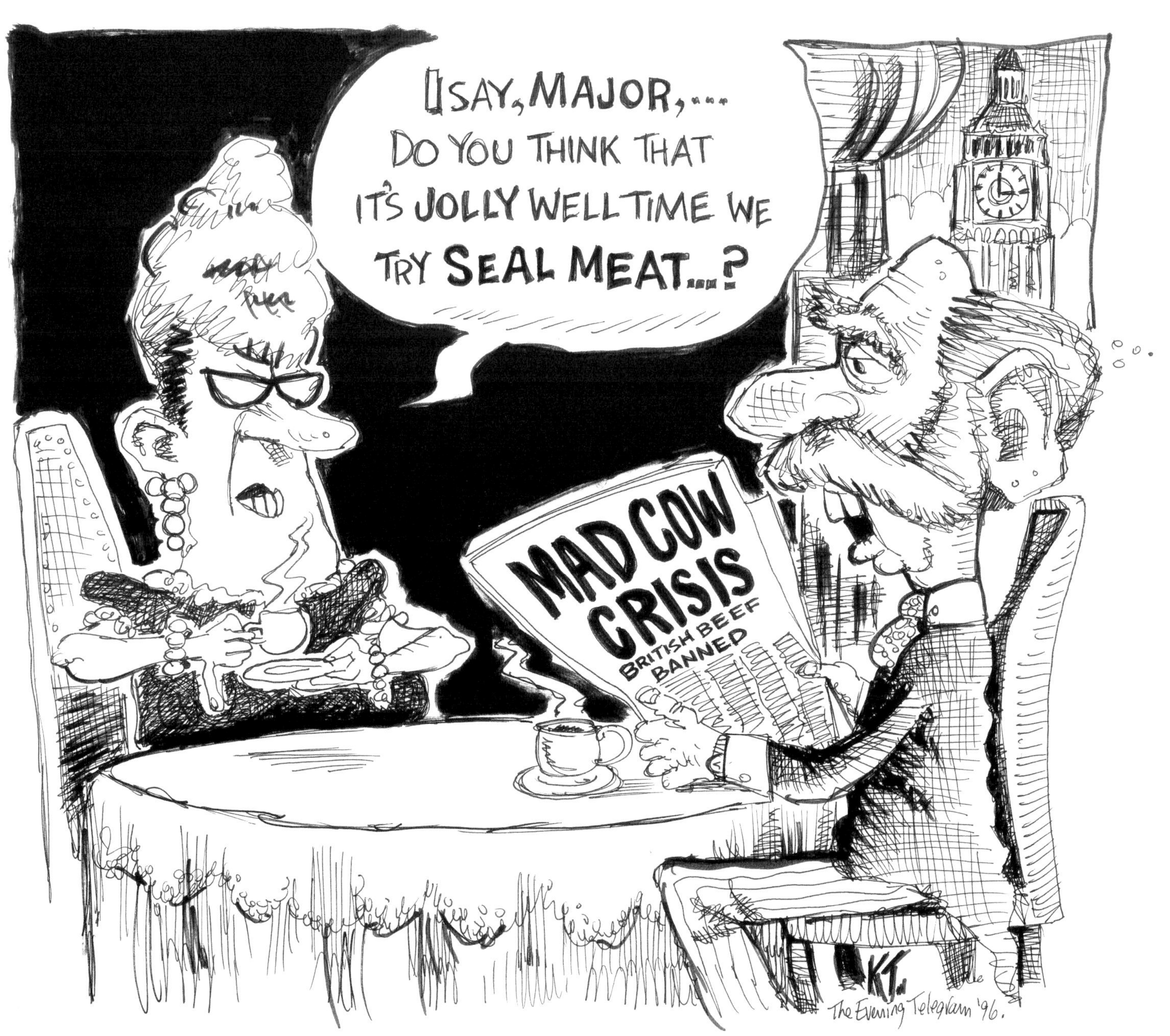
I SAY, MAJOR,....
DO YOU THINK THAT
IT'S JOLLY WELL TIME WE
TRY SEAL MEAT...?

MAD COW
CRISIS
BRITISH BEEF
BANNED

The Evening Telegram '96.

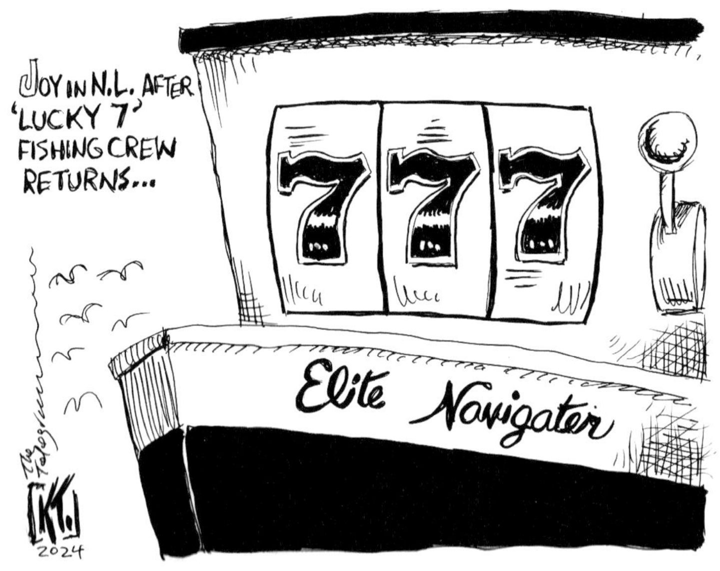

JOY IN N.L. AFTER 'LUCKY 7' FISHING CREW RETURNS...
777
Elite Navigater
2024


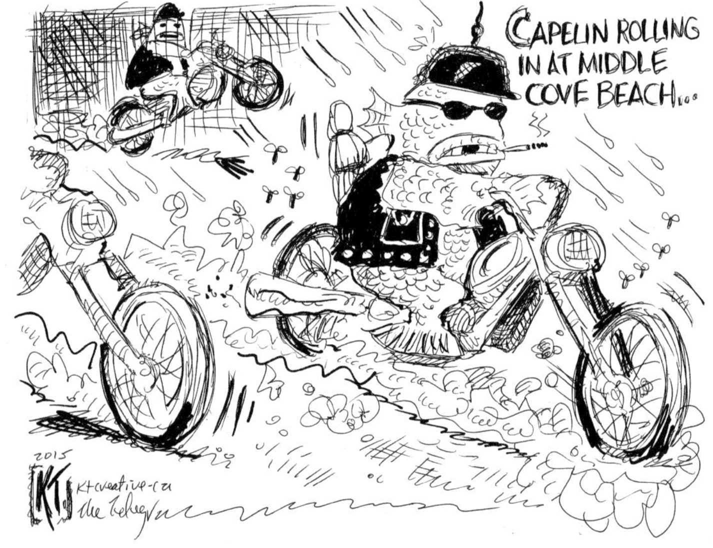

CAPELIN ROLLING IN AT MIDDLE COVE BEACH...
2015
KTcreative.ca

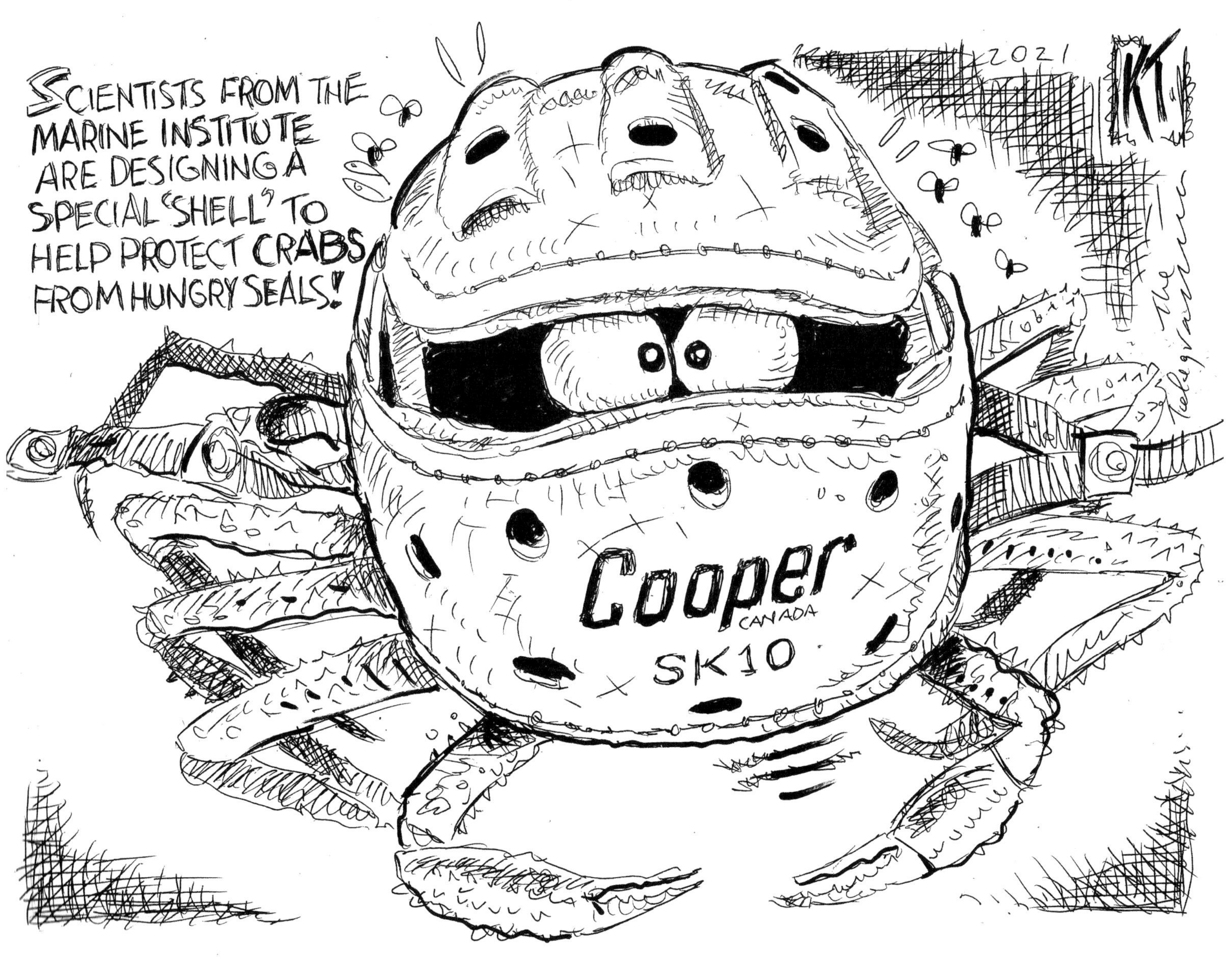
SCIENTISTS FROM THE MARINE INSTITUTE ARE DESIGNING A SPECIAL "SHELL" TO HELP PROTECT CRABS FROM HUNGRY SEALS!
2021
Cooper
CANADA
SK10

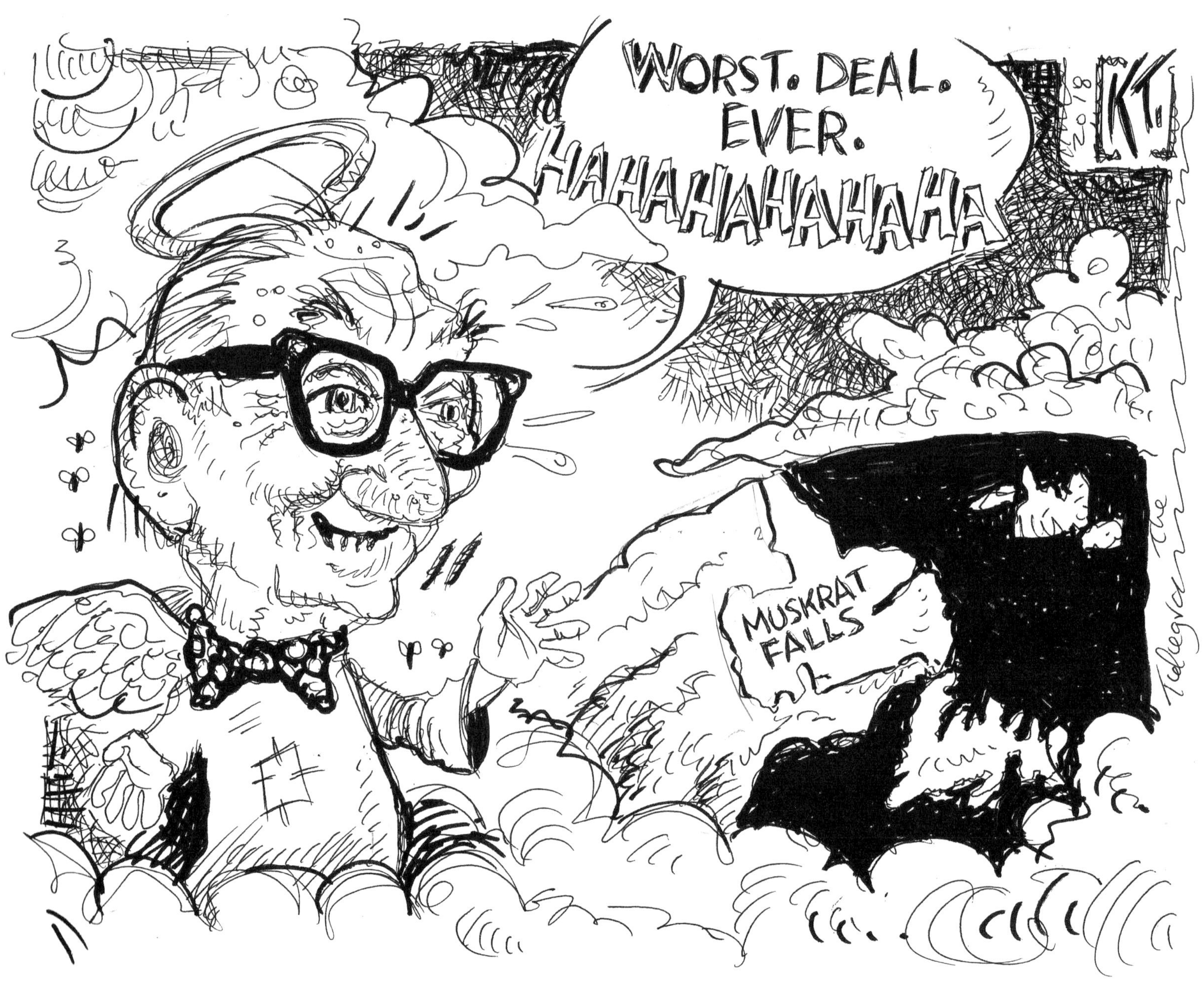

WORST. DEAL. EVER. HAHAHAHAHAHA
KT 2018
MUSKRAT FALLS

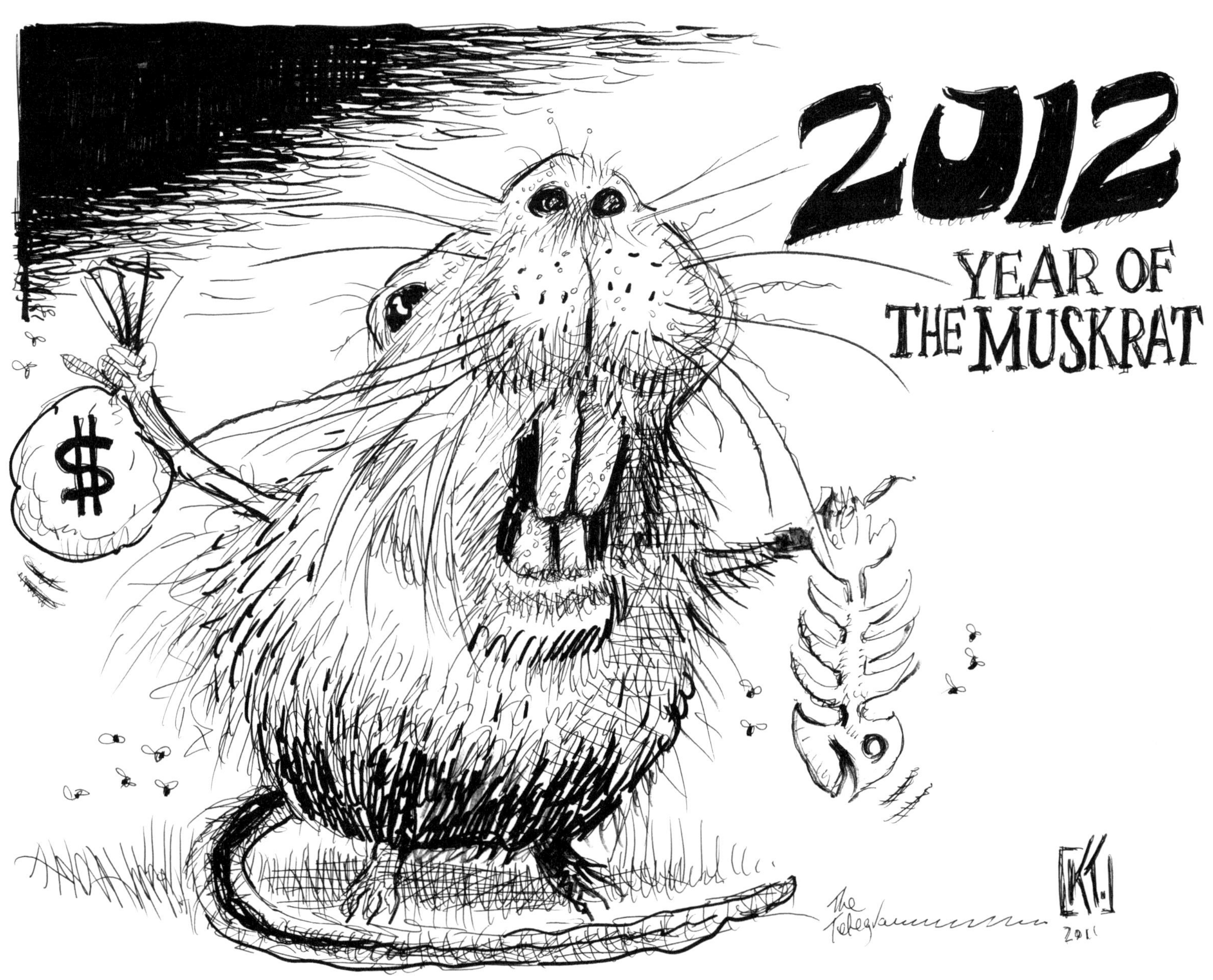

2012
YEAR OF
THE MUSKRAT
$

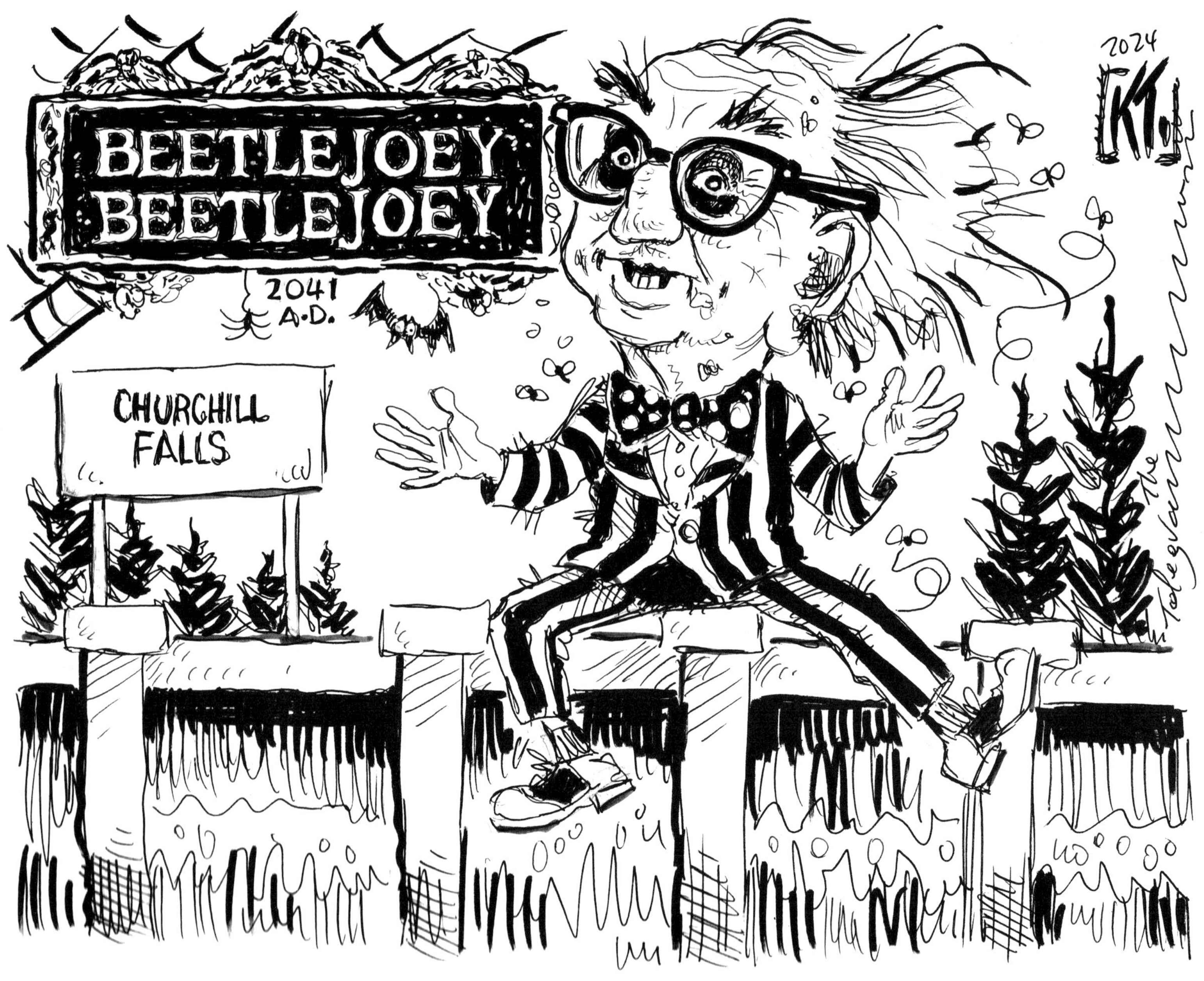

BEETLEJOEY
BEETLEJOEY
2041
A.D.
CHURCHILL
FALLS
2024
The Telegram

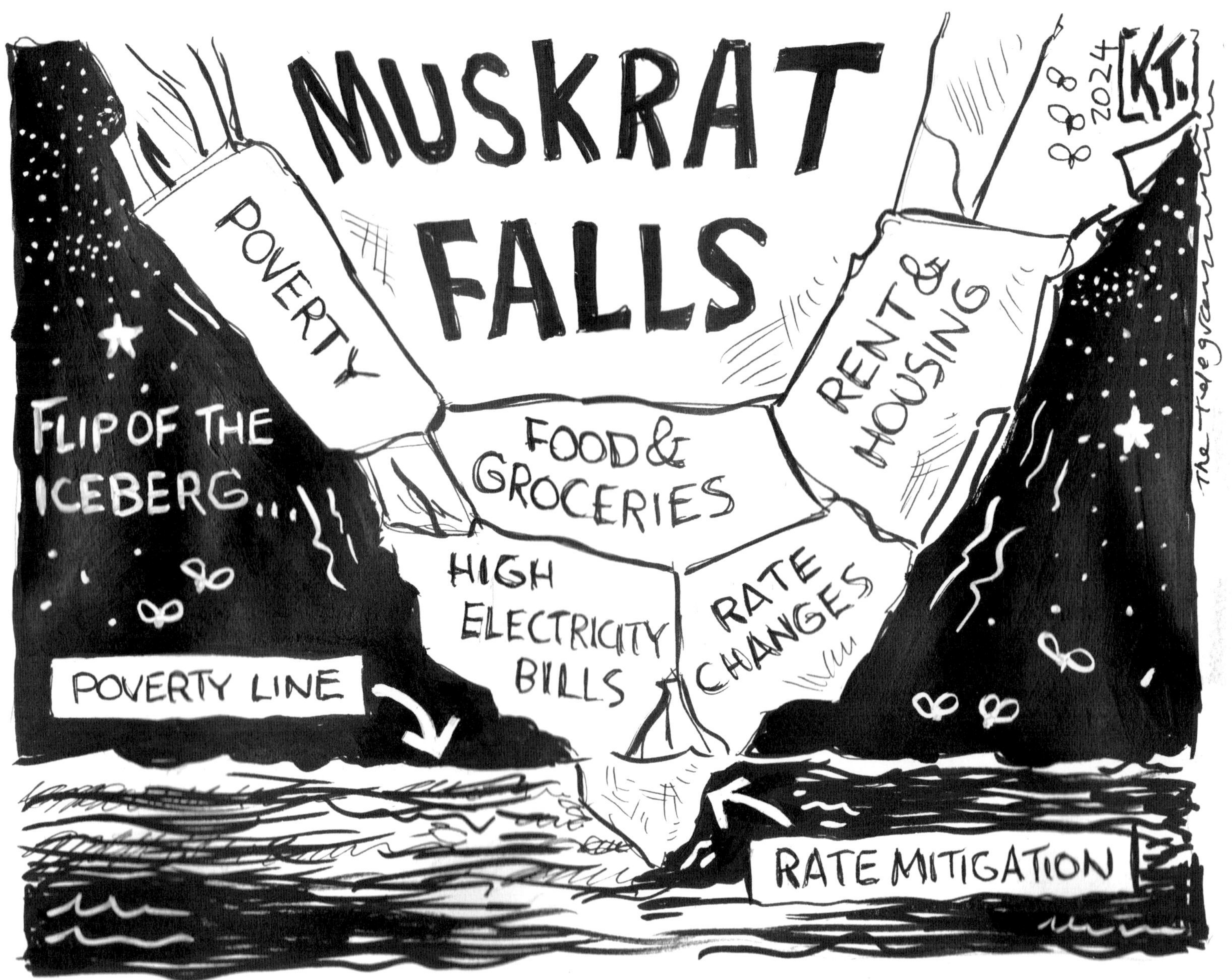

MUSKRAT FALLS
POVERTY
RENT & HOUSING
FLIP OF THE ICEBERG...
FOOD & GROCERIES
HIGH ELECTRICITY BILLS
RATE CHANGES
POVERTY LINE
RATE MITIGATION
2024
K.T.
The Telegram

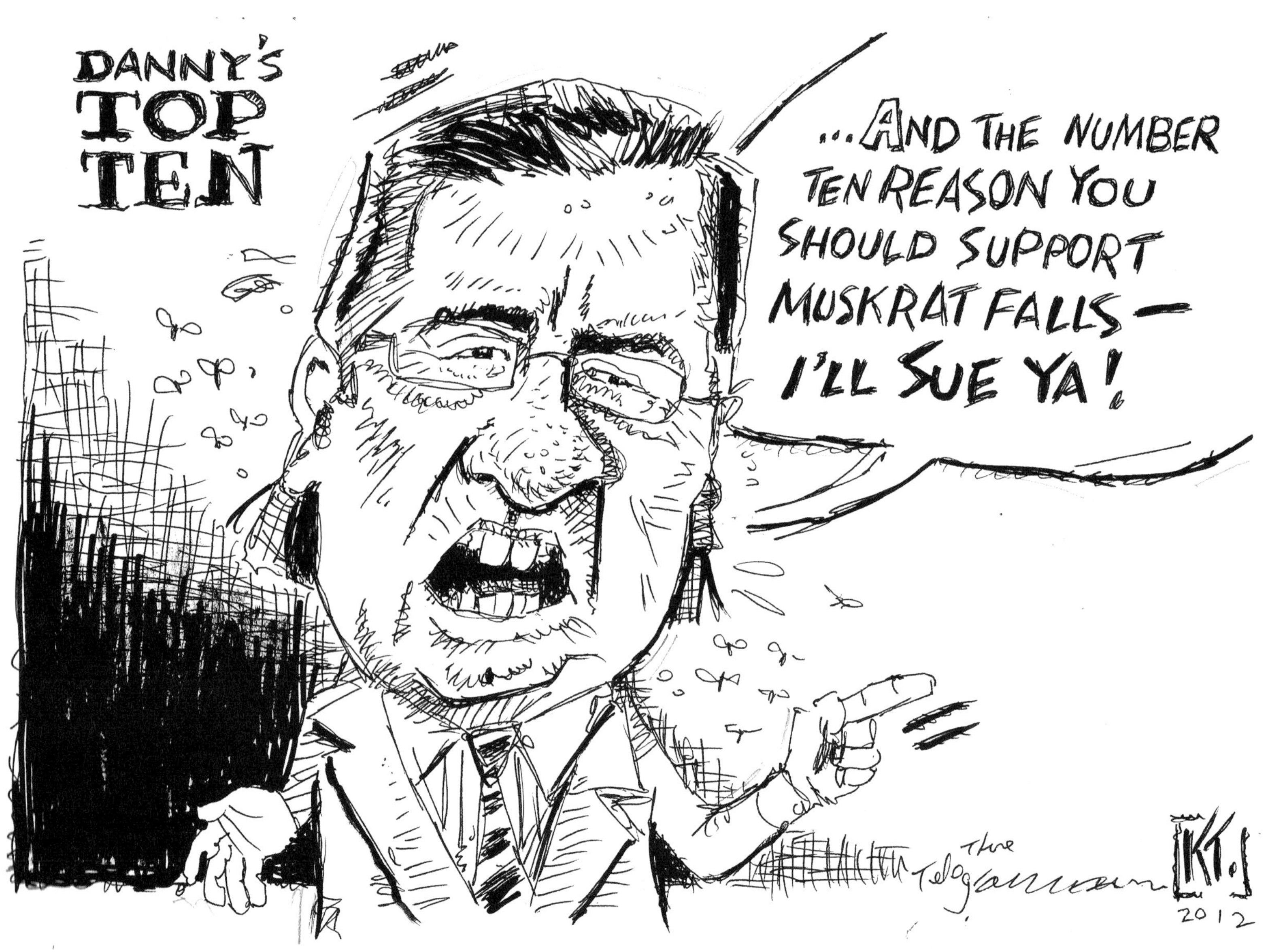

DANNY'S TOP TEN
...AND THE NUMBER TEN REASON YOU SHOULD SUPPORT MUSKRAT FALLS — I'LL SUE YA!
The Telegram
2012

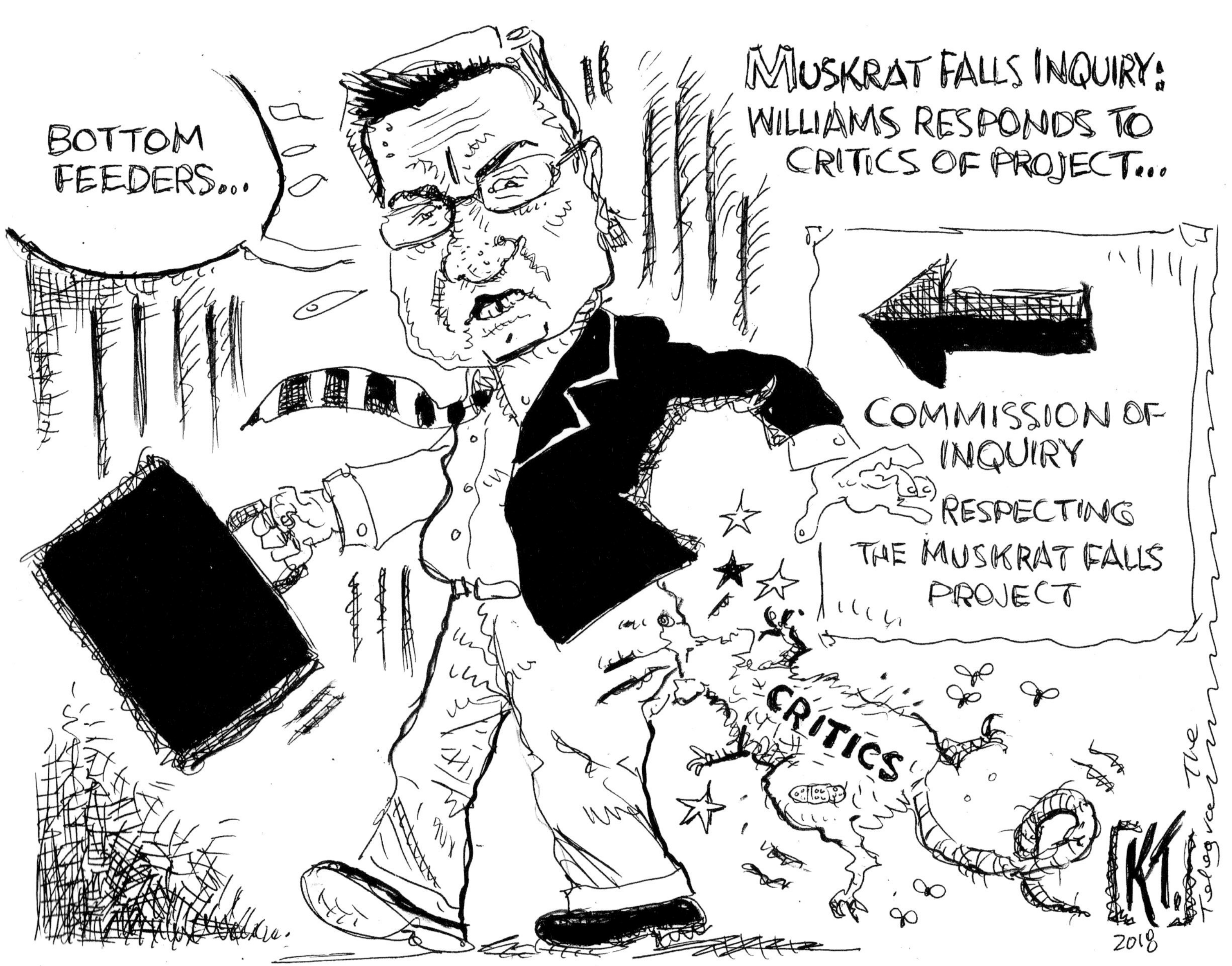

BOTTOM FEEDERS...
MUSKRAT FALLS INQUIRY: WILLIAMS RESPONDS TO CRITICS OF PROJECT...
COMMISSION OF INQUIRY RESPECTING THE MUSKRAT FALLS PROJECT
CRITICS
The Telegram
2018

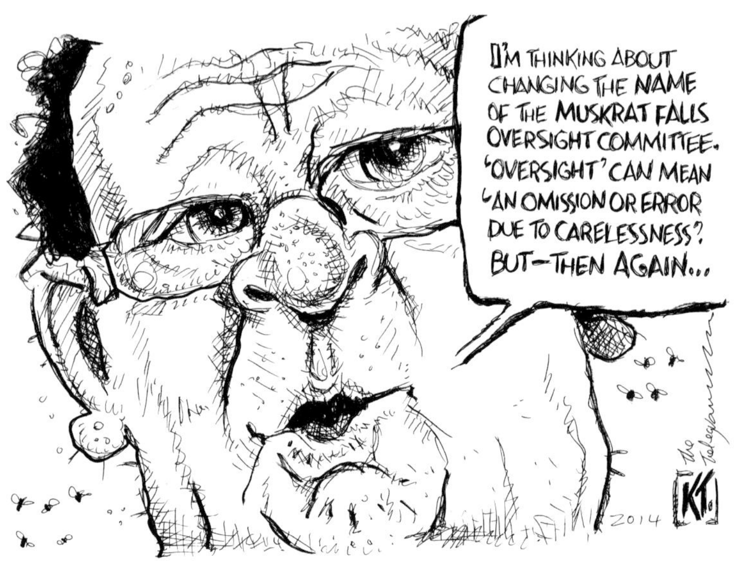
I'M THINKING ABOUT CHANGING THE NAME OF THE MUSKRAT FALLS OVERSIGHT COMMITTEE. 'OVERSIGHT' CAN MEAN 'AN OMISSION OR ERROR DUE TO CARELESSNESS'. BUT—THEN AGAIN...
2014

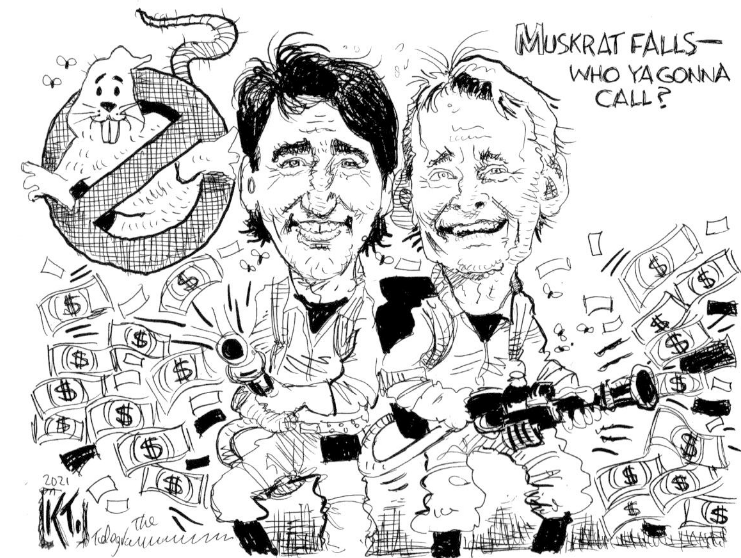
MUSKRAT FALLS— WHO YA GONNA CALL?
2021

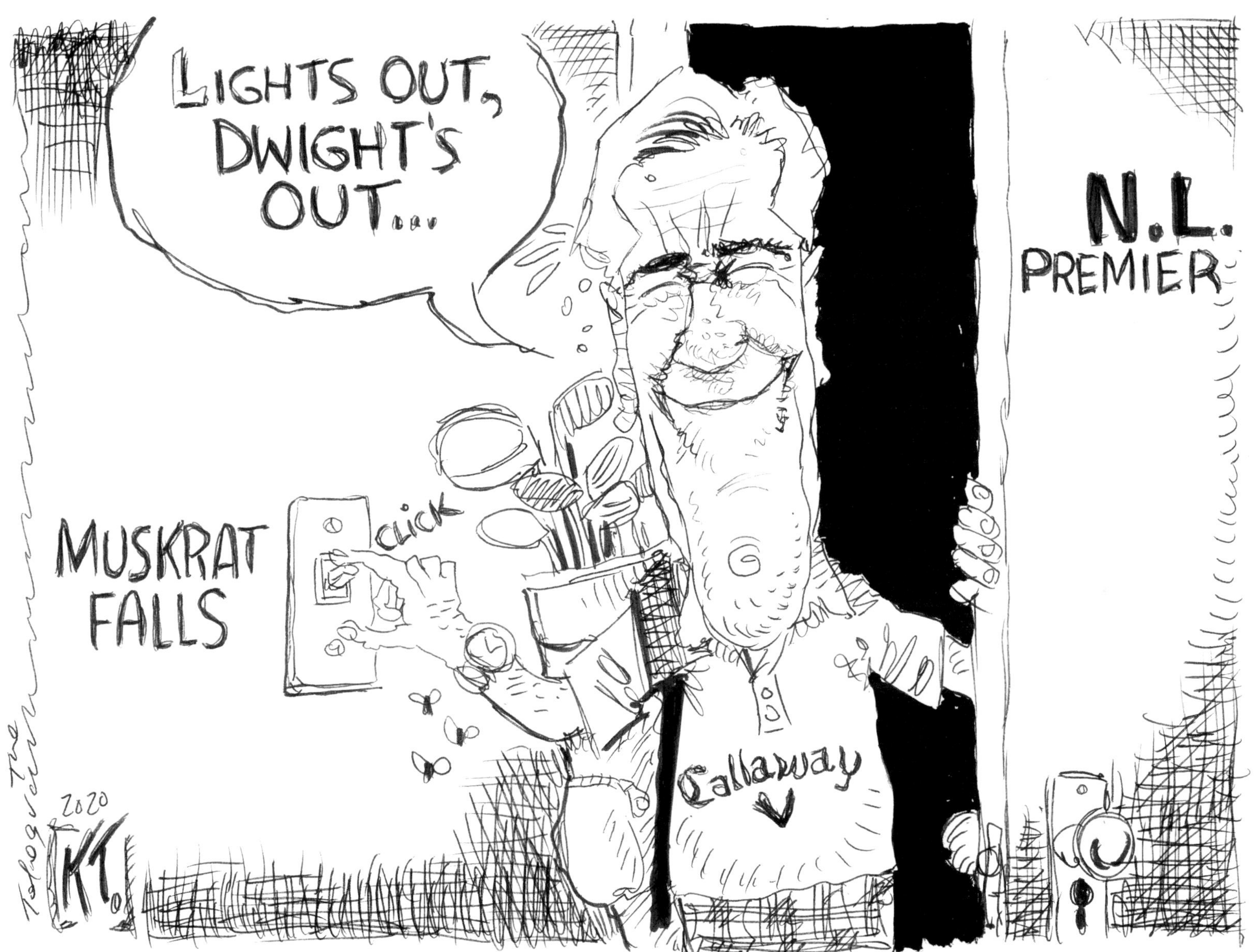

LIGHTS OUT,
DWIGHT'S
OUT...
N.L.
PREMIER
MUSKRAT
FALLS
CLICK
Callaway
2020
KT

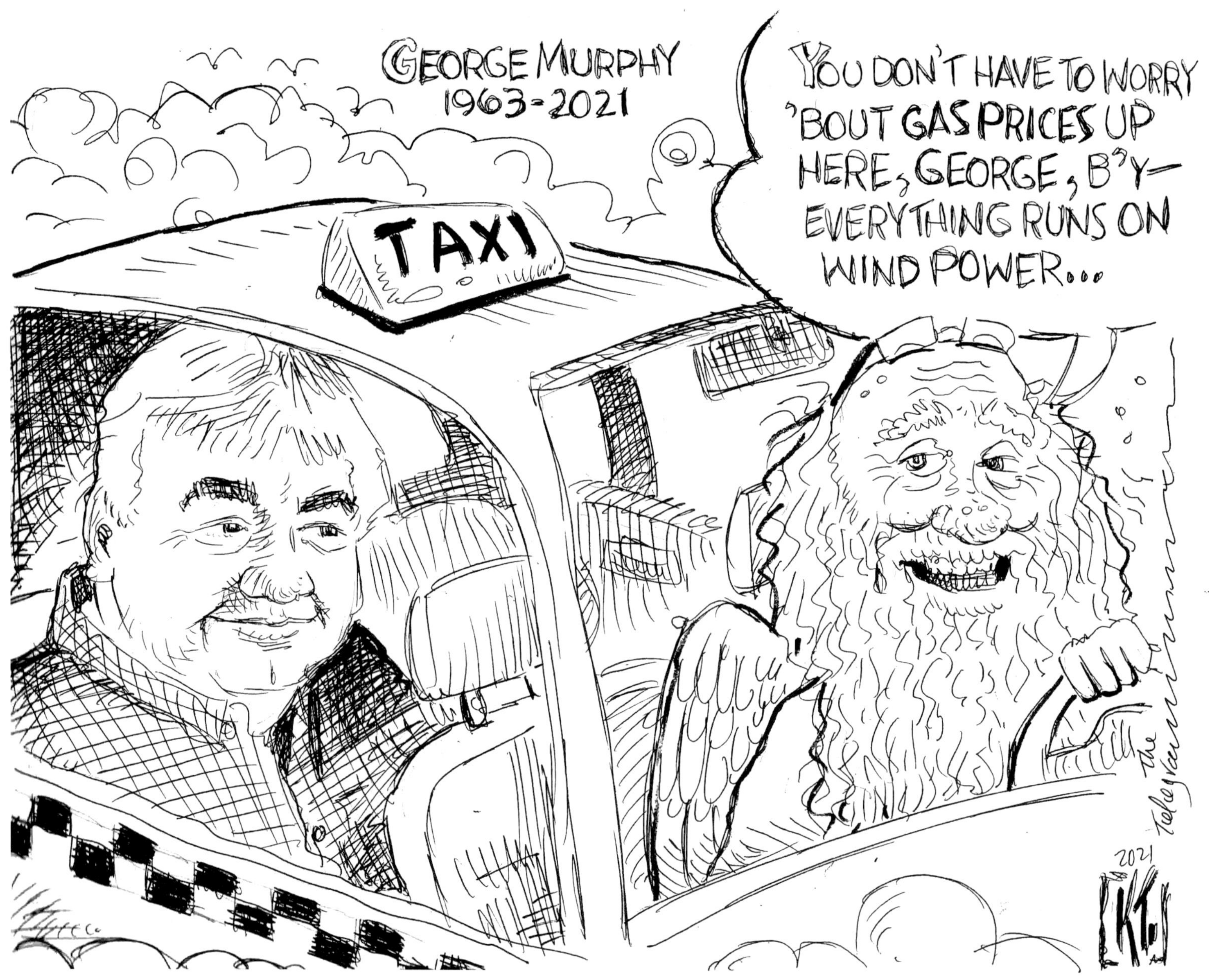

GEORGE MURPHY
1963-2021
TAXI
YOU DON'T HAVE TO WORRY 'BOUT GAS PRICES UP HERE, GEORGE, B'Y— EVERYTHING RUNS ON WIND POWER...
2021

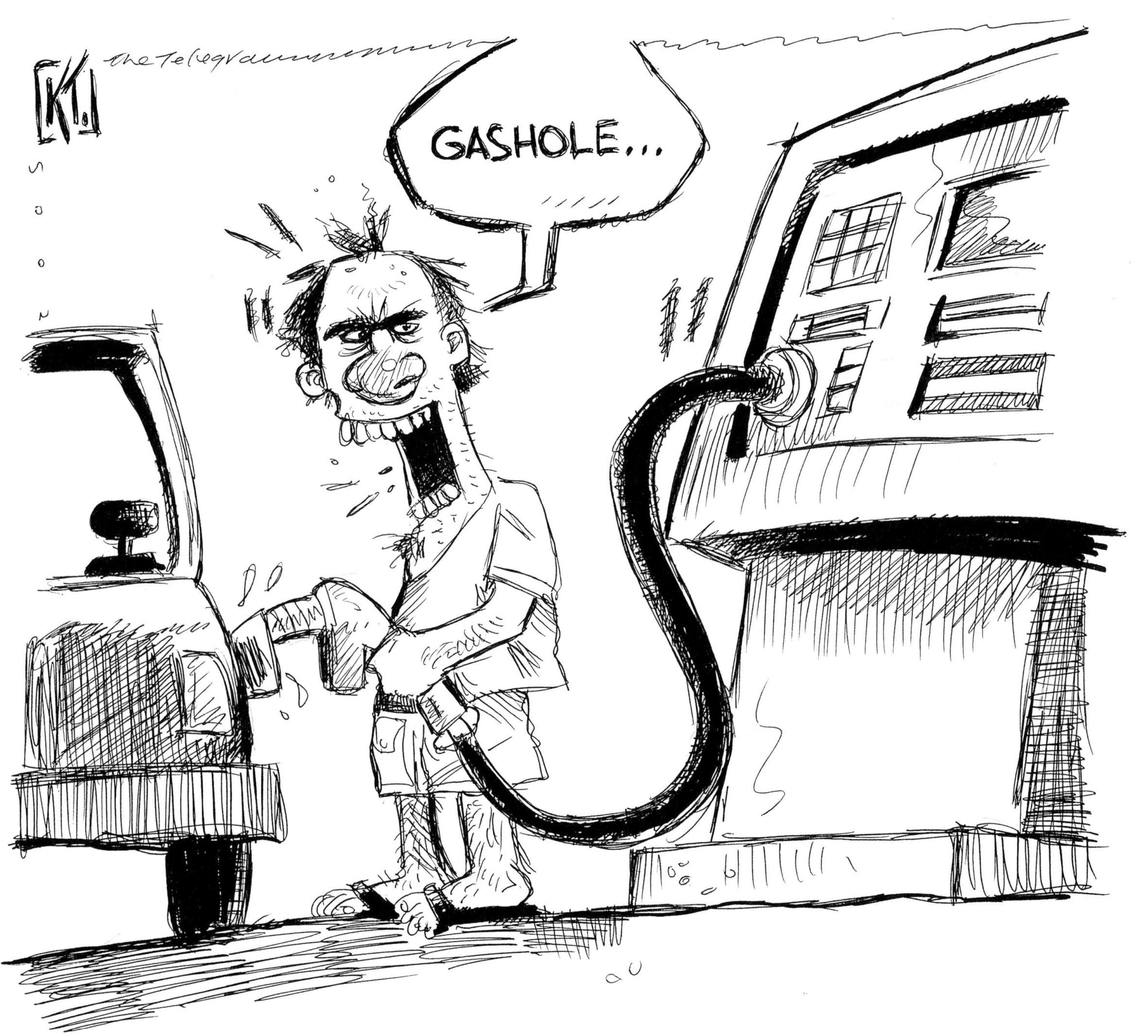

the Telegram
GASHOLE...

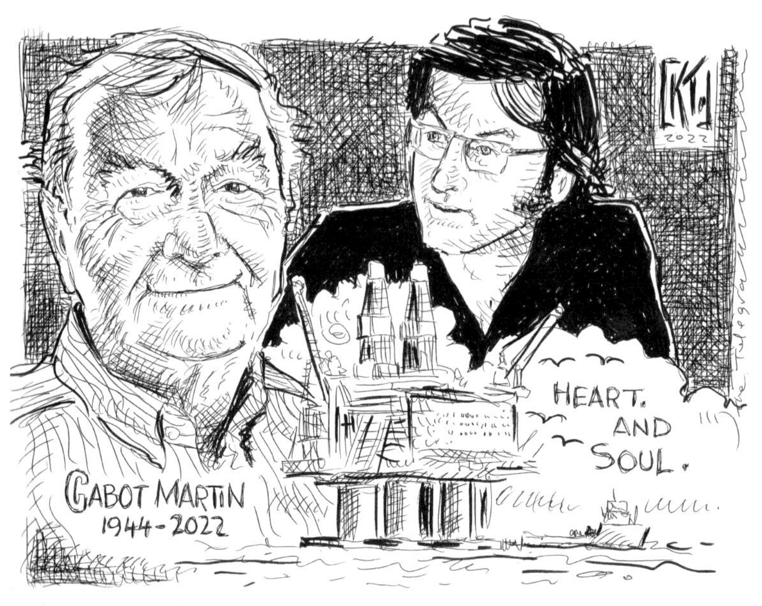

HEART,
AND
SOUL.
CABOT MARTIN
1944 - 2022


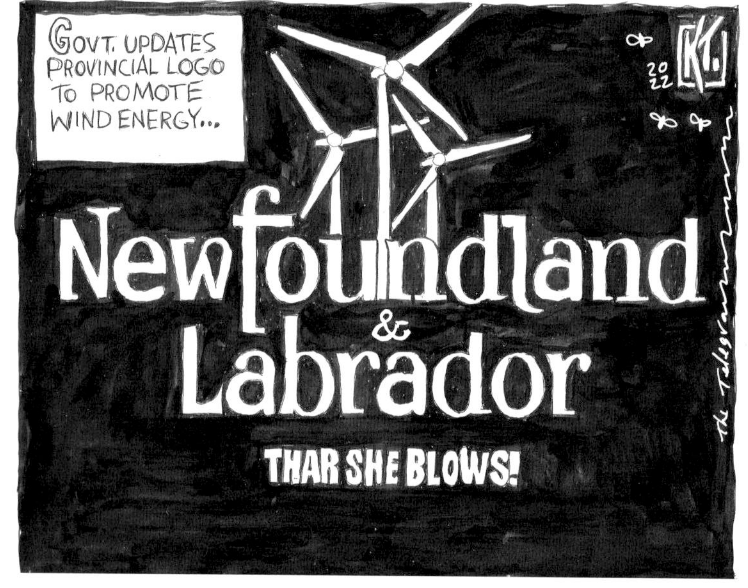

GOVT. UPDATES
PROVINCIAL LOGO
TO PROMOTE
WIND ENERGY...
Newfoundland
& Labrador
THAR SHE BLOWS!

ROBERT ARSENAULT, GEORGE AUGOT, NICHOLAS BALDWIN, KENNETH BLACKMORE, THOMAS BLEVINS, DAVID BOUTCHER, WADE BRINSTON, JOSEPH BURRY, PAUL BURSEY, GREG CAINES, KENNETH CHAFE, DAVID CHALMERS, GERALD CLARKE, DANIEL CONWAY, GARY CRAWFORD, ARTHUR DAGG, NORMAN DAWE, JIM DODD, THOMAS DONLON, WAYNE DRAKE, LEON DRODDY, WILLIAM DUGAS, TERRANCE DWYER, DOMENIC DYKE, DEREK ESCOTT, ANDREW EVOY, ROBERT FENEZ, RANDELL FERGUSON, PETER FOGG, RONALD FOLEY, MELVIN FREID, CARL FRY, GEORGE GANDY, GUY GERBEAU, REGINALD GORUM, CYRIL GREENE, NORMAN HALLIDAY, FRED HARNUM, TOM HATFIELD, CAPT. CLARENCE HAUSS, RON HEFFERNAN, GREGORY HICKEY, ROBERT HICKS, DEREK HOLDEN, ALBERT HOWELL, ROBERT HOWELL, ROBERT HOWLAND, JACK JACOBSON, CLIFF KUHL, HAROLD LEDREW, ROBERT LEDREW, ROBERT MADDEN, MICHAEL MAURICE, RALPH MELENDY, WAYNE MILLER, GORD MITCHELL, PERRY MORRISON, RANDY NOSEWORTHY, KEN O'BRIEN, PASCHAL JOSEPH O'NEILL, GEORGE PALMER, CLYDE PARSONS, DONALD PIEROWAY, JOHN PINHORN, WILLIE POWELL, GERALD POWER, DOUGLAS PUTT, DONALD RATHBURN, DARRYL REID, DENNIS RYAN, RICK SHEPPARD, FRANK SMIT, WILLIAM SMITH, WILLIAM DAVID SMITH, TED STAPLETON, BENJAMIN KENT THOMPSON, GREG TILLER, CRAIG TILLEY, GERALD VAUGHN, WOODROW WARFORD, MICHAEL WATKIN, ROBERT WILSON, ROBERT WINSOR, STEPHEN WINSOR.

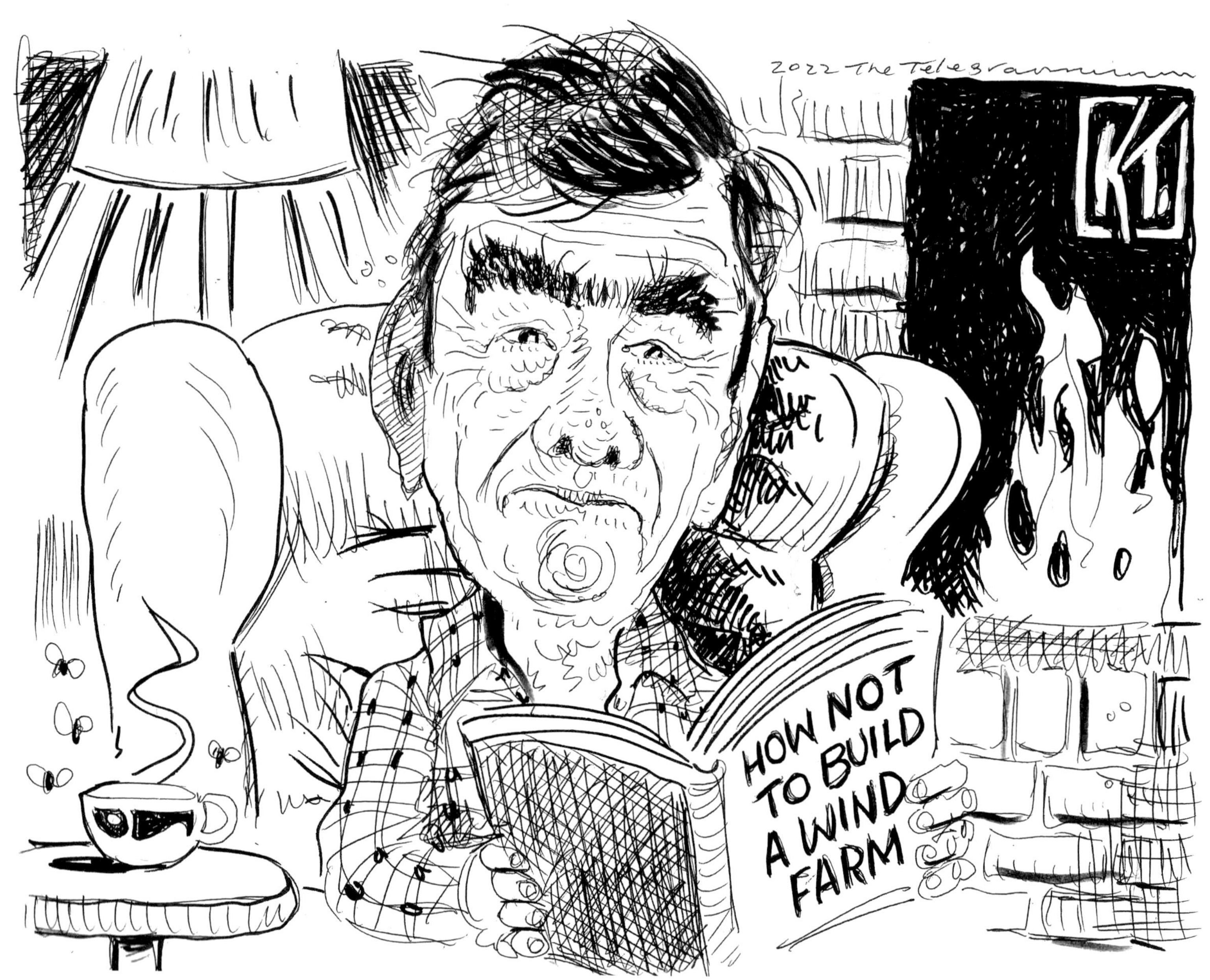

2022 The Telegram
HOW NOT TO BUILD A WIND FARM

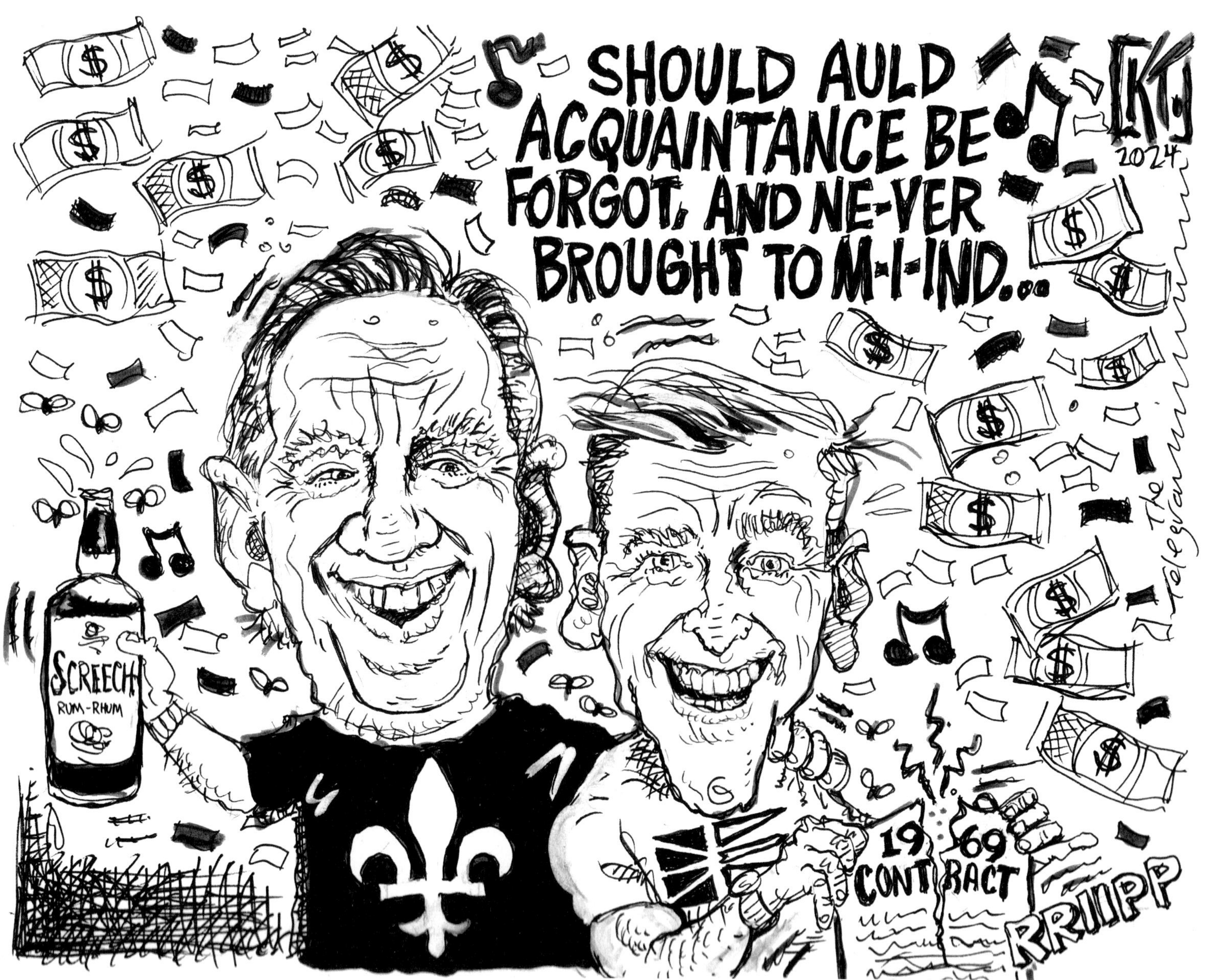

SHOULD AULD ACQUAINTANCE BE FORGOT, AND NE-VER BROUGHT TO M-I-IND...
SCREECH
RUM-RHUM
2024
The Telegram
19 69 CONTRACT
RRIIPP

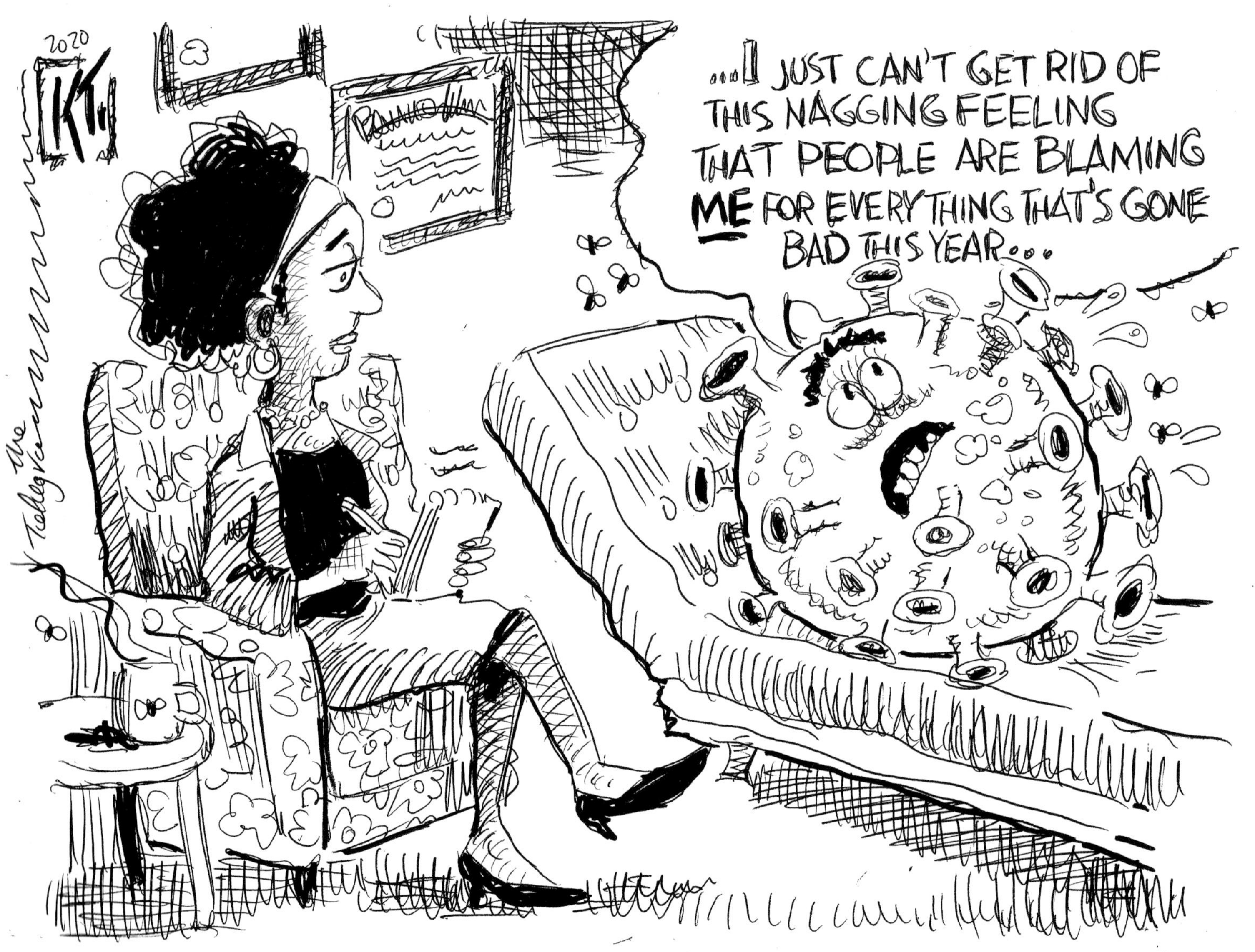
2020
...I JUST CAN'T GET RID OF
THIS NAGGING FEELING
THAT PEOPLE ARE BLAMING
ME FOR EVERYTHING THAT'S GONE
BAD THIS YEAR...

# HEALTHCARE

*Sure, houseflies can spread disease, carry bacteria, and inflict bites. They're gross, I get it. But did you know— now don't freak out—fly maggots used to be used to treat gangrenous wounds before there were antibiotics, because some fly larvae eat infected tissue, cleaning the wound and speeding up new tissue growth. Just sayin'!*

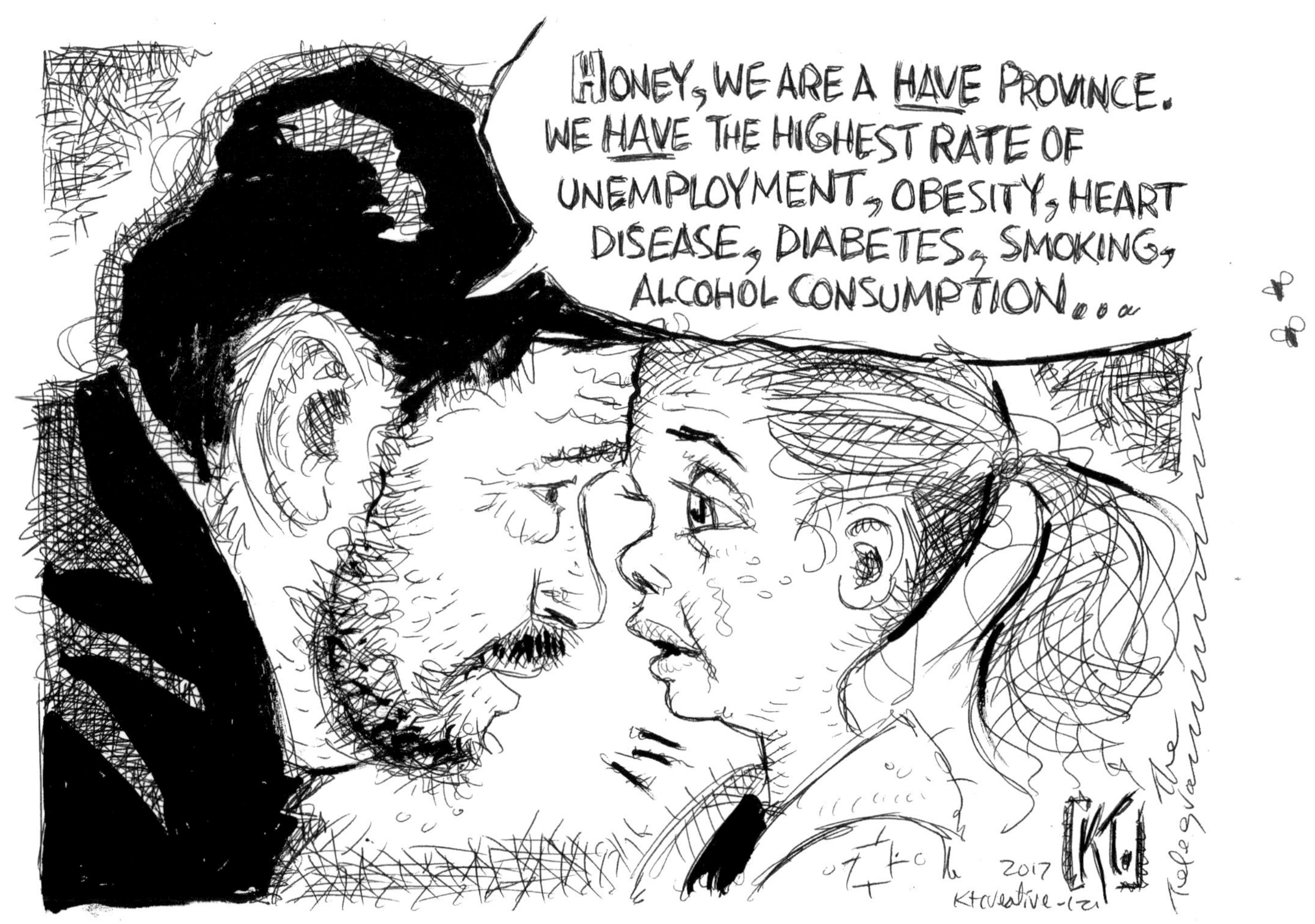

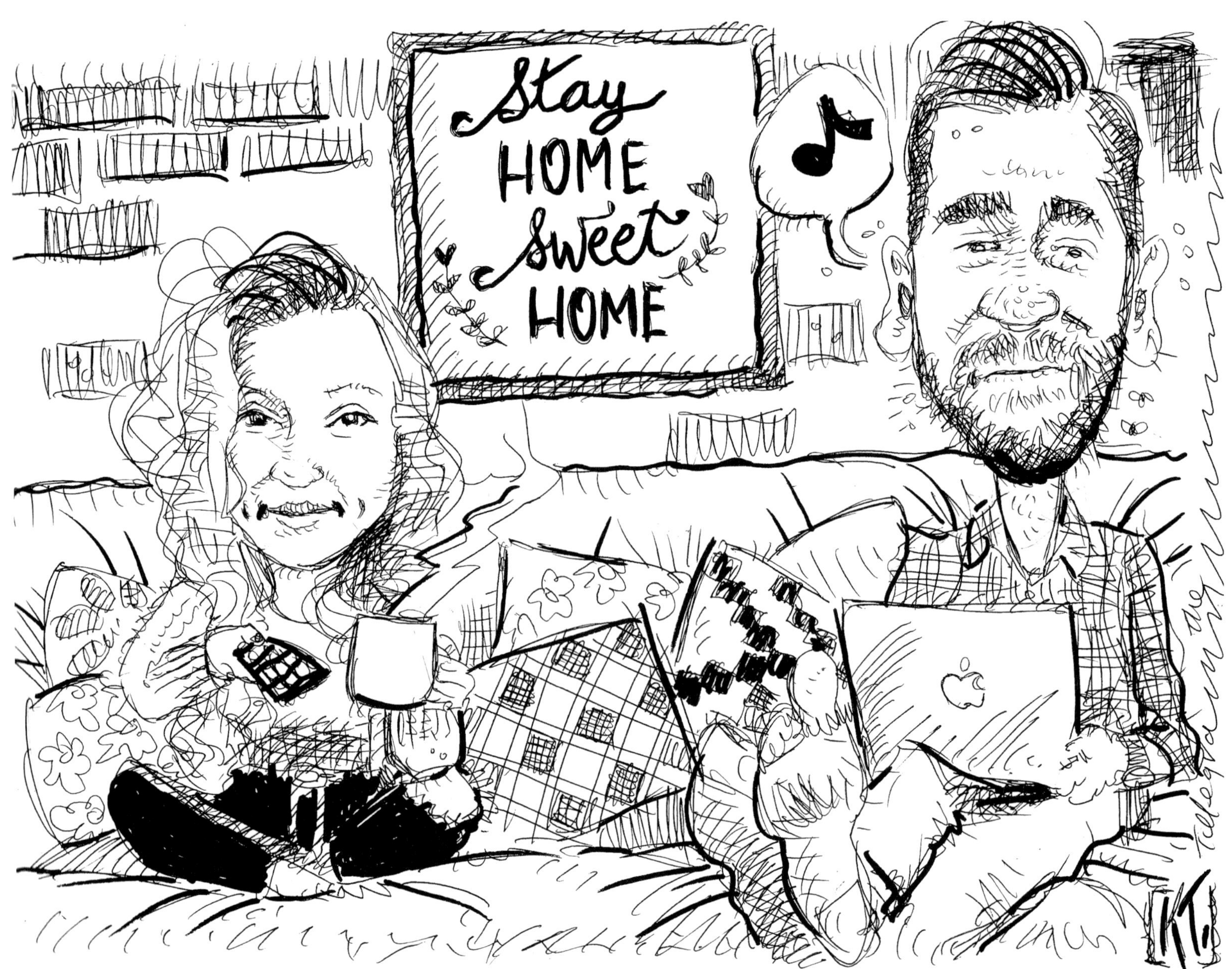

Stay
HOME
Sweet
HOME

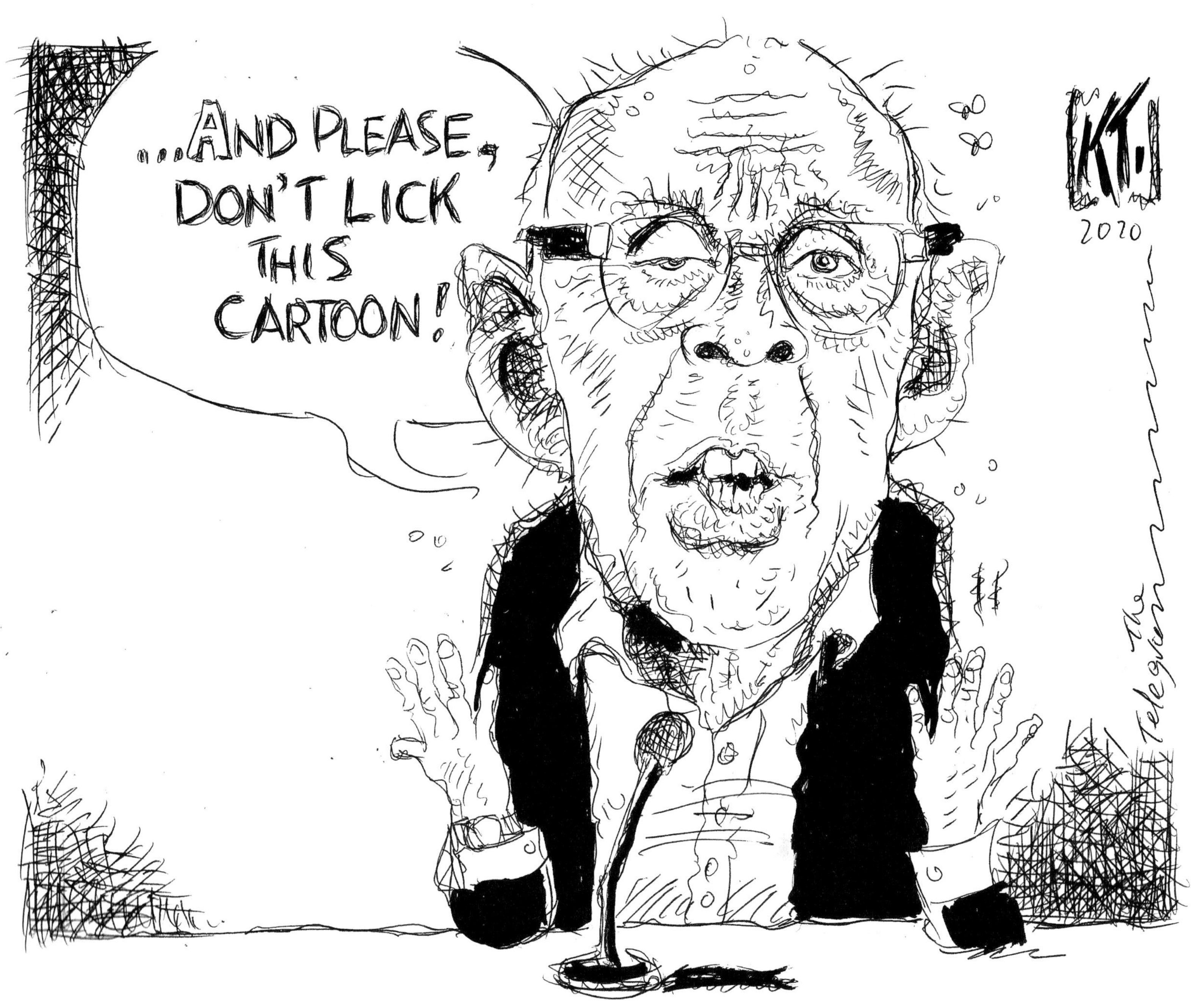


...AND PLEASE,
DON'T LICK
THIS
CARTOON!

KT.
2020

The Telegram

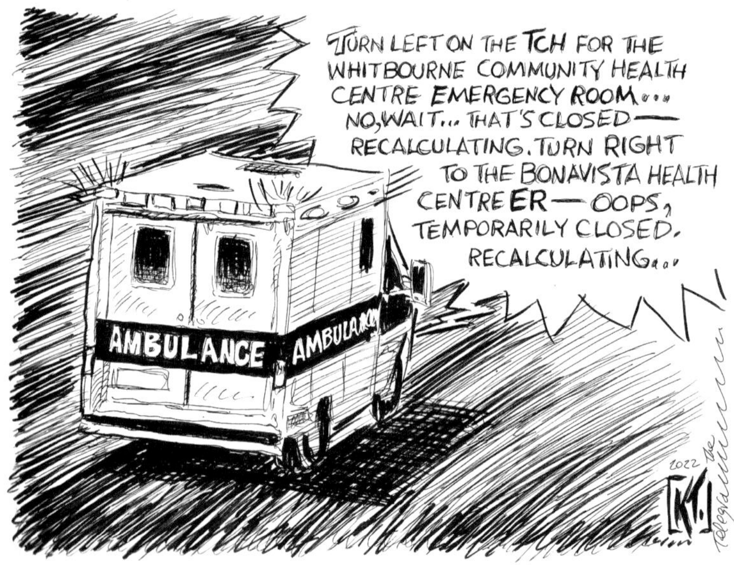

TURN LEFT ON THE TCH FOR THE WHITBOURNE COMMUNITY HEALTH CENTRE EMERGENCY ROOM... NO, WAIT... THAT'S CLOSED — RECALCULATING. TURN RIGHT TO THE BONAVISTA HEALTH CENTRE ER — OOPS, TEMPORARILY CLOSED. RECALCULATING...
AMBULANCE
AMBULANCE
2022


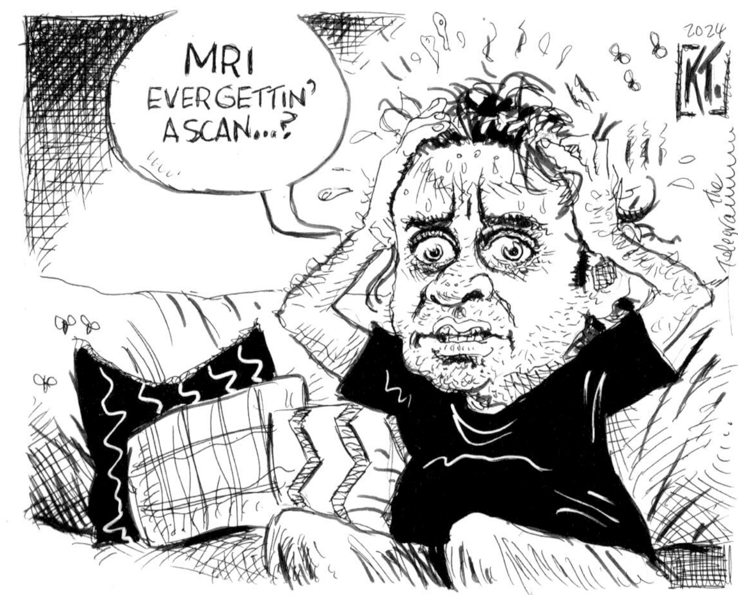

MRI EVER GETTIN' A SCAN...?
2024

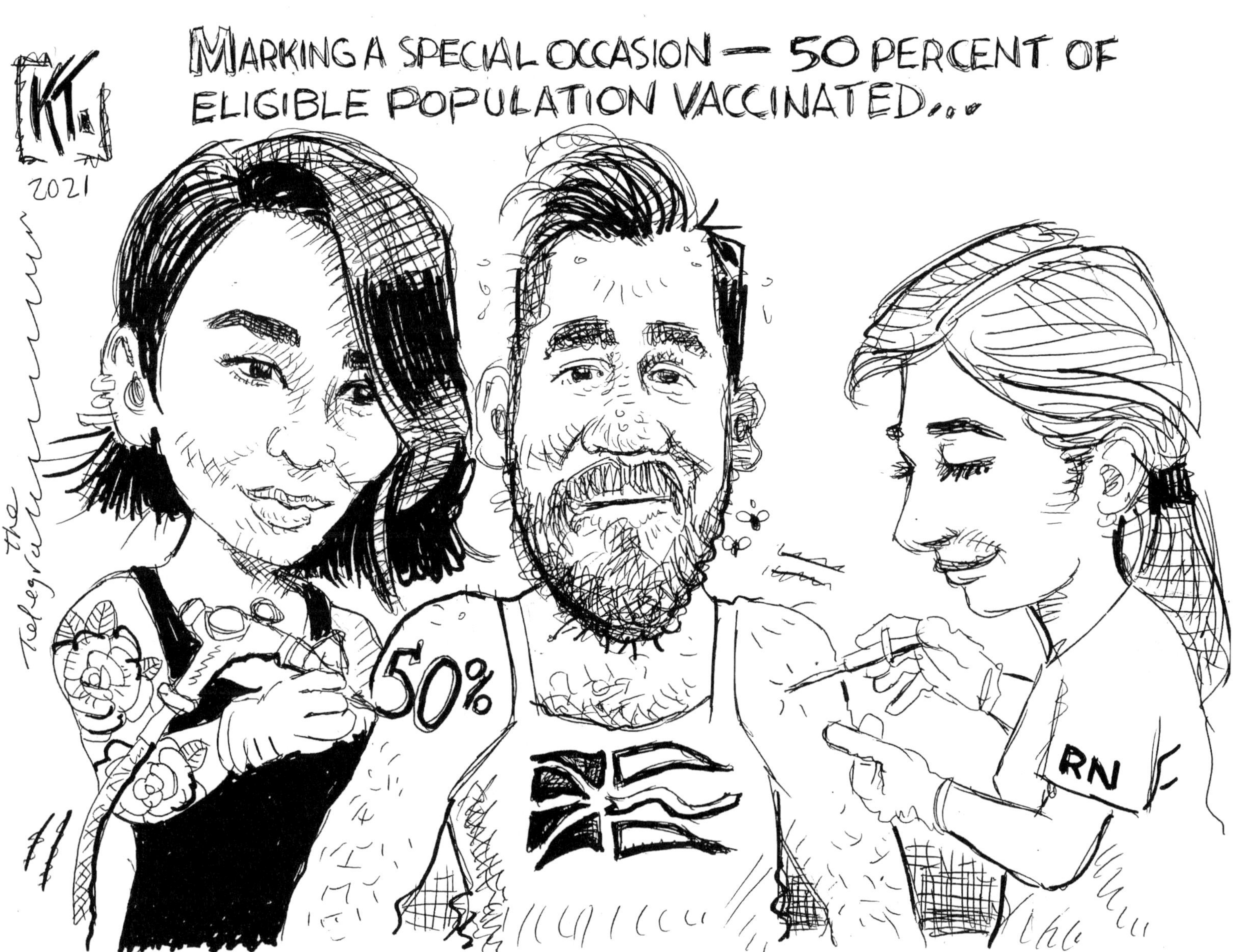

MARKING A SPECIAL OCCASION — 50 PERCENT OF ELIGIBLE POPULATION VACCINATED...
50%
RN
2021
the Telegram

# ENDANGERED SPECIES N.L.

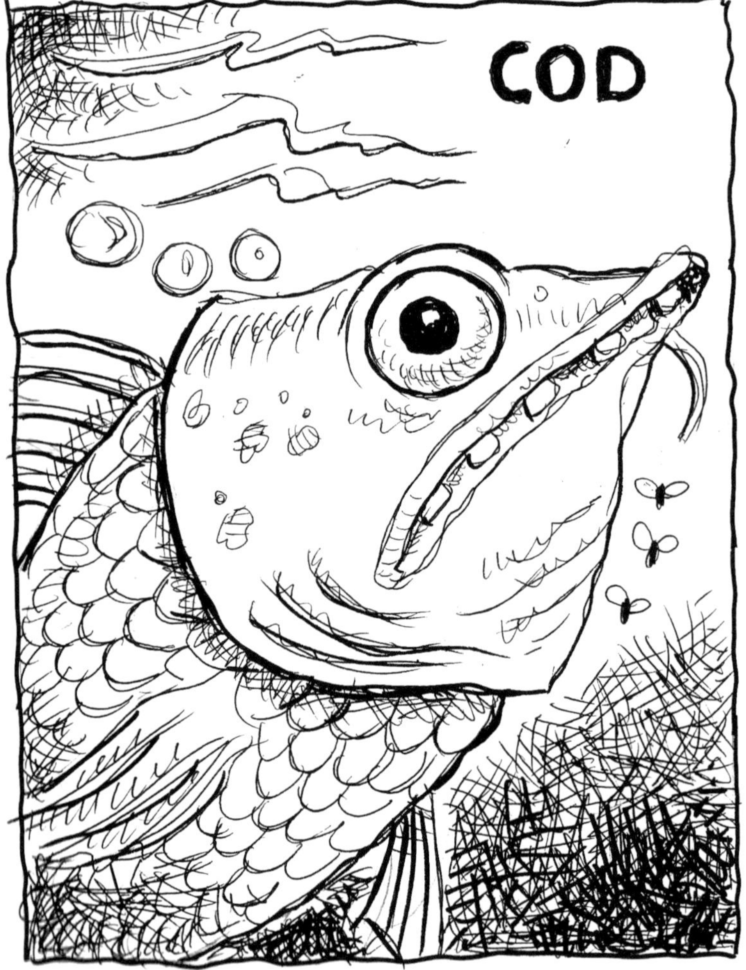


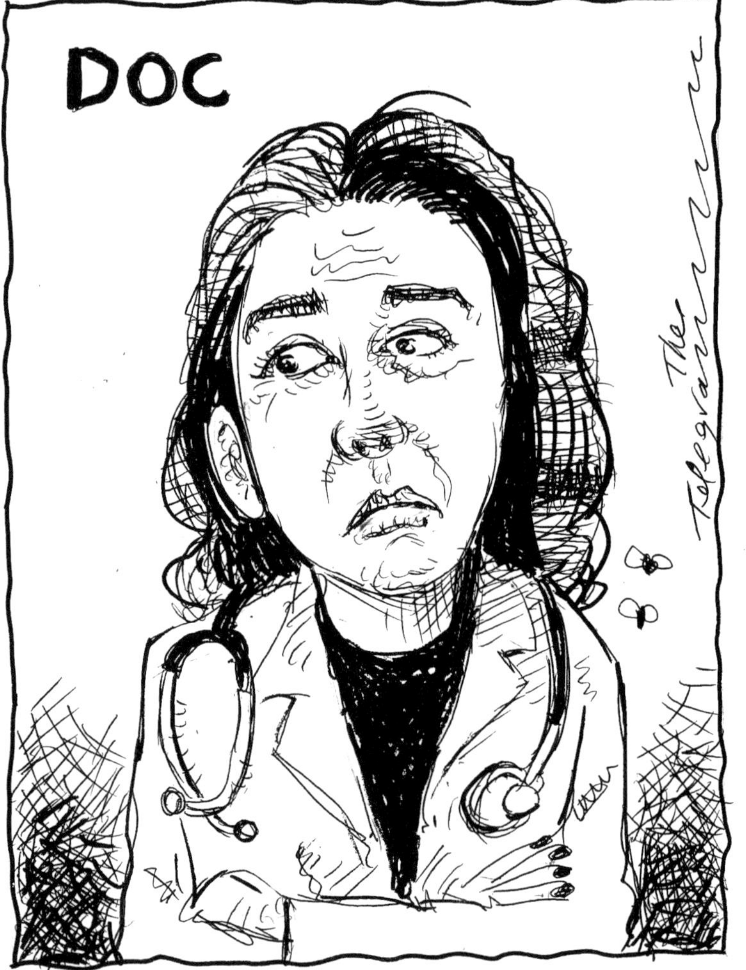

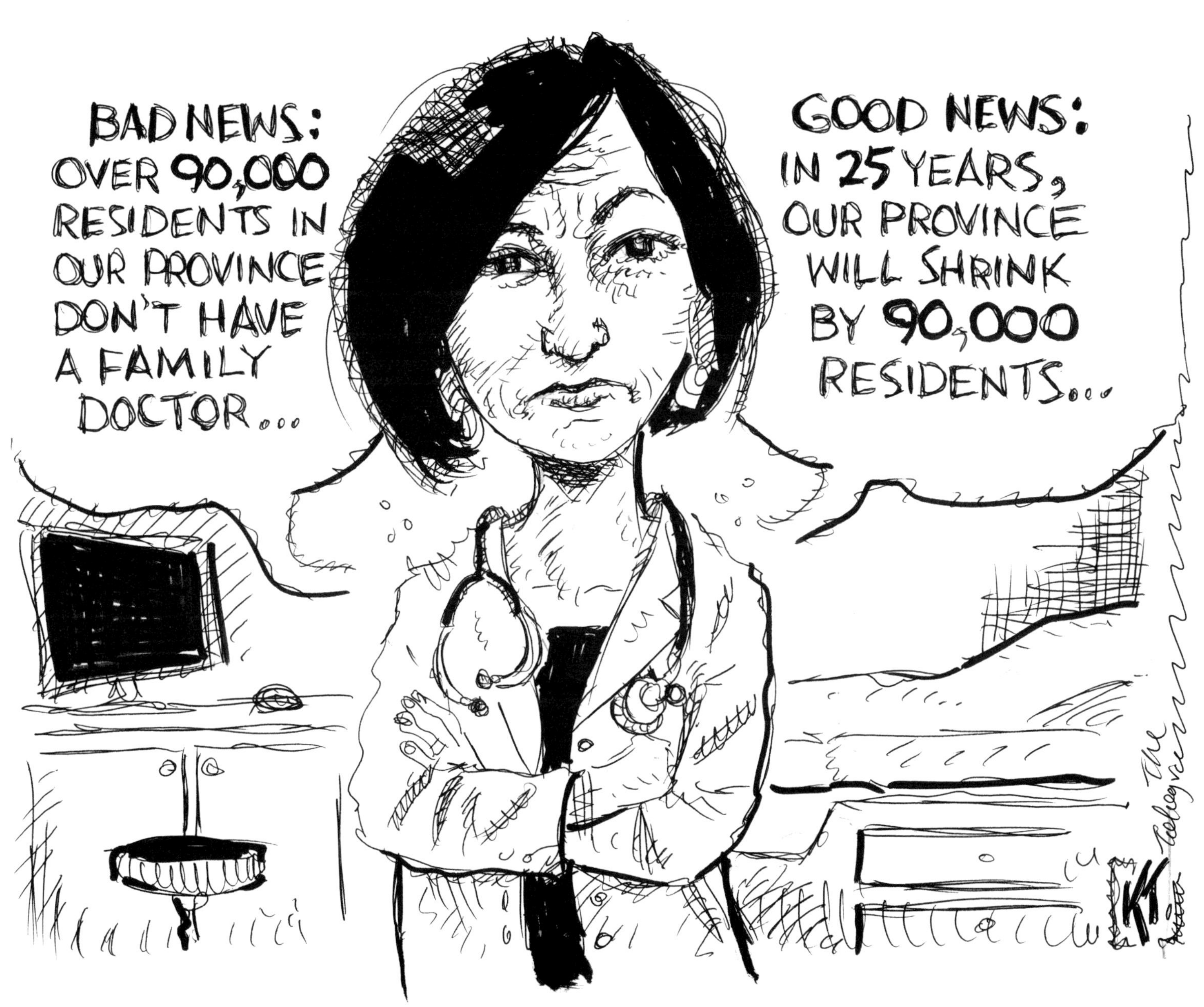

BAD NEWS: OVER 90,000 RESIDENTS IN OUR PROVINCE DON'T HAVE A FAMILY DOCTOR...
GOOD NEWS: IN 25 YEARS, OUR PROVINCE WILL SHRINK BY 90,000 RESIDENTS...

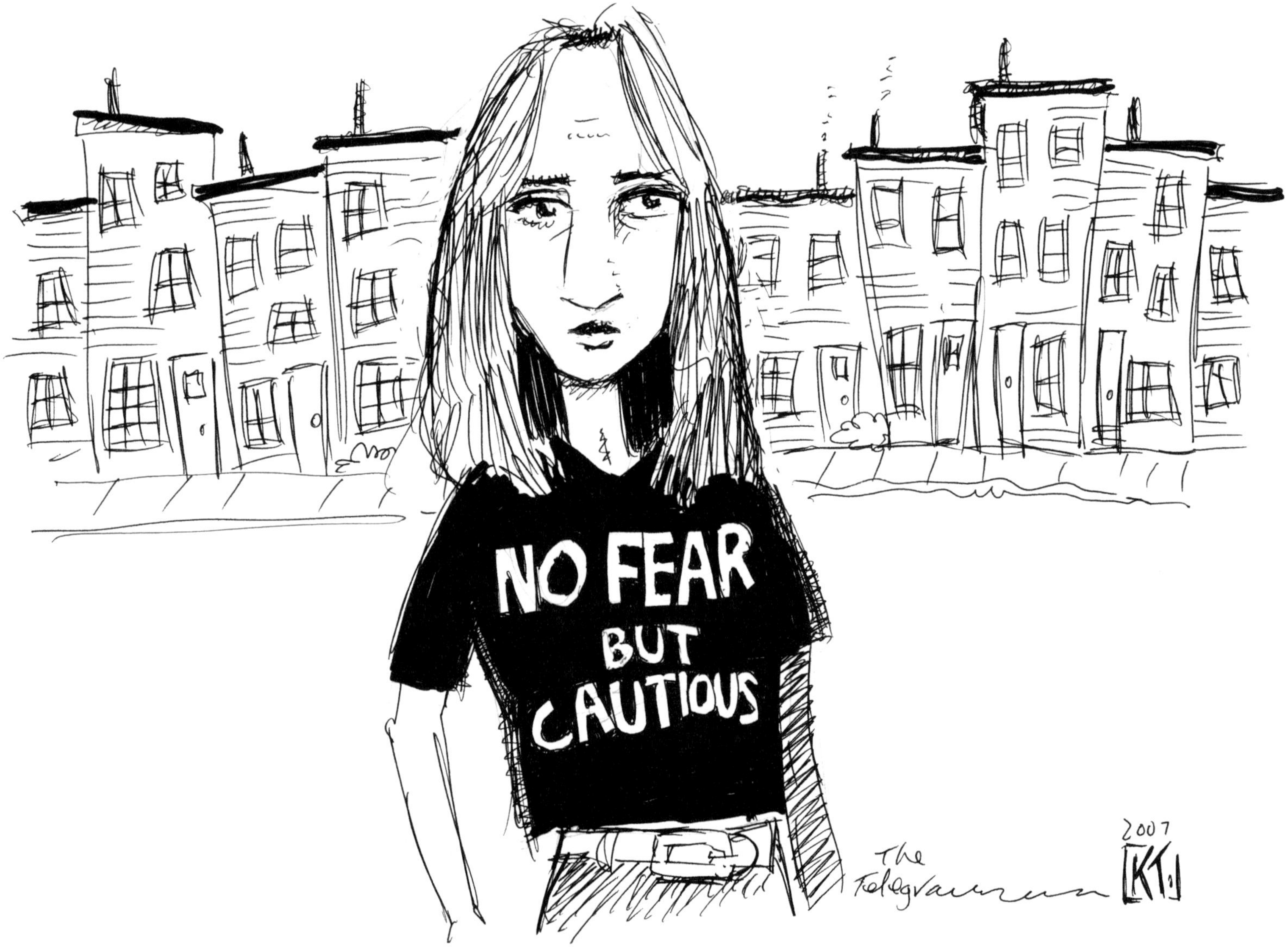

NO FEAR
BUT
CAUTIOUS

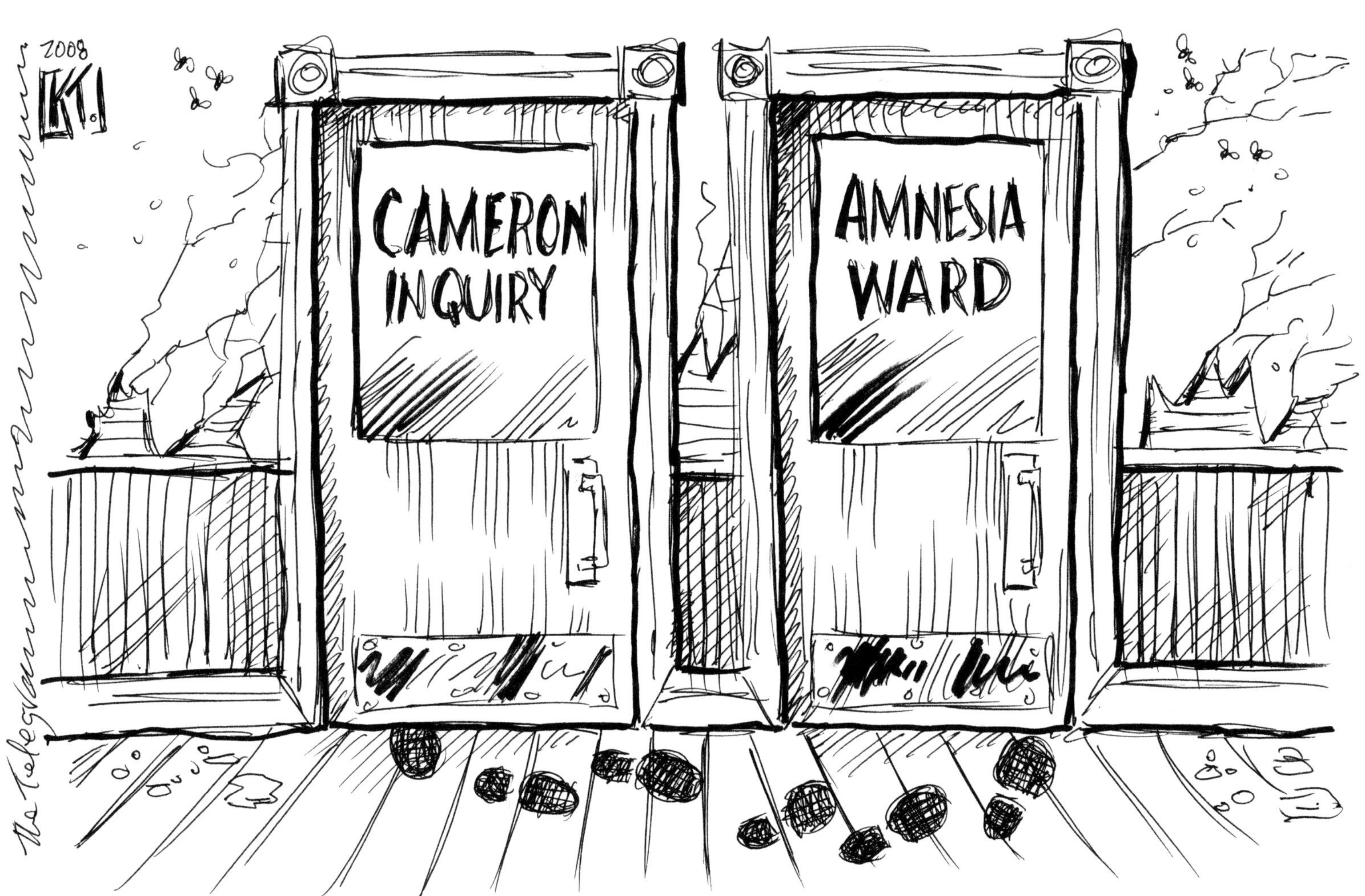

CAMERON
INQUIRY
AMNESIA
WARD

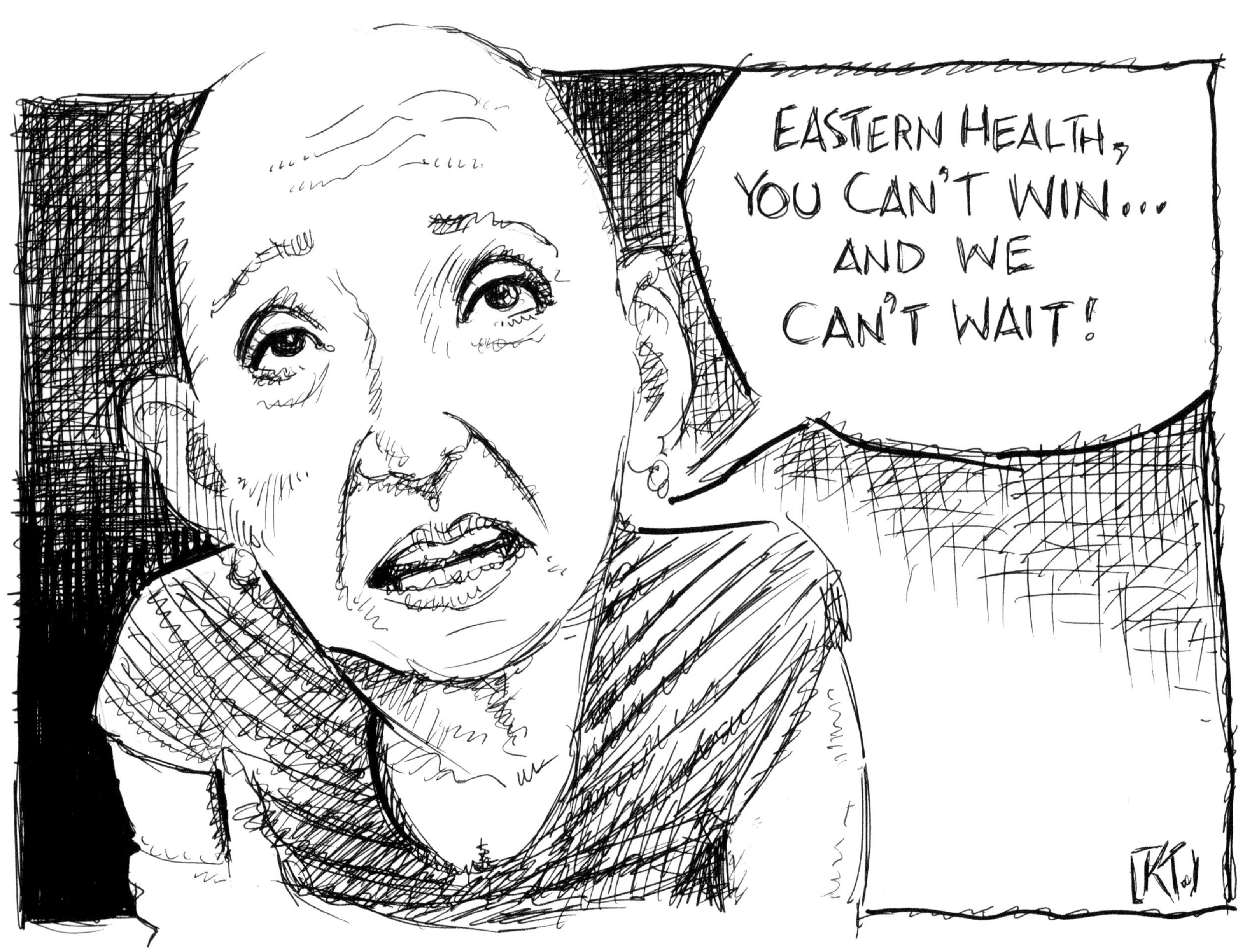
EASTERN HEALTH,
YOU CAN'T WIN...
AND WE
CAN'T WAIT!

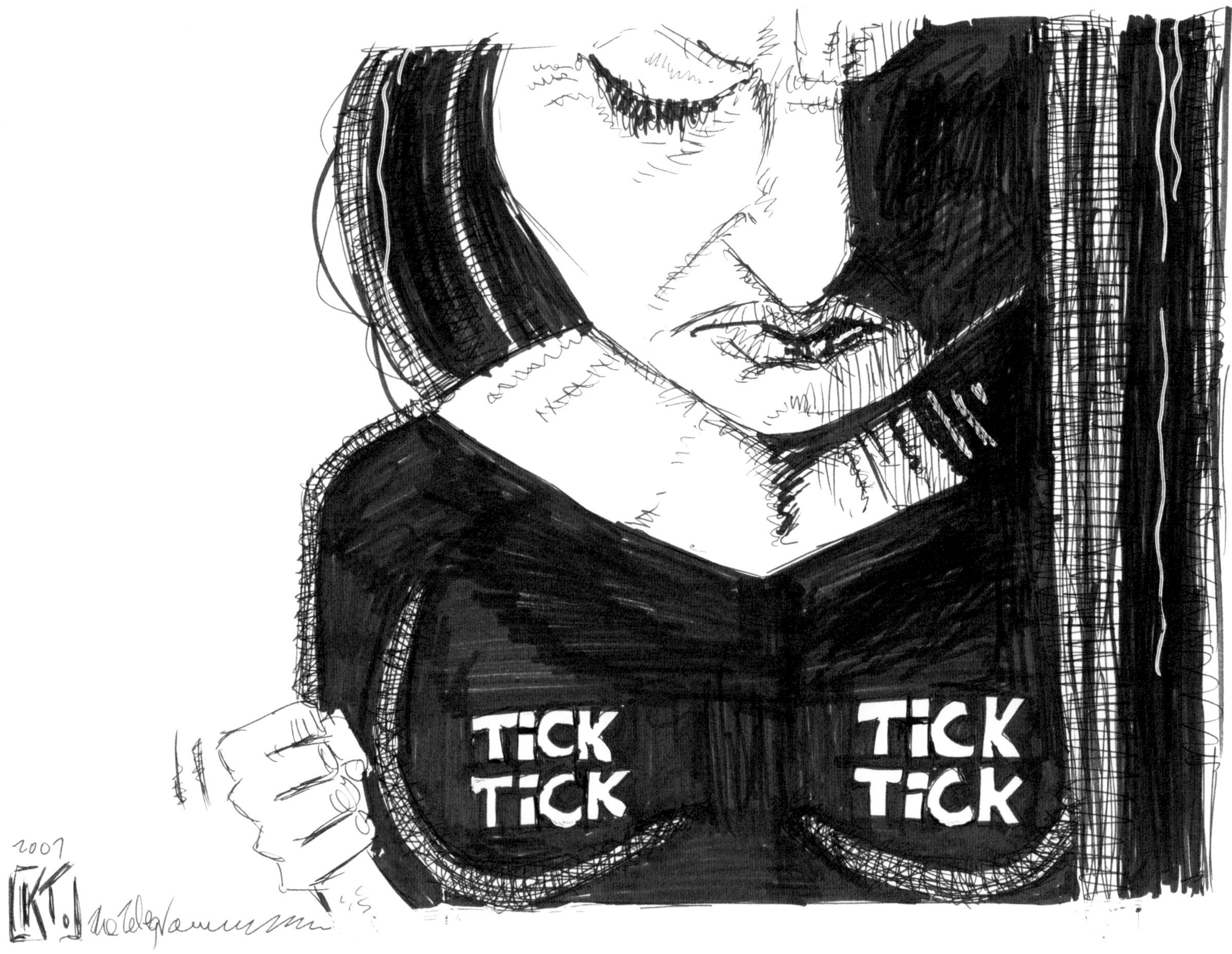

TICK
TICK
TICK
TICK
2007

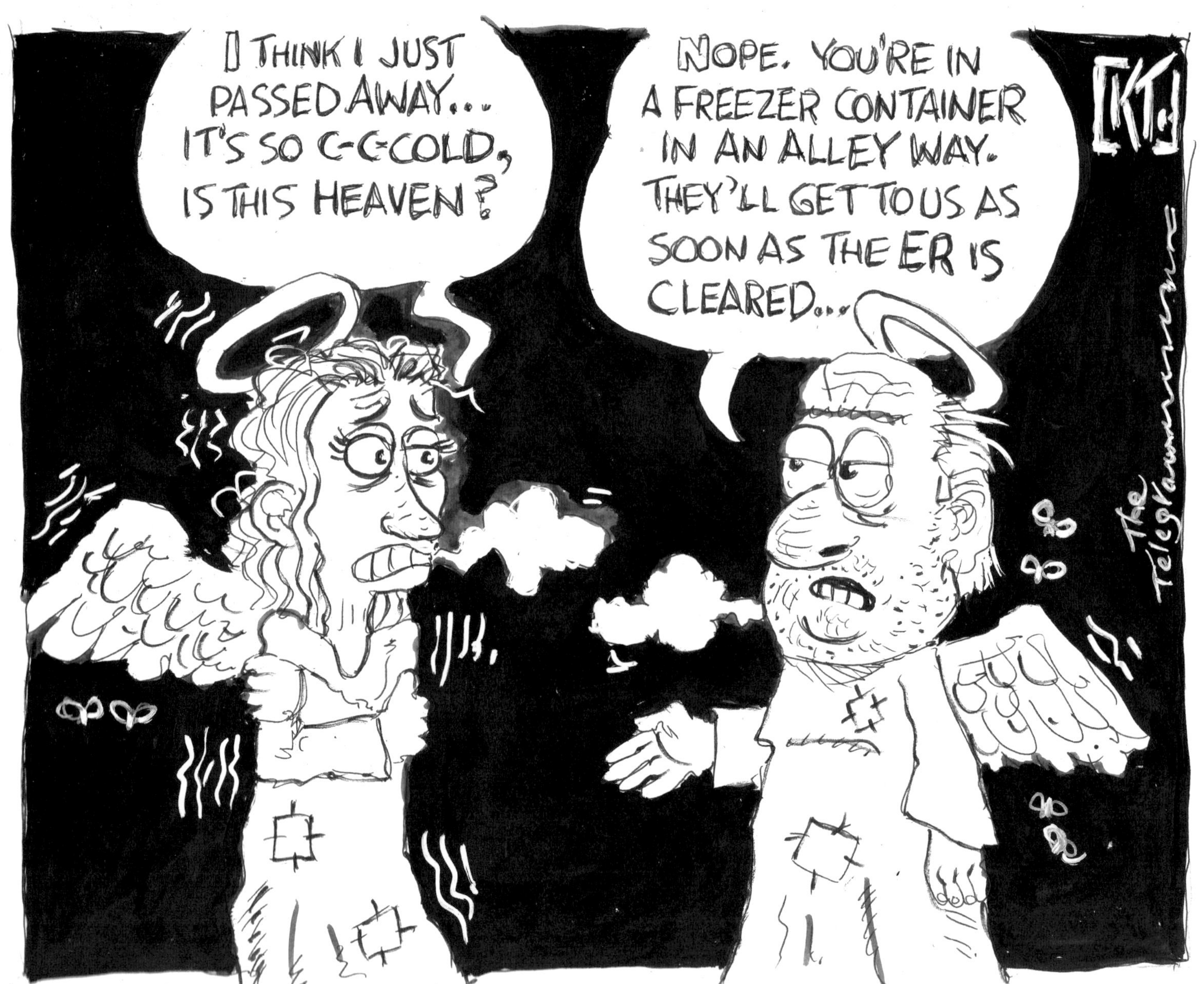
I THINK I JUST PASSED AWAY... IT'S SO C-C-COLD, IS THIS HEAVEN?
NOPE. YOU'RE IN A FREEZER CONTAINER IN AN ALLEY WAY. THEY'LL GET TO US AS SOON AS THE ER IS CLEARED...
The Telegram

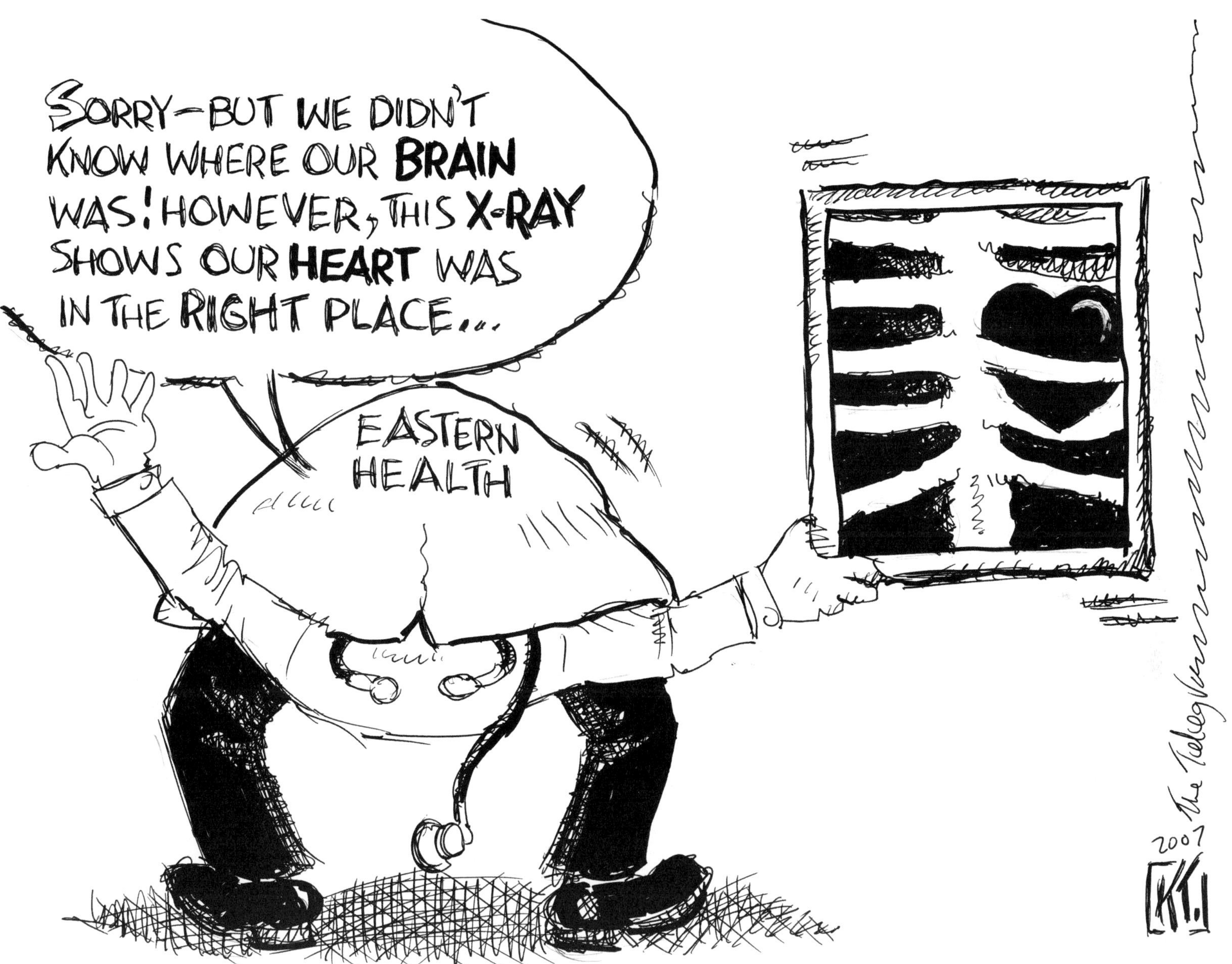

SORRY - BUT WE DIDN'T KNOW WHERE OUR BRAIN WAS! HOWEVER, THIS X-RAY SHOWS OUR HEART WAS IN THE RIGHT PLACE...
EASTERN HEALTH
2007
The Telegram

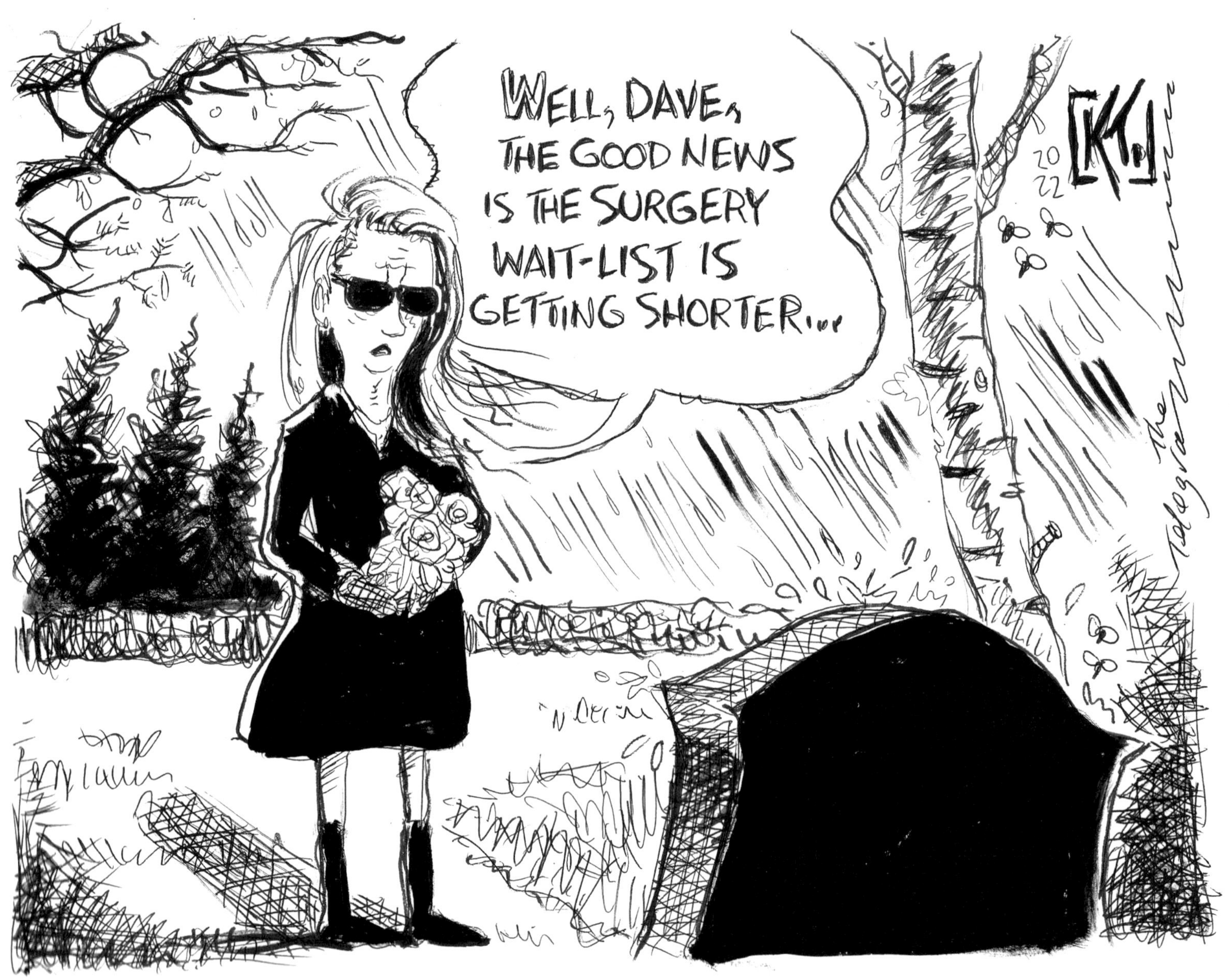

WELL, DAVE, THE GOOD NEWS IS THE SURGERY WAIT-LIST IS GETTING SHORTER...

# NEWS

*Well over a century ago, most of our breaking news was provided by word of mouth to gullible listeners. leading to the expression "There was an old woman who swallowed the news." Some years after that, it became a popular children's nursery rhyme, "There Was an Old Woman who Swallowed a Fly." These days, the gullible turn to the Internet for all their questionable information and fly's eye view of newsworthy items.*

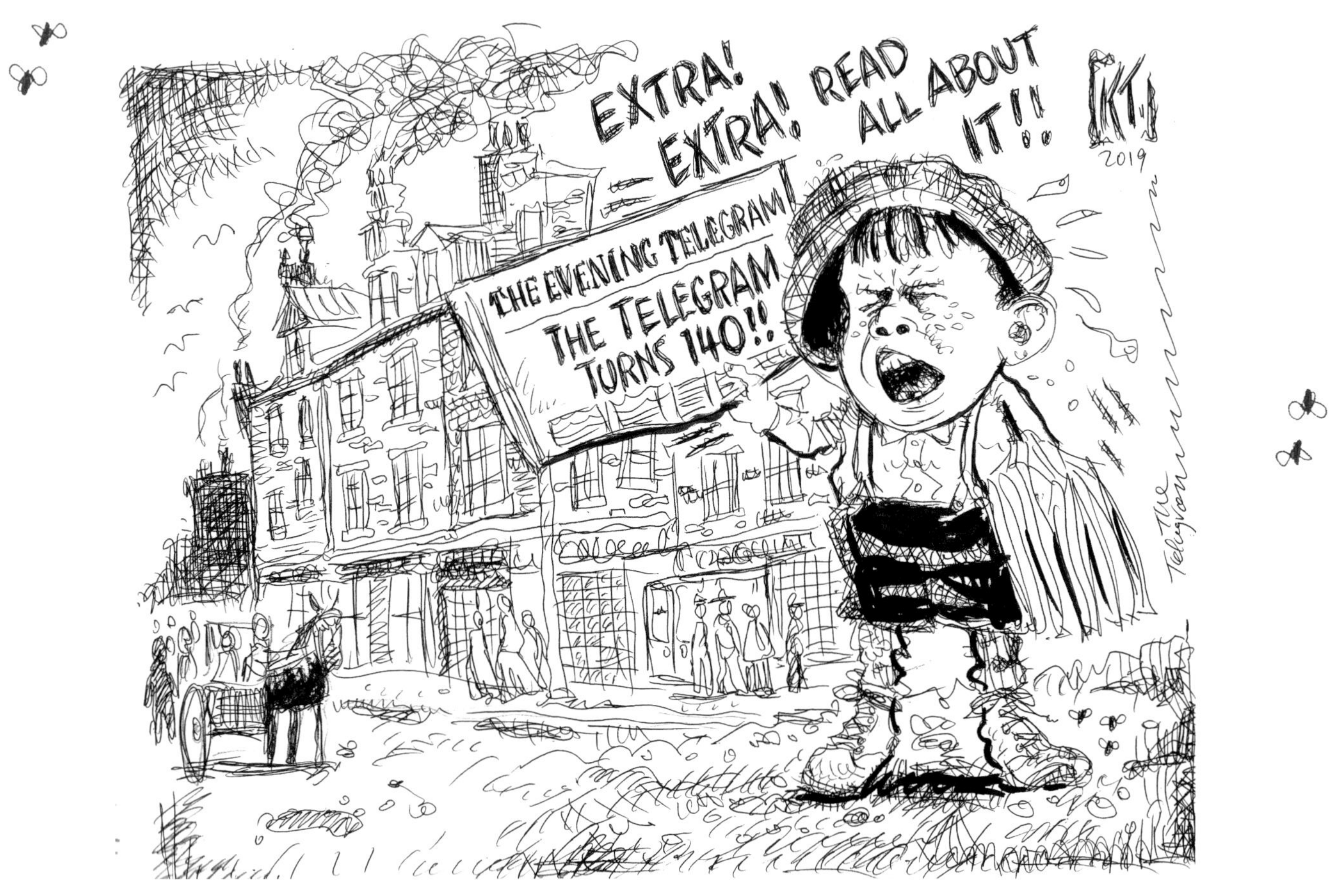

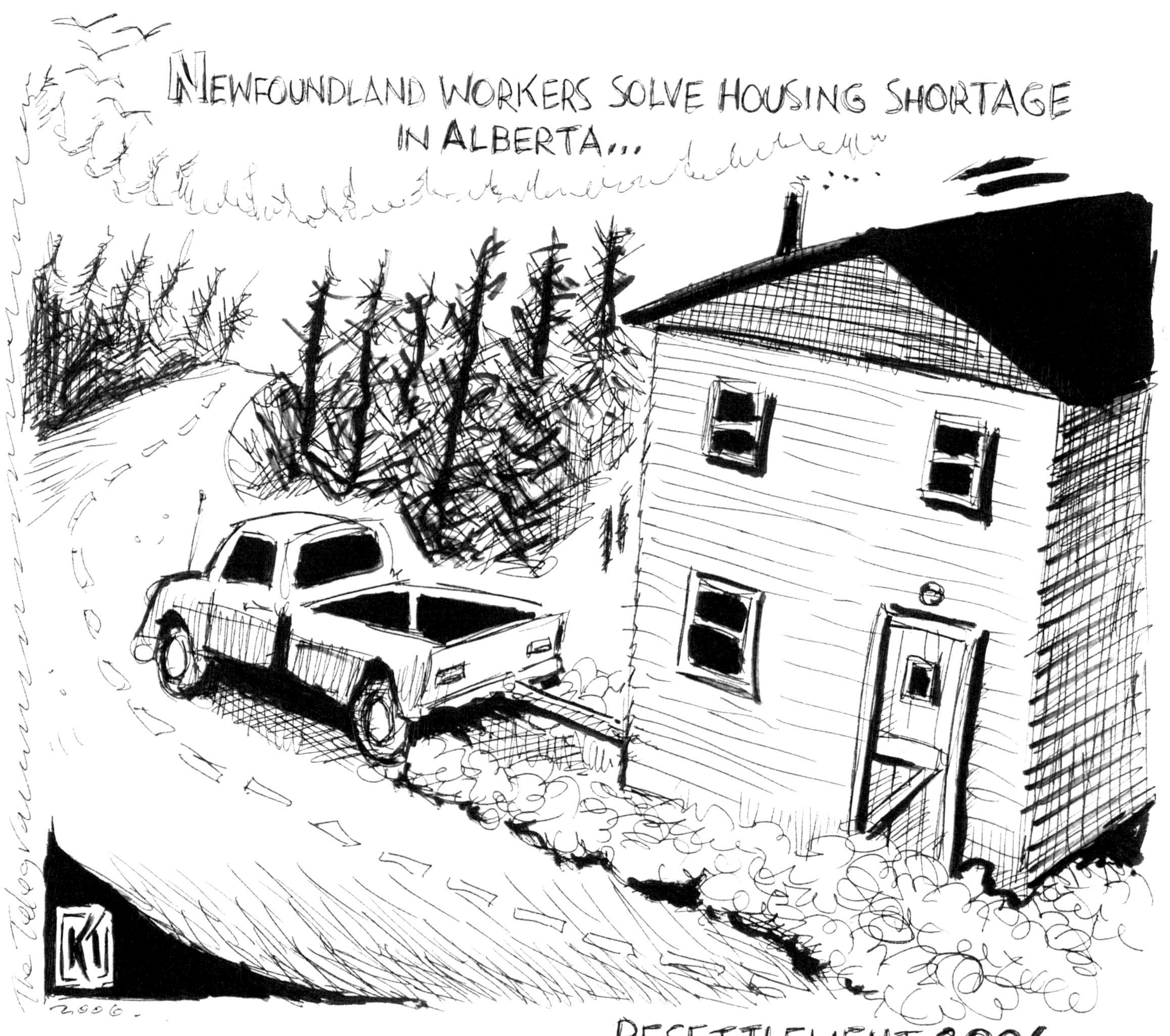

NEWFOUNDLAND WORKERS SOLVE HOUSING SHORTAGE IN ALBERTA...
RESETTLEMENT 2006...

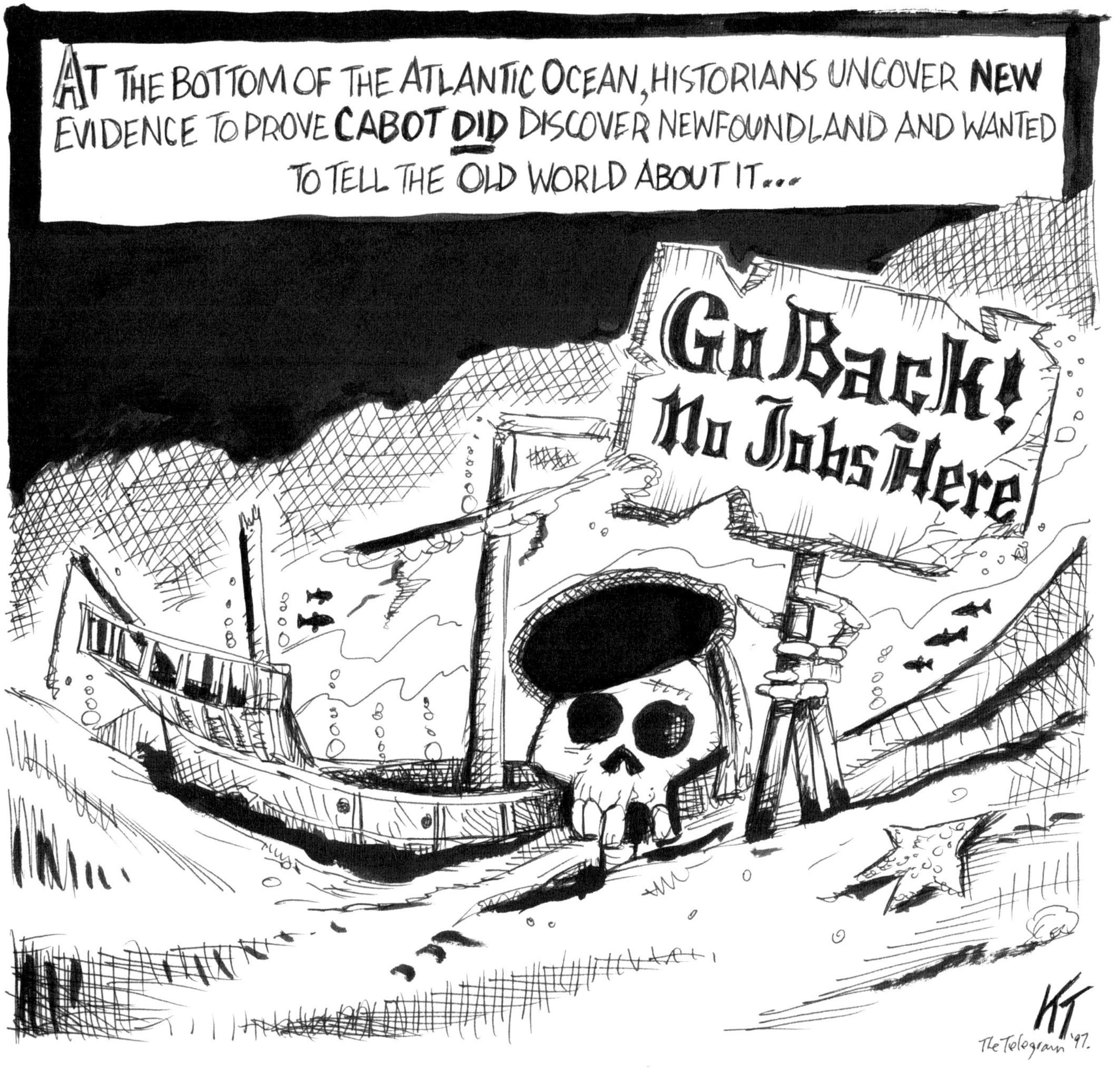

AT THE BOTTOM OF THE ATLANTIC OCEAN, HISTORIANS UNCOVER NEW EVIDENCE TO PROVE CABOT DID DISCOVER NEWFOUNDLAND AND WANTED TO TELL THE OLD WORLD ABOUT IT...
Go Back! No Jobs Here
The Telegram '97.

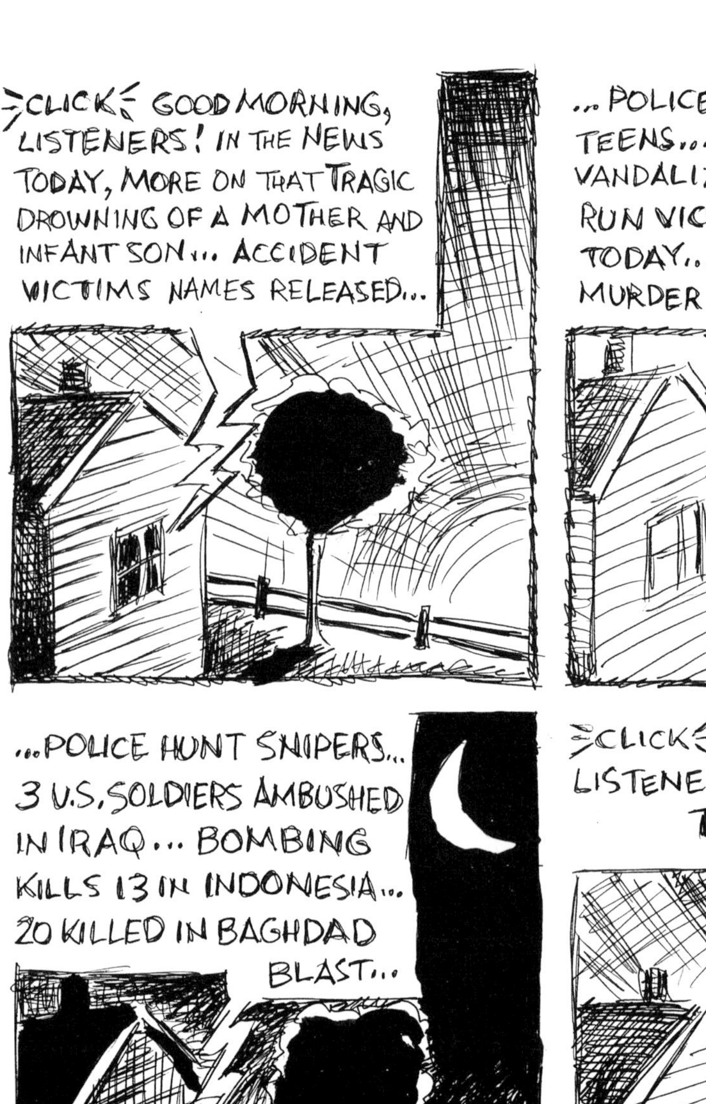

≥CLICK≤ GOOD MORNING, LISTENERS! IN THE NEWS TODAY, MORE ON THAT TRAGIC DROWNING OF A MOTHER AND INFANT SON... ACCIDENT VICTIMS NAMES RELEASED...
... POLICE SEEK MISSING TEENS... LOCAL SCHOOLS VANDALIZED... HIT-AND-RUN VICTIM BURIED TODAY... DAYLIGHT MURDER IN OTTAWA...
..POLICE HUNT SNIPERS... 3 U.S. SOLDIERS AMBUSHED IN IRAQ... BOMBING KILLS 13 IN INDONESIA... 20 KILLED IN BAGHDAD BLAST...


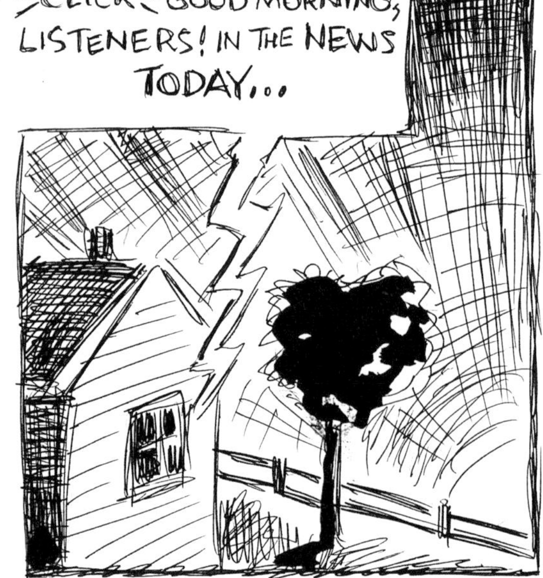

≥CLICK≤ GOOD MORNING, LISTENERS! IN THE NEWS TODAY...
2003.
The Telegram.

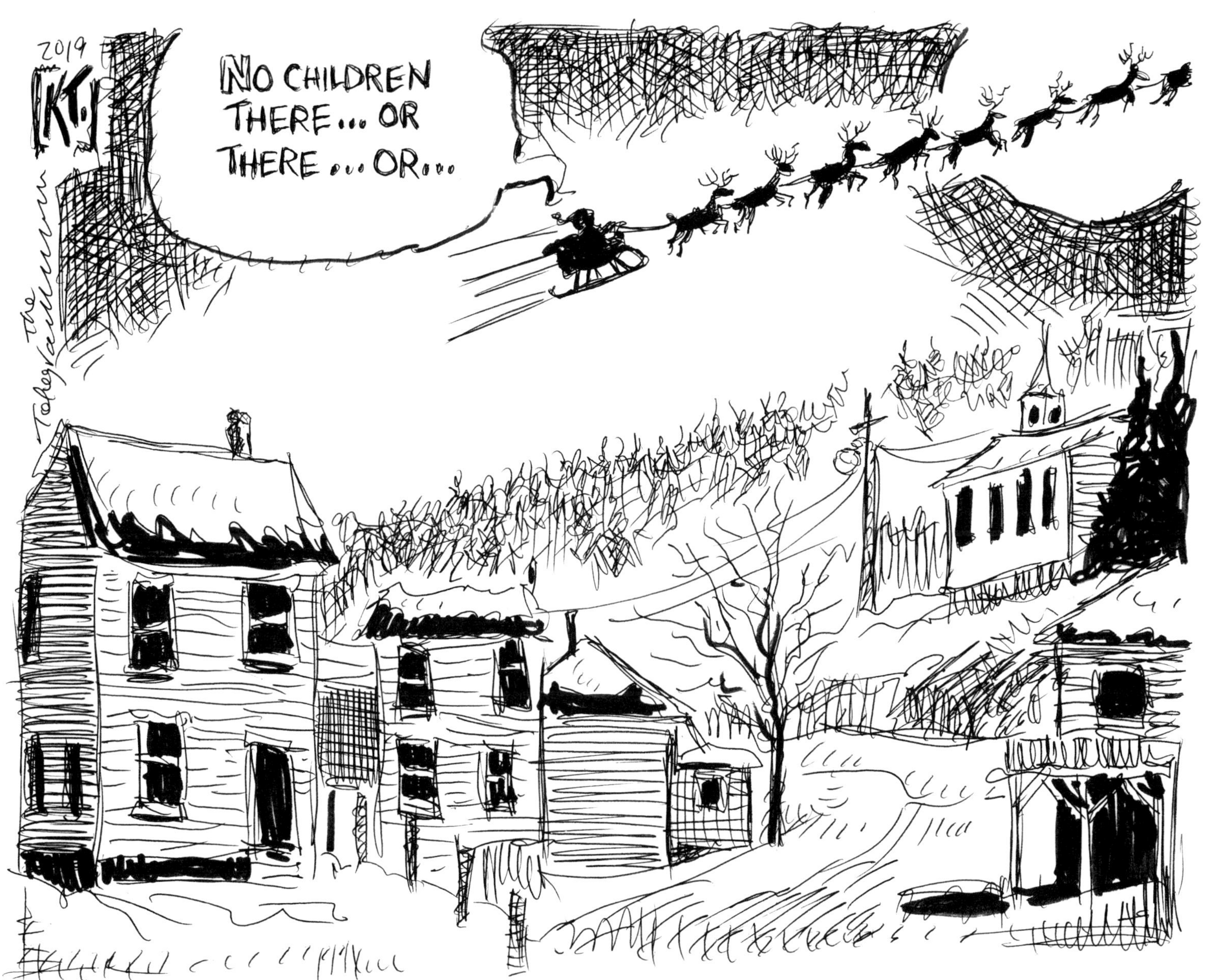

NO CHILDREN THERE... OR THERE... OR...
2019
KTJ

*Page 8*  Writer Paul Bickford and I co-created Glut The Newfoundland Humour Magazine *in 1984. We published three issues, all printed by Robinson-Blackmore in St. John's. The back cover of issue #1 featured Pope John Paul II, who visited the province in 1984, greeting the readers in the Newfoundland English dialect.*

*Page 9*  *After Glut, Paul and I also teamed up for a few editorial cartoons in 1985. I drew this cartoon after Tina Turner's comeback performance in St. John's in July 1985. This cartoon was very controversial at the time when it appeared, reaching the heated airwaves of local open line radio shows.*

*Page 11*  *Gordon Pinsent happily signed this original cartoon, "To Kevin the Great. Gordon Pinsent." A framed print of the cartoon also hangs at my favourite pub, the Duke of Duckworth in St. John's. Check it out.*

*Page 12*  *This cartoon features actor Jason Momoa from the locally produced television series,* Frontier. *I believe it has received the most "likes" of all my cartoons—over 40,000 on his Instagram page!*

*Page 52*  *This Davis Inlet cartoon received the Silver Award in Editorial Cartooning at the 1998 Atlantic Journalism Awards in Halifax.*

*Page 57*  *The Ed and Joey cartoon was published in the* Grand Falls Advertiser *in 1977. This is one of the first editorial cartoons I ever drew.*

*Page 58*  *Brian Peckford, circa 1979.*

*Page 59*  *Brian Peckford, circa 1985.*

*Page 125*  *During the* COVID *pandemic, the provincial Minister of Health, Dr. John Haggie, often made funny quips about avoiding* COVID *during media briefings. On one notable occasion, he told parents to please not let their kids lick the handles of shopping carts.*

*Page 132*  *In 2007 downtown St. John's was becoming very unsafe, especially for women, whether in bars, getting a taxi, or walking home at night. It was also common to see "No Fear" stickers in truck rear windows. At the time, I thought of my wife, my teen daughter, and her friends, and drew this cartoon reflecting all of that: A woman who has no fear, who is confident, but is nonetheless still cautious and aware of her surroundings, and what could happen—what still is happening—every day.*

*Page 155*  *The remains of an unknown First World War soldier are finally returned home to Newfoundland and Labrador in 2024.*

# SPECIAL THANK-YOUS

*Cartoonists are supposed to be solo flyers. They live in their own heads. They often dream and draw on their own. While that's true in most cases, in my 40-year journey of cartooning, I have been so fortunate to have several brilliant and quirky minds helping contribute to many of my toons.*

*In particular, special thanks to Paul Bickford, Neal Klassen, Maureen Riche, Oral Mews, Vicki Combden Murphy, Gareth Mitton, Jim Mackey, Rod Lyver, Richard Ellis, and Len Power. For many years, I have been truly in awe of your wit, humour, and silliness. Kindred spirits.*

*Many thanks to* The Telegram's *managing editor, Jennifer Vardy Little, and to Postmedia, who published my recent editorial cartoons (2024–2025) found on various pages throughout the book.*

*Rebecca Rose and the Breakwater Books team, thanks for all your guidance, knowledge, and joining forces with me to help create this particular book,* Fly on the Wall. *Many thanks to Mark Critch for writing the foreword.*

*To Matthew Keels, Linda White, and the friendly staff at* MUN *Archives, thanks for helping me select and scan several cartoons that appear in this book.*

*And to my better half, my cartoonist muse, Sherry, who's been around for the ride for 40 years, thanks for being my good sounding board, a great listener, and offering feedback when needed.*

*Finally, to the readers of* The Telegram, *thank you so much for your interest and support in my editorial cartoons for 40 years.*

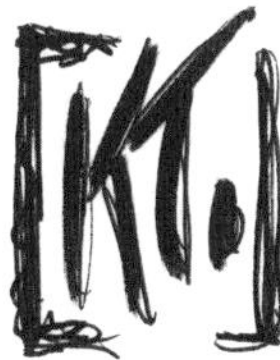

# KEVIN TOBIN

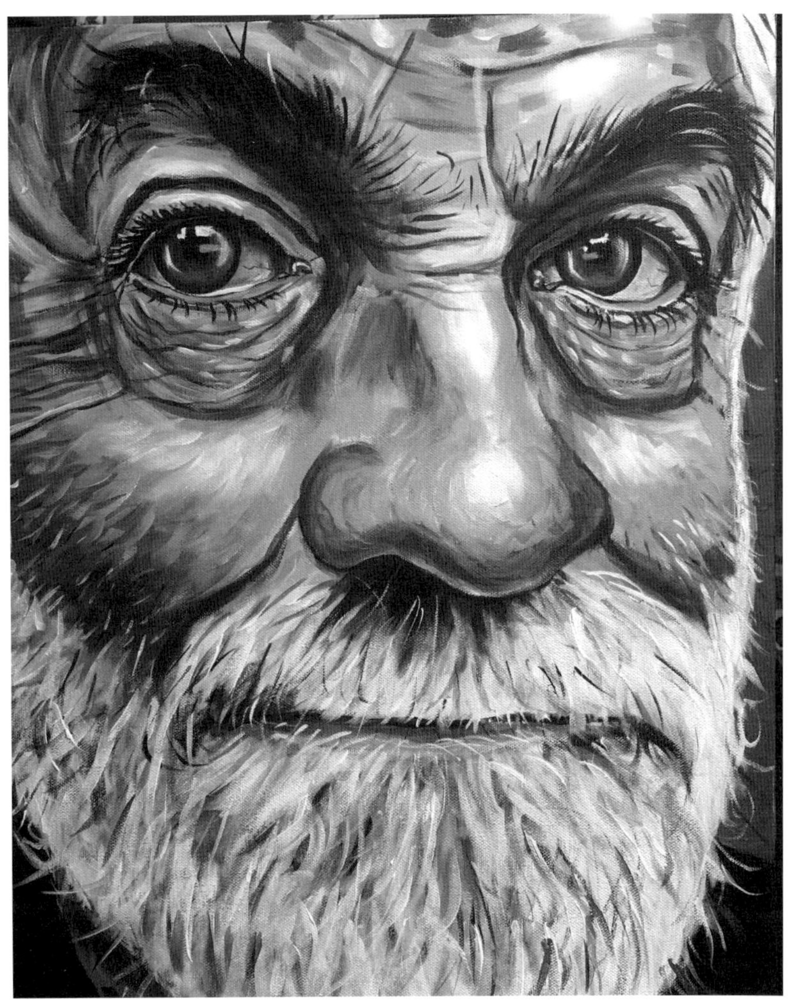

Kevin Tobin (KT) has been an editorial cartoonist for the St. John's daily newspaper The Telegram for 40 years. Since the mid-1980s he has used his cartoons to comment on local politics, provincial issues, and national events— from premiers, prime ministers, and colourful characters to the Cod Moratorium, Muskrat Falls, the recent pandemic, and everything in between. He has published 10 books of his editorial cartoons up to 2010, and has illustrated two books with the band Buddy Wasisname and the Other Fellers.

Since 2020, KT has illustrated four children's books, the "Bizzie Tizzie" series, with his daughter Jessica, a graphic designer. A self-employed artist, KT has been painting caricatures over the past decade and really enjoys the creative freedom that cartooning, painting, and illustration bring.

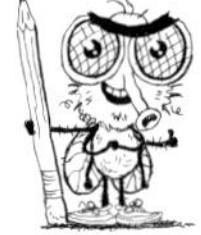